The
Lovely Treachery
of Words

STUDIES IN CANADIAN LITERATURE

Series Editor: Richard Teleky

ADELE WISEMAN

*Memoirs of a Book Molesting Childhood
and Other Essays*

LINDA HUTCHEON

*The Canadian Postmodern:
A Study of Contemporary English-Canadian Fiction*

JANICE KULYK KEEFER

Reading Mavis Gallant

ROBERT KROETSCH

*The Lovely Treachery of Words:
Essays Selected and New*

The
Lovely Treachery
of Words

Essays Selected and New

ROBERT KROETSCH

Toronto   New York   Oxford
OXFORD UNIVERSITY PRESS
1989

Oxford University Press, 70 Wynford Drive, Don Mills, Ontario, M3C 1J9

Toronto Oxford New York Delhi Bombay Calcutta Madras Karachi
Petaling Jaya Singapore Hong Kong Tokyo Nairobi Dar es Salaam
Cape Town Melbourne Auckland

and associated companies in
Berlin Ibadan

CANADIAN CATALOGUING IN PUBLICATION DATA

Kroetsch, Robert, 1927–
The lovely treachery of words

(Studies in Canadian literature)
Includes bibliographical references and index.
ISBN 0-19-540694-X

1. Canadian literature (English)—History and
criticism.* I. Title. II. Series: Studies in
Canadian literature (Don Mills, Ont.).

PS8071.K76 1989   C810′.9   C88-095286-5
PR9189.6.K76 1989

OXFORD is a trademark of Oxford University Press

1 2 3 4 – 2 1 0 9

Printed in Canada

In memory of my mother
Hildegard Weller

Contents

Acknowledgements

We begin by saying thank you; perhaps acknowledgements are preface enough.

Somewhere around 1970, while co-editing *boundary 2: a journal of postmodern literature* with William V. Spanos at the State University of New York at Binghamton, I began to think the fragments that have become these essays. It was Bill Spanos who invited me to read Heidegger against my own story of a Canadian prairie childhood. But perhaps I knew even then that the story in order to unfold has both to undo and infold itself, and I only learned by the act of reading that I had long been writing the autobiography of my refusals to be grateful to a generous world.

This is not complicated at all. It is the double mark of scandal and transgression that locates gratitude.

Since I wear geography next to my skin (and mere nakedness is never a truth, as these essays so elaborately insist)—since I speak out of the play of surfaces against and with each other, I am grateful in a literal way to the places of learning where I tried to talk some of these essays: Binghamton, Victoria, Vancouver, Edmonton, Banff, New York, Toronto, Edinburgh, Trier, Lahti (Finland), Lincoln (Nebraska), Calgary, Montreal, Brisbane, a campus in Vermont and a second one in Virginia, a beach hotel in Sicily, a museum in Singapore, Leeds, Reading, a variety of stone buildings in London, more than one place in New Hampshire, a canal in (I believe it was) Utrecht, an art gallery in Berlin, a medieval street in modern Strasbourg, Beijing, and, enduringly, Rome.

I see now that these essays are very much the consequence of extended conversation.

I am grateful also to the editors of journals who invited me to try some of these speculations on readers. Journals as various as *English Quarterly, Border Crossings, The Journal of Canadian Fiction, Canadian Literature, Dandelion,* and *Mosaic* became other versions of place. And I am equally grateful to a number of book editors for their infinite strategies in bringing versions of disorder to versions of completion. It was Richard Teleky who, over the improbabilities of high tea in the Empress Hotel, gently gave me a deadline by proposing a cover for the book.

For a first attempt at gathering together these essays I wish to thank Frank Davey and bp Nichol. They put together a special issue of *Open Letter* (Spring 1983) that they called, exactly, *Essays*. After my having essayed. And I remember with utter joy the generosity of bp Nichol, as he moved with nimble wit through my scattered ruminations.

For vaster systems of understanding, I wish to thank the Canada Council, whose Killam Research Fellowship afforded me the time to discover my way into new labyrinths of what I was guessing at, the time to narrate my sense of the narrative of an individual voice in conversation with the announced world.

That same conversation (about, and becoming, story) owes a great deal to the generous support of the University of Manitoba. Friends known and unknown found assistance for me. Colleagues were kind enough to try my speculations in that private public place that is the classroom. Dennis Cooley and David Arnason, to name only two of my critics, found caring (and sometimes comic) ways to offer correction to my extravagances.

I especially want to thank my own students, at various institutions in the United States and Canada, who were patient and instructive while I undid my own thinking towards recognitions of what they in all probability knew.

I conclude by thanking Smaro Kamboureli, who by a mystery that escapes my telling managed as wife and wise literary critic so often to steer me out of my garden (succulents and alpines, on a slope of rock, near the sea) and back to the speechless clarity of a blank page.

1

The Moment of the Discovery of America Continues

1

I was a child—I don't know how old—when my parents took me to Spring Lake, to a picnic. Spring Lake is a small, round lake, surrounded by willows and poplars; it was the centre of the community that my mother grew up in—in the parklands southeast of Edmonton, a few miles from the valley of the Battle River. I was playing in a large, shallow depression in the ground, a depression that somehow wasn't natural. My father came by, looking for me. I asked about the place where I was playing. He said, casually, that it was a buffalo wallow.

It's where buffalo rolled and scratched, he said. He could tell me a little more—the lake never went dry, he explained, the buffalo came here to drink.

What buffalo? I asked. Or wondered, if I didn't ask. I don't remember now. When? From where? . . . Even at that young age I was secure in the illusion that the land my parents and grandparents homesteaded had had no prior occupants, animal or human. Ours was the ultimate *tabula rasa*. We were the truly innocent.

There was an older boy a mile from our farm who, as we kids liked to put it, knew everything. He was so smart a lot of people thought he'd become a priest. I remember that he could recite the names and dates of kings and prime ministers from whomever was thought to be first to the latest. I asked him about buffalo wallows. He'd never even heard of buffalo wallows. But more: he made considerable show of not caring that he hadn't heard. He was educated.

My sense of the gap between me and history was growing. History as I knew it did not account for the world I lived in. Present here in this landscape, I was taking my first lesson in the idea of absence.

There was, half a mile south from our farm, a ring of stones in the prairie grass. My dad and the hired men, strangely, plowed around it. One day, again when I was a child, I ran away from home; instead of going to a neighbour's house, where I could play, I went to that ring of stones . . . and again I began to wonder. I went back home and asked my mother about those stones. She had, then, never heard of a tipi ring; she said the stones were magical. I suspect now that her notion of magical went back two or three generations to the forests of southern Germany, surviving that long transcription through Wisconsin and Minnesota to the District and then the Province of Alberta. The connection between the name and the named—the importance and the failure of that connection—is one of my obsessions.

I was that day on my way to embracing the model of archaeology, against that of history. The authorized history, the given definition of history, was betraying us on those prairies. A few years after I sat in that tipi ring and cried and then began to notice and then began to wonder, a gang of dam-builders from a Battle River site came by and picked up the stones, and my father broke the sod. If history betrayed us, we too betrayed it. I remember my father one night at supper, saying out of nowhere that he'd made a mistake, letting those men pick up those stones. For reasons he couldn't understand, he felt guilty. Where I had learned the idea of absence, I was beginning to learn the idea of trace. There is always something left behind. That is the essential paradox. Even abandonment gives us memory.

I had to tell a story. I responded to those discoveries of absence, to that invisibility, to that silence, by knowing I had to make up a story. Our story.

How do you write in a new country?

Thirty years after the experiences that I have just now described, I wrote a series of poems called 'Old Man Stories'. I had discovered the literature of the Blackfoot—the stories they might well have told along the Battle River through the many generations when that river was a kind of boundary between the Blackfoot and the Cree. The Blackfoot trickster figure was (and still is) called Old Man. And those old stories are appropriate to the new Province of Alberta:

Old Man and Fox went out hunting. They might have starved to death except that Old Man spotted four buffalo bulls lying down by a slough.

He had an idea.

'My little brother,' he said to Fox, 'there's enough meat by this slough to see us through the winter. What we have to do is this: I will pluck all the hair off you except for a tuft at the end of your tail. You will seem so funny to the bulls, they will die laughing'.

Fox, try as he might, could not think of a better plan. So he let Old Man pluck him bare, except for a tuft at the end of his tail.

First the bulls stood up to look. Then they began to laugh. Then they fell down laughing. Even then they could not keep from looking at Fox; the more they looked, the more they laughed. One by one they died laughing.

'Little brother,' Old Man said, stepping out from behind a clump of red willow, 'you were very funny. I nearly died laughing myself.' And he began to butcher the dead bulls.

It was late in the afternoon. A wind was coming up from the north. A few snowflakes were beginning to fall. 'Let it snow,' Old Man said. He was working busily while Fox sat and watched. 'We can feast until spring.'

Fox made no reply. Old Man kept on talking. 'We can dance and sing all winter. We can sleep when the blizzard blows. Cheer up, little brother.'

Again Fox did not answer. This made Old Man very mad. He turned from where he was preparing the last pack of meat. He saw Fox sitting hunched and stiff and gave him a poke. 'Wake up, we're ready.'

Fox fell over. He was frozen clean through.

2

For a young writer, beginning his career as recently as the 1950s on the prairies, there were few models. W.O. Mitchell was one. His stories of a kid and a hired man came to me as a kind of illumination, almost a vision. We sometimes had a yard full of hired men.

To my astonishment, I learned that I was living in the midst of *story* material. And this is surely a problem for a people who seldom see images of themselves in literature or art: we fail to recognize the connection between art and life. We separate the two fatally. Knowledge becomes, for us, knowledge of someone else. We become a kind of perversion—and witness our universities— a society that is reluctant to study images of itself.

My upstairs bedroom, quite by accident, looked out on the yard; I became a kind of juvenile Flaubert, staring out at a world that I would capture in words. The hired men, in turn, made no bones about telling me I was a disaster, sixteen years old and still reading books, often to be seen in the garden doing women's work when I should be out pitching bundles or working the summerfallow. I couldn't be trusted with a team of horses, partly because of a tendency to day-dream, partly because of a perverse identification with the horses, against men. Useless as the tits on a boar, the hired men said: my first introduction to the problem of language in writing about a new country.

The east room in our upstairs was the hired men's room in the wintertime. As a child I sometimes sneaked in there—I liked to read the stacks of pulp magazines that the men collected or left behind. And then, during harvest, when the bunkshack out in the yard was full, I liked to sneak out there at night and listen to stories of travel, of adventure, of hard times, of home; they were story-makers, those dispossessed men of the thirties, myth-makers. I began to recognize the archaeological sites of my own short life. Those men talked and sometimes sang and then talked again. I became, profoundly, the listener.

Somewhere in my early manhood I encountered another model: Sinclair Ross with his novel *As For Me and My House*. Where I had responded with delight to Mitchell, I remember responding with shock to Ross's portrait of a marriage, a prairie town, a prairie house. He made it possible for me, by a system of contraries, to write *The Words of My Roaring*. I had grown up in a house that was so naturally a part of my family and a part of the landscape that I was surprised, even hurt, when I found out that houses are bought and sold. I might as well have been told that arms and feet are bought and sold. Ross and his characters in his town of Horizon became a generating principle, the enabling moment that released me into a memory of the politics and the poverty, of the card parties and the funerals and the wedding dances and the sports days and the auction sales, the silences and the stories of the thirties. Ross, by some alchemy, allowed me to recognize the binary patterns that the human mind uses to construct its day and its labyrinth. But between the reading of his novel, whenever that was, and the publication of mine, in 1966, came a long learning.

3

How do you write in a new country?

Our inherited literature, the literature of our European past and of eastern North America, is emphatically the literature of a people who have not lived on prairies. We had, and still have, difficulty finding names for the elements and characteristics of this landscape. The human response to this landscape is so new and ill-defined and complex that our writers come back, uneasily but compulsively, to landscape writing. Like the homesteaders before us, we are compelled to adjust and invent, to remember and forget. We feel a profound ambiguity about the past—about both its contained stories and its modes of perception.

There are, first and always, the questions of form and language. For reasons that are not very clear, the prairies developed a tradition of fiction before developing a tradition of poetry. This seems to be contradictory to the cultural experience of most societies. I suspect it has to do with the nature of the experience—in one word, often hard (that's two words). And there was available, to record that harshness, the realistic mode of fiction.

But even as I say this I ask: Might it not be possible that we now look back on the experience as having been a harsh one because the realistic (or even naturalistic) mode of fiction pictured it so? What if the prairies had been settled—as much of the United States was in the nineteenth century—at a time when the Gothic model was easily available to novelists?

The effect of perceptual models on what we see is now the concern of social and literary critics (thanks to such books as Dick Harrison's *Unnamed Country*). I was living outside of Alberta (and outside of Canada) while writing most of my fiction and poetry. Perhaps for that reason I was constantly aware that we both, and at once, record and invent these new places called Alberta and Saskatchewan. That pattern of contraries, all the possibilities implied in *record* and *event*, for me finds its focus in the model suggested by the phrase: a local pride. (The phrase is from Williams Carlos Williams—indeed those three words are the opening of his great poem *Paterson*, about Paterson, New Jersey: a local pride.) The feeling must come from an awareness of the authenticity of our own lives. People who feel invisible try to borrow visibility from those who are visible. To understand others is surely difficult. But to understand ourselves becomes impossible if we do not see images of ourselves in the mirror—be that mirror theatre or literature or historical writing. A local pride does not exclude the rest of the world, or other experiences; rather, it makes them possible. It creates an organizing centre. Or as Williams put it, more radically: the acquiring of a local pride enables us to creat our own culture—'by lifting an environment to expression'.

How do we lift an environment to expression? How do you write in a new country?

The great sub-text of prairie literature is our oral tradition. In the face of books, magazines, films, and TV programs that are so often someone else, we talk to each other by, literally, talking.

The visit is the great prairie cultural event. People go visiting, or they go to other events in order to visit. This accounts for the predominance of the beer parlour and the church in prairie fiction. In addition, we see fictional characters going to stampedes and country dances and summer resorts—those places where we talk ourselves into existence.

Oral history is not likely to go back more than two generations—to parents and grandparents. Beyond that little remains—with huge consequences for our sense of history. Within that time-framework exists an enormous prospect of fiction-making. Individuals in a lifetime become characters. Events become story, become folklore, edge towards the condition of myth. Many of our best novels—the novels of Margaret Laurence and Rudy Wiebe especially—assert the primacy of the act of speech over the act of writing. The poetry of Andy Suknaski acknowledges a huge and continuing debt to the oral tradition. The sophisticated sound poetry of Stephen Scobie and Doug Barbour suggests that print is merely a kind of notation for speech, as a muscial score is for music.

A local pride leads us to a concern with myths of origin. Obviously, on the prairies, there has been an enormous interest in ethnic roots—that version of the myth of origin. But now, in our growing urban centres, there is a new kind of myth emerging.

Again, for writers like Laurence or Wiebe, there is available to our imaginations a new set of ancestors: the native or Métis people, Big Bear, Riel, the fictional Tonnerre family of *The Diviners*, Dumont. And I would suggest that along with this comes the urban dream that our roots are just over the horizon, in the small towns and the rural communities of the prairies. This dream of origins is already evident in Laurence's work. It is already evident in a larger Canadian context—surely it is no accident that the classics of modern Canadian writing are set in rural areas: Sheila Watson's *The Double Hook* with its setting in the Cariboo Country, Ross's Saskatchewan, Ernest Buckler's Nova Scotia in his novel *The Mountain and the Valley*. The oral tradition, become a literary tradition, points us back to our own landscape, our recent ancestors, and the characteristic expressions and modes of our own speech.

It is a kind of archaeology that makes *this place*, with all its implications, available to us for literary purposes. We have not yet grasped the whole story; we have hints and guesses that slowly persuade us towards the recognition of larger patterns. Archaeology allows the fragmentary nature of the story, against the coerced unity of traditional history. Archaeology allows for discontinuity. It allows for layering. It allows for imaginative speculation.

I am aware that it is the great French historian Michel Foucault who has formalized our understanding of the appropriateness of the archaeological method. But the prairie writer understands that appropriateness in terms of the particulars of place: newspaper files, place names, shoe boxes full of old photographs, tall tales, diaries, journals, tipi rings, weather reports, business ledgers, voting records—even the wrong-headed histories written by eastern historians become, rather than narratives of the past, archaeological deposits.

For me, one of those deposits turned out to be an old seed catalogue. I found a 1917 catalogue in the Glenbow archives in 1975. I translated that seed catalogue into a poem called 'Seed Catalogue'. The archaeological discovery, if I might call it that, brought together for me the oral tradition and the dream of origins.

4

On the prairies the small town and the farm are not merely places, they are remembered places. When they were the actuality of our lives we had realistic fiction, and we had almost no poetry at all. Now in this dream condition, as dream-time fuses into the kind of narrative we call myth, we change the nature of the novel. And we start, with a new and terrible energy, to write the poems of the imagined real place.

I don't know when I began my continuing poem. It was years ago that my Aunt Mary O'Connor, one afternoon at her house in Edmonton, handed me the ledger that had been kept by her father, my grandfather, at a watermill in Bruce County, Ontario. Up until then I'd had no idea that my grandfather and Aunt Mary and I were in complicity. I finished the poem, their poem of the ledger, and called it *The Ledger*. But their poem demanded mine of me. And one afternoon in Calgary, in the Glenbow Archives (in the old building, not the spanking new one), in the basement, I stumbled upon an old seed catalogue. I wrote the poem called 'Seed Catalogue'. The two poems spoke to each other. They changed each other. I saw what was happening. We must always go back to the shore. I wrote 'How I Joined the Seal Herd'. But the new poem created a new silence. In a huge Victorian house in upstate New York, in a room overlooking the Susquehanna River (the same river on whose banks Coleridge and Southey planned to establish their Pantisocracy), I wrote 'The Sad Phoenician'.

The continuing poem: not the having written, but the writing. The poem as long as a life. The lifelost poem.

The writing the writing the writing. Fundamentally, I mean. The having written excludes the reader. We are left with ourselves as critics. We want to be readers. The continuing poem makes us readers.

Homer's *The Odyssey*, forever being translated into new versions of the poem. How to do that without changing languages.

The self, returning from the self. Look out, Lookout.

Do not feed the apocalypse. Metamorphoses please.

Maybe the long poem replaces the old kitchen cabinet.

The seed catalogue is a shared book in our society. We have few literary texts approaching that condition. I wanted to write a poetic equivalent to the 'speech' of a seed catalogue. The way we read the page and hear its implications. Spring. The plowing, the digging, of the garden. The mapping of the blank, cool earth. The exact placing of the explosive seed.

5

Begin: Roy Kiyooka, one afternoon in Nanaimo, saying to me: the new myth of beginnings. Listen to them: Pat Lane, George Bowering, George Ryga. Listen to Gladys Hindmarch. Listen to Barry McKinnon, to Fred Wah. It's the Western Canadian myth: the artist from the distant place, from the bookless world.

I'm from a farm, I said, way hell and gone out in Alberta.

I'm from Moose Jaw, Roy Kiyooka said.

Beginnings: there were four grades to a room in the Heisler school. On one occasion, when I'd run out of books to read from the travelling library; I was permitted to go to the library table in the next room. Purely by accident, I read two books that puzzled me, fascinated me, held my imagination: because they weren't like anything I'd read, ever, before. Twenty years later, in graduate school, I chanced to discover both again. They turned out to be Joseph Conrad's *The Nigger of the 'Narcissus'* and Henry James's *The Turn of the Screw*. Recognitions. Like coyotes, howling in the night. The way the blood, then, moves differently.

Beginnings: we had a big farm, the work was done largely with horses. The hired man slept in the east room. Sometimes, in that room, I found stacks of pulp magazines: *Ten Story Western*, *Air Aces*. Stories about Doc Savage. I read those stacks:

No.

I've skipped everything.

Beginnings: I was alone. I was a dreamer. I liked to fix fence: I could be alone all day, riding the fence lines, driving a few staples, knocking a willow fencepost back into the ground. I liked round-up in the fall: finding stray cows in the rough, wild coulees of the Battle River. I almost liked working the summerfallow: the long hours of monotony that triggered my imagination, the drone of the tractor that shaped a world around my head. And best of all, I liked gardening. I planted trees and raised the garden.

Beginnings: I drove a horse and buggy to school, in the spring and fall, a horse and cutter in the winter. Four and a half miles, forty-five minutes, each way. My sisters were busy with their friends. I hated to touch a whip to a horse. Each school-horse of mine grew fat; and in its slowness I learned the seasons, with their birds, their plants, their weather. I made stories. I made stories that were continued, changed, elaborated. I invented a world complete with a town, with farms, with borders, with a river, with heroes and women. To this day I can't walk from my parked car to my office without inventing a story.

Beginnings: talk. People talked where I grew up. They talked about each other. I was a listener. I built bookshelves in my room; I sent off for books that came in the mail like ticking bombs. But there were always those other stories too; the stories that people talked.

Beginnings: a Cree from the Hobbema Reserve. A baseball pitcher. At a sports day, when the team that was on a winning streak ran out of pitchers, it was legal to send a car, driven wildly over the gravel roads, to the Hobbema Reserve. He was too old, Rattlesnake, too big to be graceful. Sometimes he was too drunk. But he pitched ball like a man possessed. I was a kid, maybe fifteen, playing first-base because I was tall and all the real players were off to war. Rattlesnake threw the first two pitches straight at my head: inside curves, coming high, breaking straight at my skull. After that I stood too far back from the plate. Only years later did I understand that I'd met The Trickster.

Beginnings: my grade twelve English teacher, Mrs Aylesworth, in the Red Deer High School. She told me I should set out to become a writer. No—stern, fierce-eyed—she dared me to become a writer. You're always writing, she explained, and I understood that too.

Beginnings: when I was almost twenty-one I received my BA from the University of Alberta and I missed the graduation ball in order to fly north to work as a labourer on the Fort Smith portage. I'd been reading Hemingway, or at least I'd read about his life, and I believed that an aspiring writer should go out and seek experience in the world beyond books. From that first year in the north I remember most clearly being taken to bed by a Métis woman who knew much more about sex than did I. I've never written about that experience until this moment.

After six years spent largely in the north I sat down in a room in Montreal to write a long novel. I wrote a short story called 'That

Yellow Prairie Sky', a story about youth, and innocence, and crops, and weather—on the prairies where I grew up. Finally, I'd learned something about experience.

Beginnings: at the age of twenty-seven I entered graduate school. I'd discovered in six years of not only seeking but finding experience that I had one hell of a lot to learn about literature. About writing. About the experience of fusing words with experience.

Begin again: I wrote my first poem when I was thirty-two. I was a graduate student in Iowa, preparing to take my comps. I had stopped writing verse when I was twenty, because at that age I sold a story, and the sale of a story made me understand that poets are god's fools, and there is no god.

Begin again: I published my first novel when I was thirty-seven. I like to think that Joseph Conrad did the same. My first novel was about my experience in the north. I made considerable use of the Narcissus theme. To this day I like to believe that one must be older in order to begin.

Begin: the body writes the poem. You must stand close to the plate: even when the ball comes straight at your skull. You must be that innocent. First things first. You must come from a distant place, a bookless world.

The tyranny of narrative. It may be, yes, that motion signifies life: but there is also the vast and complicated stillness of living. Do not carry light into the darkness; stand in the dark and learn. Thus: in other myths of origin: the poet is blind. In our myth: begin with the wonder of seeing.

Begin: each morning (*ab ovo*) from the egg. A joyful birth, into the high, sweet promise of rain and sun. Each morning: a blank page: a fearful birthing. We learn to live the two together: No.
I've skipped everything.
Thank your mother: but ask her, please, to let you out. The body writes the poem. And yet you must take the risk, finally, of loving words. Of loving words.

6

Eli Mandel comes from the Saskatchewan interior of the continent, from the literary wars of a generation that had to turn against the Moderns, from the memory of his Jewishness, from the intimacies of his uneasy body. But he is, always, the America-seeker.

It is the paradox of Columbus's perceptual moment that it cannot end. The moment of the discovery of America continues. Its re-enactment becomes our terrifying test of greatness; we demand to hear again and always the cry into mystery, into an opening. We demand, of the risking eye, new geographies. And the search that was once the test of sailor and horse and canoe is now the test of the poet.

In the epigraph of *Dreaming Backwards*,[1] Mandel asks, through Yeats, how we free ourselves of complexity. How do we purify intention? How do we who are already here in America find the astounding *here*? And the first answer, the one that must be resisted, is the attraction of the landscape itself:

> 1
> Marvel upon marvel the berries of the sun
> inflame the tumbling waters of my limbs
> I am given to such visions: wide-eyed
> luminous men walk through a hairy land
> toward a milky glade where goats bleat
>
> 2
> I put away this last unfinished poem
> to think with trouble of a friend
> who wrote me and whose words I scorned[2]

The landscape of Mandel's poems is a collage in which the pictures are placed, not beside each other, but on top of each other; each picture evokes, announces, its own violation; every violation evokes its own parodic inversion back into (up to) surface and the present (presence) as in 'On the 25th Anniversary of the Liberation of Auschwitz: Memorial Services, Toronto, January 25, 1970, YMHA Bloor and Spadina': images of Tom Mix and 'the cowboy killers' surface while the poet is 'thinking apocalypse'.

Or consider a poem as simple as 'Streetlights': 'they're not sunflowers/yet they burn on their stems . . .'

It's no accident that so radical a landscape poet should have found a model in Christopher Smart; indeed, Mandel's violent reading of that mad eighteenth-century Londoner transforms him into a North American poet, into a father (mother?)-figure for the poets of the New World; Smart is the picture behind the picture of John Berryman, betaking himself 'to ice/and death in a Minnesota morning'.[3]

We live in worlds of in and out. Mandel, like Emily Dickinson, enters the labyrinth of our daily rooms, burns through the dross with a vision of such intensity that we are left with a burden of that unfashionable stuff, truth. He dares to be wise, enigmatic, epigrammatic. Like his contemporaries Phyllis Webb and John Newlove, he dares to become the all-journeying shaman, in a time when the tradition of wisdom literature has come to mock itself. He will search the depths and the heights, he, the poet as Houdini, finding his way out of chains, and then back in again.

Journey takes us, for Mandel, into confrontations with our doubles and with place.

The short poem 'Autobiography' anticipates the attraction-repulsion of the doppelgänger.

> every night I dream I have
> wakened to find someone else
> has written and published
> my autobiography
> made of tapes of my own voice
> in words I have never spoken[4]

The figure of the double, for Mandel, signifies his own solitude. It is, at times, the rival for the Ann of the poems; the rival, that is, for wife and muse and lover. It acts out Mandel's own intricate concern with concealment, his own making of labyrinth within the labyrinth from which he seeks escape. The double is, also, the minotaur that threatens the literal self, the representation of our incompleteness, the broken world personified; it is the danger of our completion, in love or death, in politics or family. Mandel is our insistent poet of the confrontation with the double, taking us back to Goethe, forward to post-Freudian speculation. And he is the Canadian who finds always in the confrontation an edge of self-derision, self-mockery, as when the doppelgänger says:

> when I make love with your wife
> she will moan and praise you
> asking you never to leave
>
> where shall I say you have gone?[5]

In his love-quarrel with Estevan, Saskatchewan, Eli Mandel is also one of our insistent, profound poets of place. Lacking in the certainty of a Williams or an Olson about self-location, Mandel speaks for his generation, possibly for his country, with his punning title *Out of Place*. To find ourselves in the present, we must to the edge of madness dream backwards, as did the Montreal poet A.M. Klein, as did the fictional traveller Don Quixote, those earlier doubles for the presenting poet.

In that dreaming backward to find America, Mandel goes to Spain, even as the Italian navigator Columbus went there to commence his searching. In the poem 'Locality' the speaker-poet, living in Spain, begins:

> new year's eve my friend from Utah
> remarks a cubist view of our village
> from his apartment
> > church
> pine tree
> > white tilted homes
> 'our village' I said

and ends:

> late alone I remembered
> it was not Spain but Estevan,
> that home, I meant[6]

The poetry of Eli Mandel locates the complexity of Canadian poetry. The maps overlay the maps. He is at once conscience and explorer, living with mind and body the changes from disaster, into courage and family and love, into disaster. He hears, uneasily, his own laughter. But he is unwilling either not to laugh or not to look. He seeks and accepts the total implications of the lived moment, the occasion of the poem, the occasion of blood. 'The moon has no language,' he tells us. He speaks.

7

Henry Kelsey, in 1691, wrote in his diary, 'this plain affords Nothing but short Round sticky grass and Buffillo.'[7] Kelsey, with his European bias, looked at the Great Central Plain and saw mostly 'Nothing'. 'Canadian prairie fiction', Dick Harrison begins his fine book *Unnamed Country*, 'is about a basically European society spreading itself across a very un-European landscape. It is rooted in that first settlement process in which the pioneer faced two main obstacles: the new land and the old culture.'[8]

For a long time, the EYES did not have it.

Among Harrison's first words: basically, rooted, first, new. Not origins, but beginnings. Origins recede into history, history into myth. Beginnings recur. We often begin again in our culture by moving from one place to another. The homesteaders, we now know, were often people who had, before that, homesteaded. Prove up. Sell out. Head west.

Most of the first writers of the west came from versions of the east—versions of elsewhere. Dick Harrison recognizes and explores the implications. He analyses, brilliantly, early wood engravings of the west. The artists saw not what they were seeing but what they had seen. Or, better still, what they would like to have seen: Eden.

Vico, *The New Science* (1744): 'Doctrines must take their beginning from that of the matters of which they treat.'
     The plow itself was a failure of form.
     The poets waiting for Andy Suknaski to find in a kind of rhapsodic belly-aching a version of form. Eli Mandel, in his cosmic journeying 'out of place', finding, in the double, himself. Those two Saskatchewan poets: framing a choice.
     Framing. By taking away the frame, reframing. Arrest those men, officer, we were framed.

The first prairie novelists gave us the frames without the pictures. Then it struck more than one writer that the faceless face in the frame was the father. 'The disappearing father', says Harrison in writing of contemporary prairie fiction, 'is far more universal than the prairie patriarch ever was, and his range of significance correspondingly broader' (p. 188).

And with that insight he sets off on a re-evaluation of history, language, and archetype as they are imagined in prairie literature. One must read again Suknaski, read again Mandel, read again Mitchell, read again Wiebe. And the critics: we must consider again the landscape of Laurie Ricou's criticism, the landscape of Dave Carpenter's translations of George Bugnet.

Paradigms of meaning, the faltering form: Dumont, the warrior leader of the tribe, listening to (for) the shaman to speak. But the shaman leader was doubting his language. Riel and Grove: their spirits met in Manitoba. Language: the word as EYE. Riel, studying the languages of the Old World. Grove, studying the languages of the New World. Dumont, his gun loaded, waiting for the word. Margaret Laurence: discovering how to speak what she sees.

Something as simple and as difficult as: How to see what Kelsey didn't. What is the nature of prairie realism? What about pop culture in the west? The mountie as hero. The rodeo as folk ballet. The hockey game as sacred ritual. The radio revivalist as prophet. . . . The content and the method of Harrison's *Unnamed Country* point towards new studies. Beginnings.

His chapter 'Archetypes of Ruin' made me remember:

It was in the early 1930s. The hayrack and the team of horses turned in at our lane a little after sundown. There was a water barrel on the back of the rack; I was six years old and that impressed me, not the household goods, the old mattresses and furniture and boxes, the scraps of farming equipment. The man sat on the side of the rack, his feet swinging almost to the ground. At first I didn't see the woman; she was seated, almost comically, in an old chair.

My parents didn't know the couple, but the man's father and my father's father had been close friends back in Ontario. It was that kind of elaborate web of assistance. My mother made supper. The men fed and watered the horses and bedded them down, and filled sacks with feed, and refilled the water barrel.

They were going to the Peace River Country, those two people, my mother explained; they'd been dried out in southern Saskatchewan. I didn't understand, really; they'd travelled a couple of hundred miles to our central Alberta parklands farm; they had a few hundreds of miles left to go. Their children were waiting, with a neighbour back in Saskatchewan.

I was allowed to stay up late that night. Or possibly I was just ignored, in the intense talk that went on late around the kitchen table. And possibly the couple stayed more than one night, resting themselves and the horses.

But one morning I awoke and the visitors had gone. Only then did I grasp it: I had met homeless people. I had met refugees. And I remember walking out our lane, almost secretly, to stare; I remember the literal weight of the sun's heat, the silence of the road.

The mapping. The naming. The unlearning so that we might learn: the *un*named country. How to see the vision, how to imagine the real. I wanted Harrison to tell more about the concept of space, and maybe he did.

The world does not end. It's hard to make a literature out of that realization. But at least the father disappears. And that, out west (as opposed to down east), makes everything possible.

Harrison, *Unnamed Country*: 'The habit of beginnings, of starting again, is deeply ingrained in the western consciousness, and comedy is its necessary expression' (p. 179).

8

The trick is just this: to *hear* a pub. To look at the interior of a prairie pub is merely a pleasure; to listen is to recover our story, is to dwell at the centre again. Drink, one day, from early afternoon to closing time: rejoice in the flow of sound, the building from quiet, from silence even, to the closing crescendo. Or go on a pub crawl: rejoice in the modulation from performance to performance, the nuance of soliloquy and diatribe. But always *listen*.

Glen Sorestad, the poet, the wanderer, listens to the farmers in the Sturgis pub as they 'talk of final payments / and income tax dodges';[9] he listens to the shuffleboard player in Langham who sights along the waxed hardwood and says,

> I've gotta knock one'a them ass-forward
> and the other ass-backward, know what I mean? (p. 10)

Sorestad hears the laments, the tall-tales, the ironies, the indignation, the resignation, the sentimentality—but he hears it all together, finally. He hears, in the beer-talk of our daily lives, the shape of our living.

Our endless talk is the ultimate poem of the prairies. In a culture besieged by foreign television and paperbacks and movies, the oral tradition is the means of survival. The bastards can't keep us from talking. Sorestad tunes in on that survival. We must listen as carefully to his poems as we do to a beer-parlour story:

> One time I drive de fencepost
> wit de sledgehammer you know
> and de rattle, he comes up behind me (p. 64).

The rattler comes up behind you, in a Sorestad poem. At a sound, the ordinary world is charged.

Drinking beer is a ritual act, a sharing with each other of values, of pleasures, of aspirations, of suffering. There is a profound truth in the old saying, 'You don't buy beer, you rent it.' Sorestad understands that. Art too is a ritual act, a recurrence, a recognition of continuity.

These poems confront a central poetic dilemma. On one hand, our language, our story, only uses the poet in order to speak itself. On the other hand, we expect to hear from the poet whatever it is we mean by originality. Sorestad accommodates to the dilemma by coming on low-keyed. He refuses to dramatize his own presence in the scene. Quite often he is submerged in the pronoun 'we'. Glen Sorestad, a magnificent drinker, a man who makes an art of bending an elbow, whether to write a poem or to raise up the barley, surrenders his ego to the voices in the room. Again he is the master of listening.

In this rare abnegation of self, he announces that a beer parlour is a sacred place. The True Drinker knows that to enter in through those doors, off the street of a small town, is to enter a place where time is suspended. In the sacred place of the beer parlour, we are allowed to change identities—in our laughter, in our silence, in the stories we tell, in what we remember from the past. In a beer parlour we are as equal as our politics insist we are—or as equal as the price of draught can make men be. We are God's blessed creatures, seeking a prairie version of ecstasy, sharing the poet's divine madness.

I want to pay Glen Sorestad the supreme compliment, the supreme prairie compliment, the beer-parlour compliment—he is a bullshit artist. That is how he acknowledges his debt and obligation to our oral tradition. Then we, as listeners, can say with the shuffleboard player in Langham:

Should we have another? What the hell
the old man can damn well wait (p. 10).

9

There are these two sides to language: *langue* and *parole*. *Langue* is
the great-given, the sum total of words and grammar and literature and concluded speech. *Parole* is what one of us says, the uniqueness of the speaking (writing) person. If you are unlucky, the
great-given swamps you, and even when you speak, you are
silent. If you are incredibly lucky, and if you work your ass off, the
great-given sounds, not over, but *in* your unique speaking. If that
happens, then you have found a Voice.

'Where is the voice ccoming from?' Rudy Wiebe dares to ask. His
terror at the answer quakes him into a million words.

The voice of the body. There is no voice of the body, only the voice
of the body. That isn't what I mean.

Is the poet more complex than his creation? I should say not. We
invent speakers greater than ourselves. Shakespeare is a small
man beside King Lear. Melville is a quiet lunatic beside Ahab. The
poet is just that person who invents the Greater-Than-Himself. He
does it by finding Voice. He/She.

Listen to the voice of the blackbird, my dear friends. When you
hear not one phoneme, not one morpheme—not one smidgen of
sound—that is familiar: then you will cease to be afraid of your
own Voices.

You must acknowledge the angel's face at your window. See the
silence. Reply to it.

Persona is a beginning. Persona is how, warily, we talk our way
towards Voice. Two would-be lovers. They meet in the tongue.

Notes

[1] Eli Mandel, *Dreaming Backwards* (Don Mills: General, 1981).

[2] 'The Milk of Paradise', ibid., p. 40.

[3] 'Two Dream Songs for John Berryman', ibid., p. 62.

[4] 'Autobiography', ibid., p. 64.

[5] 'the doppelgänger', in *Out of Place* (Erin, Ont.: Press Porcépic, 1977), p. 47.

[6] 'Locality', *Dreaming Backwards*, p. 69.

[7] Henry Kelsey, quoted in Dick Harrison, *Unnamed Country: The Struggle for a Canadian Prairie Fiction* (Edmonton: University of Alberta Press, 1977), p. 3.

[8] Harrison, ibid., p. ix.

[9] Glen Sorestad, *Prairie Pub Poems* (Saskatoon: Thistledown Press, 1976), p. 77. Further references will appear in the text.

2

Disunity as Unity:
A Canadian Strategy

The organizers of this conference,[1] by a narrative strategy that fills
me with admiration, juxtapose the completion of the CPR tracks
across Canada with the hanging of Louis Riel, in 1885. Two narratives, here, come into violent discord. In 1885 the completion of
the railway seemed the dominant narrative, an expression of, as
the journalists would have it, the national dream. The story of the
Métis leader, Louis Riel, with his rebellion or uprising or resistance—the troubles in the northwest—seemed at best a sub-plot.
In the Canadian imagination one hundred years later, the story of
the railway has turned into a nasty economic scrap in the name of
something called The Crow Rates, while the Riel story has become
the stuff of our imaginative life, with fifty-some plays, for example, making use of Louis Riel's uncertain career.

My concern here is with narrative itself. The shared story—
what I prefer to call the assumed story—has traditionally been
basic to nationhood. As a writer I'm interested in these assumed
stories—what I call meta-narratives. It may be that the writing of
particular narratives, within a culture, is dependent on these
meta-narratives.

An obvious example is the persistence of The American Dream,
with its assumptions about individual freedom, the importance of
the frontier, the immigrant experience, as it functions in the literature of the United States. Even the cowboy story, and the American
version of the detective story, are dependent on that meta-narrative.

To make a long story disunited, let me assert here that I'm suggesting that Canadians cannot agree on what their meta-narrative
is. I am also suggesting that, in some perverse way, this very fall-

ing-apart of our story is what holds our story together.

In the 1970s the Conseil des Universités of the government of Quebec invited the French critic Jean-François Lyotard to write a report on the state of universities in the western world. Lyotard's reflections were published in English in 1984 under the title *The Postmodern Condition: A Report on Knowledge*. In that report Lyotard writes: 'Simplifying to the extreme, I define *postmodern* as incredulity toward meta-narratives. . . . To the obsolescence of the meta-narrative apparatus of legitimation corresponds, most notably, the crisis of metaphysical philosophy and of the university institution which in the past relied on it. The narrative function is losing its functors, its great hero, its great dangers, its great voyages, its great goal. It is being dispersed in clouds of narrative language elements. . . .'[2]

I am suggesting that by Lyotard's definition, Canada is a postmodern country.

The high modern period is a period that ended at some time during or shortly after the Second World War. T.S. Eliot, living in London in the 1940s, was writing his great modernist text *Four Quartets* at the same time that William Carlos Williams, in New Jersey, was writing his great postmodernist text *Paterson*. In Eliot I hear still a longing for the unity of story or narrative. In Williams I hear an acceptance of, even a celebration of, multiplicity. The stories that gave centre and circumference to the modern world were losing their centripietal power. As Yeats observed, the centre does not hold.

It was this very decentring that gave a new energy to countries like Canada. Canada is supremely a country of margins, beginning from the literal way in which almost every city borders on a wilderness. The centredness of the high modern period—the first half of the twentieth century—made us almost irrelevant to history. I remember the shock, after the Second World War, of reading a popular history of that war and finding Canada mentioned only once—and that in connection with the Dieppe raid. Yet as a high-school student during the war years I, with my community, was obsessively concerned with the war. In a high modern world, with its privileged stories, Canada was invisible.

Lyotard attributes the decentring to developments in science. I feel that the movement away from the European-centred empires to the current domination by America and the USSR has had an equal impact. In fact, I suspect that those two empires, in attempting to assert or reassert their meta-narratives, turn all other societies into postmodern societies.

Timothy Findley in his novel *The Wars* gives an account of the particularly Canadian experience. His protagonist, Robert Ross, in the course of being destroyed by and in a marginal way surviving the First World War, acts out for the colonial society the destruction and the loss of its European centres, cultural, political, economic. For Findley, form and content speak each other's plight in *The Wars* as the traditional authority of the novel itself begins to falter. He resorts to an archival approach, using letters, photographs, interviews, family history, to recover the story, allowing the reader in turn to wonder how the fictional narrative centre relates to the writer writing. A doubt about our ability to know invades the narrative. What we witness is the collapse, for North American eyes, of the meta-narrative that once went by the name Europe. Europa. Findley's more recent novels, *Famous Last Words* and *Not Wanted on the Voyage*, in their titles and in their stories remind us of Lyotard's observation that in postmodern writing there appears a scepticism or hesitation about the meta-narrative's great voyages, its great goal.

The centre does not hold. The margin, the periphery, the edge, now, is the exciting and dangerous boundary where silence and sound meet. It is where the action is. In our darker moments we feel we must resist the blind and consuming power of the new places with their new or old ideas that now want to become centres. In our happier moments we delight in the energy of the local, in the abundance that is diversity and difference, in the variety and life that exist on any coastline of the human experience.

This willingness to refuse privilege to a restricted or restrictive cluster of meta-narratives becomes a Canadian strategy for survival. We must, in Mikhail Bakhtin's terms, remain polyphonic, and the great Russian theorist was in his carnivalesque way a great master of survival. We are under pressure from many versions of the meta-narrative, ranging from Star Wars to programs like 'Dynasty' and 'Dallas'—and again we hear the shorthand of the meta-narrative in the naming. The trick is, I suppose, to resist the meta-narrative and still to avoid Riel's fate. Or did he, rather, by his very strategies, trick the privileged centre into allowing and even applauding his survival? *Sir* John A. Macdonald becomes a failure, even as villain. Louis Riel, the outcast, the halfbreed, the man from the periphery, becomes, as villain or hero, the stuff of myth.

Rudy Wiebe, in his novels *The Temptations of Big Bear* and *The Scorched-Wood People*, explores the process by which we reject the meta-narrative and assert the validity of our own stories. Rudy, as a Mennonite, the first Canadian-born child of exiles from Russia, living on a bush farm in Saskatchewan, then in a small town in southern Alberta, experienced the margin and its silence and its compulsion to speak its own validity. But what I want to do now is to look at some of the implications operating behind his and similar texts.

In this postmodern world, we trust a version of archaeology over the traditional versions of history. History, in its traditional forms, insisted too strongly on a coherent narrative. Timothy Findley speaks for many Canadians when he uses an archival method in *The Wars*, trusting to fragments of story, letting them speak their incompleteness. There is resistance to this mode, of course. A great Canadian architect like Arthur Erickson is at heart a modernist. A great Canadian critic like Northrop Frye is at heart a modernist, trying to assert the oneness, the unity, of all narrative. But the writers of stories and poems nowadays, in Canada, are not terribly sympathetic to Frye and his unifying sense of what a mythic vision is. Against this *over*riding view, we posit an archaeological sense that every unearthing is problematic, tentative, subject to a story-making act that is itself subject to further change as the 'dig' goes on.

One of the functions of art, traditionally, is the location and elaboration of the meta-narratives. Canadian writing is obsessively about the artist who can't make art. That model is securely established by Sinclair Ross and Ernest Buckler.

Ross, in his novel of the Saskatchewan prairies during the Depression, *As For Me and My House*, has a minister's wife tell the story in the form of her diary. Her husband is a minister who doubts his ministry and who wants both to paint and to write and who succeeds at neither. The book is in effect a powerful novel about the inability to make art—it is a novel as a set of diary entries about an unwritten novel. The meta-narratives—religious, artistic, social, economic—do not hold. Even the great European meta-narrative about 'nature' does not hold here, as nature turns into wind and moving dust and an unreachable horizon.

Ernest Buckler sets his novel *The Mountain and The Valley* in Nova Scotia. His protagonist, David Canaan, is a young man who wants to write great stories and who dies with his ambition unrealized. The meta-narratives of art, of family, of love, don't hold. The narrative itself turns into brilliant and static passages of description, speculation, repetition. The story quite simply cannot *move*.

Both these novels are set on geographical margins—the prairies, a rural area in Nova Scotia on the Bay of Fundy. Both deal with lives that the people themselves see as marginal—in both novels the ambition is obsessively to move into a bigger city. David Canaan gets into a car that will take him there, then gets out when he sees it's actually going to happen. Mrs Bentley in Ross's novel—and we never know her first name or her family name—believes she and her husband are going to succeed by opening a secondhand bookstore in a city—and again, I hear Ross mocking this metaphoric (or is it metonymic?) representation of the meta-narratives.

In both it is a kind of archaeological act that succeeds, against the traditional narrative. Mrs Bentley does keep a journal, and in that journal, without recognizing it, she makes her art. In *The Mountain and The Valley* it is David Canaan's grandmother, hooking a rug out of the scraps of clothing that represent traces of family history, who is the successful artist.

In this model of narrative, the generalizations are tentative. In traditional narrative, a new detail fits into the story. Here, a single new detail can alter the possible story—as when, at the end of *As For Me and My House*—a question of paternity shakes our very sense of whatever narrative it is we've been reading. Instead of answers we have questions. Instead of resolution we have doubt. The endings of both novels are hotly and endlessly debated. While not outlining the debate, I want to suggest that the debates themselves—is Mrs Bentley a good woman or a wicked woman?—is David Canaan an idealist or a self-deceiving failure?—are what create 'unity'. We come to a Bakhtinian version of the dialogic, in which the possibility of a single or privileged voice announcing the *right* version of the narrative is talked away. The unity is created by the very debate that seems to threaten the unity.

Do the provinces or does the federal government deserve the revenue from oil? Was Riel the hero, or was it really Gabriel Dumont? Why is the expression 'The CPR' a curse in Western Canada?

Given the failure of ends, of goals—and it's interesting to look at the hesitancy built into the ends of Canadian novels—process becomes more important than end. The novel that acts out this concern for process with greatest effect might well be Margaret Laurence's *The Diviners*.

Again, the protagonist of the novel is a writer, Morag Gunn. Morag is an orphan. She lives on geographical margins—she is born in a small town in Manitoba and when we see her writing she is in a cottage on a river in rural Ontario. She is aware of other margins—through her Celtic background she is reminded of threatened mythologies and of a language that she has in fact lost. She is a writer obsessively concerned to locate the meta-narratives of her own life and of Canada—and what she finds, over and over, is a set of contradictions, sets of variations. As an archaeologist of her own stories, she finds traces, lies, misreadings, concealments, fragments.

There is a moment in *The Diviners* that has become a touchstone passage in Canadian writing. Morag Gunn, living in London, meets a Scottish painter, Daniel McRaith. Morag had gone to London expecting to find a centre. Instead, she finds her closest friend (and lover) in an artist who is as uncertain as she about the centre. And, like her, he does his best work by remaining decentred. But Morag goes on believing she might still find a centre if she goes to Scotland, to what she believes must be her true 'home'. McRaith takes her there:

> McRaith points across the firth, to the north.
> 'Away over there is Sutherland, Morag Dhu, where your people came from. When do you want me to drive there?'
> Morag considers.
> 'I thought I would have to go. But I guess I don't, after all.'
> 'Why would that be?'
> 'I don't know that I can explain. It has to do with Christie. The myths are my reality. Something like that. And also, I don't need to go there because I know now what it was I had to learn here.'
> 'What is that?'
> 'It's a deep land here, all right,' Morag says. 'But it's not mine, except a long long way back. I always thought it was the land of my ancestors, but it is not.'
> 'What is, then?'
> 'Christie's real country. Where I was born.'

McRaith holds her hand inside his greatcoat pocket. Around them the children sprint and whirl.[3]

One of the important elements in meta-narratives is the story of the place and moment of origin. In the American story we hear of the apparently infinite crowd that was aboard the 'Mayflower', we hear of the moment in July 1776 when there seems to have been no opposition at all to the impulse toward revolution and, regrettably, little toleration for peoples who want to emulate that moment. In Canada we cannot for the world decide when we became a nation or what to call the day or days or, for that matter, years that might have been the originary moments. If we can't be united we can't be disunited. Our genealogy is postmodern. Each move of a generation back into time doubles the number of ancestors instead of refining itself toward a sacred moment. (I remember vividly, as a student, hitting on Lord Raglan's *The Hero*, and for the first time being made aware of the mathematics of genealogy.) Morag Gunn is there but she isn't there, she isn't there but she's there. Margaret Laurence attempts some counting of ancestral sources—and her heroine gets stories from the official histories, from the mouths of the veterans who actually fought in the trenches, from the survivors of the trek from the Scottish villages, from her Métis lover in Manitoba, from the professor of English to whom she is married for a while, from her own daughter who has songs of her own to sing. The abundance, the disunity, is her saving unity. Christie Logan is indeed of and in the 'real country' of Canadian art and story. He is a garbage man who 'reads' what he finds in the nuisance grounds, and as such he is the ultimate archaeologist of that old new place called Canada.

The attempt at allowing versions of narrative might explain the extreme intertexuality of Canadian culture. Where the impulse in the US is usually to define oneself as American, the Canadian, like a work of postmodern architecture, is always quoting his many sources. Our sense of region resists our national sense. I hear myself saying, I'm from *western* Canada. Or, even beyond that— because I was born in Alberta and now live in Manitoba—people ask me, seriously, if I think of myself as an Albertan or a Manitoban. We maintain ethnic customs long after they've disappeared in the country of origin. We define ourselves, often, as the cliché has it, by explaining to Americans that we aren't British, to the British that we aren't Americans. It may be that we survive by being skilful shape-changers. But more to the point, we survive by working with a low level of self-definition and national definition. We insist on staying multiple, and by that strategy we accommodate to our climate, our economic situation, and our neighbours.

Morag Gunn works this experience through by encountering the many versions of herself as artist, ranging from shaman and prophet to fool and clown. In Canadian writing there is little sense of a privileged self at the centre. Contrast Morag Gunn in *The Diviners* with Jay Gatsby in F. Scott Fitzgerald's *The Great Gatsby*. Fitzgerald's hero, we are told, springs from the Platonic concept of himself. Morag Gunn springs from a multiplicity of stories.

At the centre of any meta-narrative is a traditional hero. Canadians, uncertain of their meta-narratives, are more than uncertain of their heroes. We have no 'dearly loved' leaders. The Fathers of Confederation tend to be an anonymous bunch. When Canadian TV producers tried to find an equivalent of America's frontier hero Daniel Boone, they came up with Radisson and Groseilliers. How they thought they would make a single hero out of that pair of look-alike fur thieves I don't know.

The struggle with the concept of hero illuminates much about the faltering meta-narrative in Canadian life. The western story, in Canada as in the US, seems to offer the best possibility for a fresh and genuine story. In the American west, the 'free' or the 'criminal' figure becomes heroic—the cowboy or the outlaw. In the Canadian west, the figure of authority is often the fictional protagonist. A remarkable number of school teachers ride into town—in the fiction not only of a comic writer like W.O. Mitchell but also in the near-tragic writings of Gabrielle Roy or in a novel like Martha Ostenso's *Wild Geese*. In this kind of fiction the authority figure as good guy ends up being treated parodically. The best example is Sinclair Ross's *As For Me and My House*. In that novel the 'stranger' who 'violates' the order of the town is the new minister, Philip Bentley. We first see him when he is unpacking. Or rather, when he is sleeping instead of unpacking. It is obvious from the first page of the story that his wife has the faster gun-hand. 'He hasn't the hands for it,' Mrs Bentley says. 'I could use the pliers and hammer twice as well myself . . .'[4]

Philip is white-faced and tight-lipped, quick, mostly, at drawing shut the door—of his study or of the bedroom. In this truly magnificent novel, the potential hero, Philip, has his role usurped by his nameless wife, the endlessly fascinating woman who, by quietly keeping a diary, creates the work of art that her artist-minister-husband cannot create. Perhaps the TV producers were right in looking for a doubled hero in the Canadian psyche. They might have fared better, however, had they turned to Louis Riel and Gabriel Dumont, those paired leaders who in their division of action and meditation, gun and book, act out the disunity that becomes our dance of unity.

Rudy Wiebe tried to find a single hero in the great Plains Cree leader of the nineteenth century, Big Bear, and in a way he succeeds profoundly. Big Bear refused to be baptized and he refused to settle his people on a reserve. In his refusals, in his resistance to the temptations, he resisted a whole new set of meta-narratives. In a sense he became the archetypal Canadian by refusing to become a Canadian. The divisions within him became the mark of his unified 'Canadianness'. Wiebe makes of Big Bear a powerful and attractive figure who in his defeat asserts his values—and the stories that carry those values. Again, here, it is the authority figures—the Queen's representatives, the agents of the Eastern Canadian government—who ride in from the east and begin to parody what they claim to stand for. In this new world, the old stories break down. The systems of law, being used to take the land away from the Indians, become a parody of law. The systems of writing, up against the elaborate oral codes and traditions of the Indians, become a parody. Justice itself becomes a parody of justice. And yet the parodic forms, in their single-mindedness and in their greed, triumph; in the final inversion the forces of 'civilization' destroy a prospering civilization that was based on a buffalo economy and the complex inter-relatedness of tribal life and geography. The railway, in Wiebe's book—the iron horse of 1885—announces the arrival of a new story—of immigration, of dustbowl economics, of life and death on the reservation—and in this new story, by that ambiguous process we call art, the defeated Big Bear is transformed into an emblem of what the new story claims to cherish. In this near-hopeless separation of hero from communal behavior, the Canadian psyche, once again, both survives and flourishes.

One of the most fascinating studies of the hero in recent Canadian writing is that in Michel Tremblay's novel *The Fat Woman Next Door Is Pregnant*. The nameless woman at the centre of this story is the mother pregnant with the author who is writing the book. She is largely silent. She is almost immobile. To go back to Lyotard's definition, she is a kind of vast inversion of the traditional hero who goes out on a quest and who explores the implications of that quest, encounters great dangers and incredible trials. Tremblay is one of the most effective writers we have in the telling of our urban story.

A great deal of Canadian writing centres on the small town or the isolated community—and I suspect this is revealing in the ways it announces the hesitation we feel about our meta-narrative. In Sheila Watson's *The Double Hook*, the young man who murders his mother in an isolated community in the interior of BC manages to escape from that community to a town where he might catch a train. Again, the ubiquitous train. Again, the train that might offer freedom, but does not. Young James Potter gets back onto his horse and rides back to his community. He, like David Canaan in Buckler's novel, cannot or will not break out of the circle, into a larger story.

Michel Tremblay confronts us with the same predicaments and the same impulses, in the urban setting of Montreal. The resemblance between his urban story, written in French, and that of the English-language writers is unnerving. Tremblay's characters, too, resist the meta-narratives—of war, of religion, of the consumer society represented by the downtown Eaton's store in Montreal—and in that resistance they are kept apart and brought together. Tremblay, like Sinclair Ross, uses the house as the place of this diabolic and heavenly exchange. Ross has two people, man and wife, in a small house in a small prairie town, next to the church which they never seem quite to enter. Tremblay packs his house with generations, with the past and the present, with the natural and the supernatural. Yet in both novels there is, at the centre, not the traditional hero, but rather the unborn child. That child is at once an enormous potential and a terrible, obsession-making absence. At the centre of the story is zero. The story is decentred. All the reality of the story, the speech against the silence, is on the circumference. The margin. We live a life of shifting edges, around an unspoken or unspeakable question. Or, at best, in asking who we are, we are who we are.

It is no accident that the hero of the Canadian story, often, is the artist. David Canaan, writing or not writing. Mrs Bentley, writing about her husband's not writing or painting. Margaret Laurence's Morag Gunn, growing old, still learning. Michel Tremblay's writer, waiting to be born. In a rock-bottom situation like ours, in which the very shape of story itself falters, the artist in the act of creating art becomes the focus.

The nameless woman in Margaret Atwood's *Surfacing* is an artist, an illustrator of children's books who can't make her illustrations match the folk-tales she's trying to illustrate. A second character in *Surfacing*, David, back in the fifties wanted to be a minister and tried selling Bibles door-to-door to put himself through theological seminary. Now he's trying to make a film, with his friend Joe. At the end of the story, the nameless heroine exposes their film and drops it into a lake. By the end of the story, she has mated with Joe, who is on the way to becoming a bear-like creature, and she *might* be pregnant. The story becomes that minimal for Atwood. In making that minimal statement, she has become for many the quintessential *Canadian*, not just the Canadian artist. She locates our story by not finding it. The missing father is the central metaphor in *Surfacing*, the central metaphor in a failed and successful quest that is full of cryptic messages and languages that yield up their meaning by not speaking. Again, all is periphery and margin, against the hole in the middle. We are held together by that absence. There is no centre. This disunity is our unity.

I can suggest other novels that deal with the same paradox or strategy. Michael Ondaatje's *Coming through Slaughter*, the story of a black American jazz musician, Buddy Bolden, who left behind no record of his music. Alice Munro's *Lives of Girls and Women*, the growing-up into artist of Del Jordan, a girl in a small town in Ontario, born into the silence of a small town, learning the fragments of story that make her life cohere. The *künstlerroman* is basic to the Canadian search for and rejection of meta-narrative. Audrey Thomas's *Latakia*, the search of a woman writer that takes her back to the place where the alphabet is supposed to have developed, only to discover the chaos of unreadable maps, languages she can't understand, an archaeological site that yields up only a bewildering multitude of fragments.

Let me end, however, by glancing at one meta-narrative that has asserted itself persistently in the New World context—and that is the myth of the new world, the garden story. The dream of Eden.

That dream, and the falling into fragments of the dream, haunts Canadian writers from nineteenth-century figures like Thomas C. Haliburton, berating his fellow Nova Scotians for their failures, from Susanna Moodie, arriving from England into Quebec and Ontario, to Stephen Leacock, making his comic readings of life in a small town, to contemporary writers like myself. It haunted the politicians like Sir John A., building his railway in the name of a slogan (from sea to sea); like Louis Riel, proclaiming his Métis nation; like Tommy Douglas, again in the west, announcing the formation of a socialist party; to John Diefenbaker of Saskatchewan, dreaming his further dream of the Canadian north.

Perhaps it is the novelist Frederick Philip Grove who most tellingly explores that Eden dream. He was a German novelist, Paul Greve, who faked his suicide and managed his own rebirth as a Canadian writer, as a teacher, living on the prairies of Louis Riel. In his novel *Settlers of the Marsh*, he takes his characters from Sweden and Germany and England, from the United States and Ontario, to the promised new world of Manitoba. Grove, in that setting, shows that life in the new world meant mind-numbing and body-breaking work. And, more than that, he shows, before our eyes, the collapse of the stories the settlers of the marsh brought with them. In the opening of the story, two Swedish immigrants are walking through a blizzard, lost. The narrator tells us: 'Both would have liked to talk, to tell and to listen to stories of danger, of being lost, of hairbreadth escapes: the influence of the prairie snowstorm made itself felt. But whenever one of them spoke, the wind snatched his word from his lips and threw it aloft.'[5]

Perhaps the literal word is being dispersed, as Lyotard would have it, 'in clouds of narrative language elements . . .'

In this silence the two men are unhooked from their old stories, and from the unified world-view (whatever its virtues and vices) that those stories allowed. There, on the old hunting-grounds of Louis Riel's Métis, delivered to this place by railway, the two immigrants enter into the Canadian story. And the hero is, again, two, as if the disunity is so radical that it physically splits the hero. And yet, out of that division comes the discovery of unity.

The unnaming allows the naming. The local pride speaks. The oral tradition speaks its tentative nature, its freedom from the authorized text.

Notes

[1] Tenth Annual Conference of the British Association for Canadian Studies, Edinburgh, 9-12 April 1985.

[2] Jean-François Lyotard, *The Postmodern Condition: A Report on Knowledge*, trans. Geoff Bennington and Brian Massumi (Minneapolis: University of Minnesota Press, 1984), p. xxiv.

[3] Margaret Laurence, *The Diviners* (Toronto: McClelland and Stewart, 1974), pp. 318-19.

[4] Sinclair Ross, *As For Me and My House* (1941; rpt Toronto: McClelland and Stewart, 1970 [New Canadian Library]) p. 3.

[5] Frederick Philip Grove, *Settlers of the Marsh* (1925; rpt Toronto: McClelland and Stewart, 1966 [New Canadian Library]), p. 16.

3

Reciting the Emptiness

An emptying out is fundamental to any making of art. That emptying is at once painful and exhilarating. It calls for abandon and concentration, blindness and perception, both in the individual artist and in that artist's culture as a whole.

I propose to read two portraits of that eliminatory process. One of those portraits is Tom Thomson's 'The Jack Pine'. The other is Russell Drysdale's 'The Drover's Wife'. I think it is fair to say that both have achieved, one in Canada, the other in Australia, the status of icons.

Those two iconic configurations are so complex, so allusive and elusive, so determined to work by encodings that at once reveal and conceal, that I am tempted to lose them in the silence of praise.

It was the Canadian poet Doug Barbour who told me about Drysdale's painting. Doug and I were on the spectacular campus of Griffith University, in Brisbane. His mention of the painting made me remember I'd read about it in an essay by Brian Edwards, who at the same time had mentioned the fiction of the Australian writer Murray Bail.

I come more and more to suspect that art proceeds by quotation and misquotation. I had not read Bail when I read Brian's essay. I found a copy of Bail's collection of short stories in Melbourne. *The Drover's Wife and Other Stories*[1] has on its cover a reproduction of Drysdale's painting, in colour—a reproduction that is reproduced, in black and white, as an epigraph to the title story.

I have never seen Drysdale's painting, only reproductions. I had seen dozens of reproductions of Thomson's 'The Jack Pine' (including one on a postage stamp, if my memory serves me correctly) before I went into the National Gallery in Ottawa and saw the huge original—it measures 50 3/4 inches by 55 inches. It was the campus of Griffith University that made me think of 'The Jack

Pine'. Griffith University is set in a national forest, and the morning sight of gum trees filled me with a longing that I may never satisfy or understand. My pervasive sense of garden itself turned into 'gap'.

As you may have gathered by now, we have entered that postmodern condition where the gap tells us more than does the bridge. The icon itself can be read as a reciting of the gap, a reciting of the emptiness.

Let me quote a quote that appears in Nick Waterlow's introduction to the catalogue of The Biennale of Sydney 1986—an art show that in itself would justify a trip across the Pacific. Waterlow quotes Daniel Thomas, who wrote about Dick Watkins for still another catalogue:

> In Australia it is widely accepted that art has come to us secondhand through reproductions, but hitherto this has been considered as a disadvantage—an unfortunate by-product of our physical and cultural isolation. Now we are beginning to recognise this as an advantage. We have been protected from 'originals'— from their 'aura', their surface and their authority. Furthermore the dot-screen of mechanical reproduction has rendered all images equivalent, interchangeable, scaleless and surface-less: for the Australian artist it has made art in the reproduced form the perfect material for 'bricolage'.[2]

This is the exciting predicament of the artist who works on the periphery, not at the centre. The quoting or misquoting of the 'original' renders it 'surface-less'. The icon is permitted to speak the 'gap' which it is presumed to close.

Waterlow goes on to say, 'Jean-François Lyotard, had he been more aware of Australia, might well have dubbed it rather than Japan "the post-modernist sublime".' I hasten to add that had Waterlow been more aware of Canada, he would have recognized that the Pacific Ocean, the periphery of that ocean, or that ocean as an immense periphery, is a postmodern occasion that begins now to reshape our narrative of ourselves.

But I have undertaken to discuss the narrative implications of these two icons, 'The Drover's Wife' (1945) and 'The Jack Pine' (1916).

In Drysdale's rather smallish picture (20 x 24 inches), the wife dominates the left side of the canvas, the hat of the large woman almost touching the top of the canvas, her right shoe bordering on the lower edge of the canvas. The horizon, very flat, passes well below the middle of the picture, serving to accentuate the looming size of the woman, who stands still, a bag in her left hand, staring out at the viewer. Far behind her, on the right of the picture, is the wagon, and the tiny figure of the drover, tending his horse. Leafless trees, almost on the horizon, divide the man from his wife; more leafless trees, like pegs, draw the horizon line taut.

What surprises the Canadian observer first of all, I suspect, is the presence of people in the landscape. In Tom Thomson's painting there is not a trace of human presence. Or at best there is the implied painter, not being confronted, as he is by the woman in Drysdale's painting, but rather being affirmed in his invisibility. Nature is complete without him, made incomplete by his attention. Meaning, for the Canadian artist of 1916, precedes human presence. The text, as nature, is complete, until the reading act begins. For the Australian artist, it would seem, only a human presence can make nature readable.

In Thomson's painting the huge and looming tree—as opposed to the figure of the woman in Drysdale—is pretty much on the right side of the painting, on the shore of a lake, with far behind it a line of purplish-blue hills. In both paintings there is a vast and empty middle distance. The emptiness of desert landscape in the Drysdale is matched by the emptiness of the lake in the Thomson. In both paintings, the colour of the empty middle distance reflects the colour of the sky. Difference simply will not assert itself.

The geography of middle space is a peculiar problem in these two countries, which both like to talk so much about great distances. The middle space becomes, if you will, unquotable. Quotation of course implies gaps, the quotation cannot be a quotation of the whole, it must become fragment. But here the gap is in the middle.

Both paintings set an almost preternatural darkness against a preternatural light—the darkness of the woman and her uncertain shadow against the luminous twilight or morning of the Drysdale painting; the darkness of the horizon hills and the branches of the jack pine against the giddy light of sky and water in the Thomson painting. Each painting, in its appalling stillness, somehow suggests an approaching storm, the one emotional, the other meteorological. This sharp contrast of dark and light intensifies and repeats the sharp contrast of foreground and background. In another sense, there is no realized middle distance.

In both paintings still another gap exists—between left and right, right and left, in the middle of the picture. The wife on the left in 'The Drover's Wife', the tree to the right in 'The Jack Pine'—each opens a gap rather than filling the centre.

Both these paintings with their empty middles are post-colonial, and speak to us of genealogical anxieties. The originary occasion has gone blank. With Margaret Atwood we have learned to enter the lake in search of the missing father. With Australian writer Peter Carey in *Illywhacker* we watch the deaths of fathers, the search for new fathers.

We need not call to mind any Byzantine icons, with their centred male heads, to recognize the death of the father. But what about that other paradigm of the colonial experience, the mother-child relationship?

Drysdale iconographs that too. He turns the looming figure of the drover's wife into mother as well as wife. But the small figure in the background, the man become child, is hardly protected. He hesitates on the edge of his own vanishing. Where the female, threatening to become mythic as well as real, is about to step out of the picture, forward, into the world, the male is about to fall backwards into the picture, over the horizon. Mothers and fathers threaten to go their separate and isolate ways.

Sex, that reputed conjoiner, is in trouble in both paintings. The drover's wife hesitates relentlessly on the boundary of the canvas, at once tempted and tempting. But is not the man tending the horse, positioned between horse and wagon, now become the traditional woman? Has not the woman at the front of the painting, travelling bag in hand, seized hold of the traditional male narrative?

But what about Thomson's tree? Surely the tree, in this post-Freudian world, unlike Drysdale's ambiguous and disappearing drover, is secure in its maleness.

But, alas, not so. O Canada. The jack pine, here—*Jack* Pine—wearing its clusters of nubile circles, pretends to a kind of hermaphroditic godliness. Proposing itself at once masculine and feminine, it hints grandly, against the plain insistence of lake and sky, at its own completeness. This is the new self-reliance of the New World.

Except that to the tree's right, on the left of the painting, is a cleft in the purple-blue hills, offering an escape—or an entrance. That cleft is repeated in the foreground by a bent or arched tree that shapes itself into an open or gaping circle. In the suppressed narrative of this painting, the implicit female energy is as threatening and omnipotent as it is in the explicit narrative of Drysdale's painting. In both, the male impulse toward a self-contained hermaphroditic condition is resisted by a potent femaleness that can only remind us of the eternal return of The Terrible Mother. Or to put it another way: Hey, guys. Empires end.

These icons speak not so much of nature as nature as they do of the question, How does one quote nature?

The artist, or at least the male artist, in Canada and Australia, insists that the middle ground is unreadable. In Thomson's painting that middle becomes the lake—the surface of the lake that in its mirroring of the empty sky refuses to mirror us. In Drysdale's painting it becomes not the woman but the unshaped shadow of the woman. But the lake and the shadow, both and equally, represent, at the very middle of things, the presence of absence.

Drysdale and Thomson establish iconically the problem: how do we quote the unreadability that is in the middle of our . . . project? I've hinted that the feminist endeavour must no doubt help us to speak the unspeakable. I want to look briefly at two other possible responses, one general, one specific.

Canadian literature has in a number of ways quoted the gap by concentrating on the experience of the migration across the Atlantic. This is a version of quotation that I find myself questioning, warring with. Perhaps the immediate task is to write our way not through the Atlantic narrative, but into the Pacific narrative.

Canada, for all its talk of sea to sea, has been slow to recognize that one of its shores is the Pacific Ocean. There has been almost no narrative that allows us to make that recognition. Alexander Mackenzie, the first European to cross the continent on what is now Canadian territory, hardly paused long enough at Bella Coola to paint his name on a rock before turning back. The railway story, as told by people as various as E.J. Pratt and Pierre Berton, sees the completion of the trans-Canadian railway as the *completion* of the story, not its opening.

It was left to George Bowering, in *Burning Water*, to make a major breakthrough. Anticipated by writers like Daphne Marlatt and Michael Ondaatje and Fred Wah, it was nevertheless he who was able to 'kill off' Captain Vancouver in the middle of his trans-Atlantic return. It was Bowering who drowned the captive Eden, the shipboard Eden, when the stillness turned to storm.

The discovery of the Pacific connection, most dramatically in the works of Herman Melville, in many ways liberated American writing into its own voices. Perhaps a similar thing has already happened in Australian writing.

One of the most exciting novels I've read in years is Peter Carey's *Illywacker*. Carey's magnificent hero, Herbert Badgery, acts out an epic or at least mock-epic version of the switch from the Atlantic to the Pacific narrative. Badgery loses the father who, hauling a cannon across the Australian landscape, pretended to be or was an Englishman—Badgery is something of a liar—and finds a 'new' father, the wonderful teacher of magic—the man who teaches him to disappear—the Chinaman, Goon Tse Ying.

Patrick White in *Voss* tells the story of the man Voss, a foreigner who becomes an archetypal Australian by disappearing into the gap that is the actual place and surviving in its narrative. Johann Ulrich Voss and Laura Trevelyan become embodiments in the shadow in Drysdale's painting—or do they only re-enact that shadowness? . . . At any rate, we have in Canadian history an abundance of explorers, but so far the narrative has surrendered them entirely to Thomson's absolute and 'empty' landscape.

Murray Bail, in his novel *Homesickness*, has his characters become homesick for Australia, not for their many countries of origin. His characters set out, not toward, but away from Australia—and never make the escape. They are, wittingly or unwittingly, embedded in the Pacific story.

But I'll turn to Bail's short story 'The Drover's Wife' to find a particular example of how the silence *recites* itself in Australian writing.

Bail's is an act of reciting and revisioning, of quoting and misquoting. His story is based on a painting that is in turn based on a story written by Henry Lawson (1867-1922). All three bear exactly the same title. Brian Edwards announces the complexity of this retelling when he writes:

> Through Bail's story we read Drysdale's painting . . . and its predecessor text, Lawson's 'The Drover's Wife,' icon of Australiana with its version of nineteenth-century outback life and considerable responsibility in fixing identikits of the laconic Aussie wanderer, whose absence can't be helped, and the battling woman who waits. A proliferation of texts, of reading frames.[3]

In his act of postmodern repetition, Murray Bail insists not on unity but on disunity. He repeats the story, and in his repetition insists that the gap is wider, more atrocious, than anyone has guessed. 'The parody is clever,' Brian Edwards goes on to say, 'deconstructing the earlier story by reversing the main props: whereas Lawson's female hero battles the odds and dreams of the city, Bail's Hazel has left the city for the bush . . .'

Bail's multiple quotation is what makes the icon an icon. Yet he insists radically that the longed-for coherence of the story is not available. The story is precisely the story of its own disruption, that dwelling *with* the gap in the middle ground.

That gap may have something to do with how we do or don't read nature. It may have something to do with the collapsed narrative of empire. It may have a lot to do with notions of sexuality and the erotic in two supposedly 'macho' societies. It may have a lot to do, not with the stories we share, but with our attempts at sharing stories. . . . Whatever the case, I can only conclude my speculations by quoting to you the opening of Bail's own version of 'The Drover's Wife'—

> There has perhaps been a
> mistake—but of no great importance
> —made in the denomination of this picture. The
> woman depicted is not 'The Drover's Wife'. She is my wife.
> We have not seen each other now . . . it must be getting on thirty
> years. This portrait was painted shortly after she left—and had
> joined him. Notice she has very conveniently hidden her wedding
> hand. It is a canvas 20 x 24 inches, signed l/r 'Russell Drysdale'.
> . . .
> It is Hazel alright.

Notes

[1] Murray Bail, *The Drover's Wife and other stories* (St Lucia, London, New York: Queensland, 1975; rpt 1980, 1984). First published as *Contemporary Portraits and other stories*.

[2] *ORIGINS ORIGINALITY + BEYOND*, art catalogue of the Sixth Biennale of Sydney, 16 May-6 July 1986 (Sydney: The Biennale of Sydney Limited, 1986), p. 11.

[3] Brian Edwards, 'Alberta and the Bush: The Deconstruction of National Identity in Postmodernist Canadian and Australian Fiction,' *Line*, Six (Fall 1985), pp. 72-82.

4

No Name Is My Name

In a new place, and in its literature, the Adamic impulse to give name asserts itself, as it did in the New England of Emerson and Thoreau and Hawthorne. Writers in a new place conceive of themselves profoundly as namers. They name in order to give focus and definition. They name to create boundaries. They name to establish identity.

Canadian writing is the writing down of a new place. Indeed, Northrop Frye tells us in his now famous statement that the Canadian sensibility 'is less perplexed by the question "Who am I?" than by some such riddle as "Where is here?"'.[1]

Frye's insight is basic to the unriddling of whatever it is to be a Canadian. Yet it slights a question that is at least manifest, if not central. The interest in the question of identity speaks its presence in a curious way. That presence announces itself as an absence. Or, more specifically, one of the peculiarities of this new literature is the recurrence of major fictional characters who have no names.

This resistance to a speakable name occurs early in Canadian writing. Thomas Haliburton, in a series of newspaper pieces begun in 1835 in Nova Scotia and published together in 1836 under the title *The Clockmaker*, invented the wilful and eloquent character to whom he gave the name Sam Slick. That same Sam Slick, that first great Canadian literary character, is not a Bluenose at all but, rather, a New Englander, a Yankee clockmaker. The narrator of the story, the incipient Canadian (this is before Confederation), refuses to name himself.

The two men travel together on horseback as they ride circuit, one a clock peddler, the other a lawyer. (And travel itself, is, of course, a form of escape from name; Canadian writing is obsessively about travel.) On this ride, Sam Slick does most of the talking. The other man tells about the talking; he is at once at a remove from the action and its mediator. And he is, by fascinating design, anonymous.

We are in Episode XI before the matter of his anonymity is confronted. It is suppertime. The narrator is approached by the hostess of Pugwash's inn: 'Approaching me, she said, with an irresistible smile, "Would you like, Mr—" Here there was a pause, a hiatus, evidently intended for me to fill up with my name. . .'[2]

The irresistible smile of the hostess is, it turns out, resistible. And the narrator gives us a longish paragraph on why. He says of his name:

> but that no person knows, nor do I intend they shall; at Medley's Hotel, in Halifax, I was known as the Stranger in No. 1. The attention that incognito procured for me, the importance it gave me in the eyes of the master of the house, its lodgers and servants, is indescribable. It is only great people who travel incog (p. 43).

He names himself by giving a name that leaves him nameless. He is, or was, the Stranger in No. 1. But even that was somewhere else, not here in Pugwash's inn. This narrator has discovered a version of privilege in anonymity. He is not above a little deceit. His delight is almost naïve. But the lawyer-impulse in the narrator makes him attempt at least a partial description of the indescribable: 'State travelling is inconvenient and slow; the constant weight of form and etiquette oppresses at once the strength and the spirits. It is pleasant to travel unobserved, to stand at ease, or exchange the full suit for the undress coat and fatigue jacket' (p. 43).

The man who wants to be recognized for his importance wants also to go unobserved. This comes close to contradiction. We see here an early manifestation of the Canadian personality. The man who exploits social hierarchy by being falsely named into it wants also to be free of it. He wants to have a system that gives him identity and stature, but he wants to be free of that system. This man is surely ready to enter into the Canadian Confederation. Having created his own coffin and climbed into it, he now manages, by some wonderful sleight of hand, to nail it shut:

> Wherever, too, there is mystery there is importance; there is no knowing for whom I may be mistaken; but let me once give my humble cognomen and occupation, and I sink immediately to my own level, to a plebeian station, and a vulgar name; not even my

beautiful hostess, nor my inquisitive friend, the Clockmaker, who calls me 'Squire', shall extract that secret! (p. 43)

This remarkable and sort-of anonymous man fears that by naming himself accurately he will, in a mind-boggling paradox, sink immediately to his own level. Perhaps this is at the heart of the enduring Canadian crisis about the federal state: I would never join a country that would have me as a member.

It is better, much more desirable, the narrator insists, to be *mistaken*. And yet this same narrator is fascinated by—captivated by—the person who admits to and even proclaims for himself a plebeian station and a vulgar name.

Sam Slick is the double and opposite of Haliburton's narrator. He is the named man who fearlessly and proudly, and with his own kind of shrewdness, speaks his own name. For all his 'soft sawder', Sam speaks direct truths. He is, in a certain way, the carnivalesque destroyer of the hierarchy that the narrator both admires and wishes to escape. He deals in actual clocks and profane time and the randomness and the chance and the poetry at the edge of *law*. The nameless narrator meets his alter ego and both hankers for the freedom of Sam's sly directness and clings to the legalistic indirectness of his own being 'incog'. Not even his beautiful hostess, he says (and her charms, he lets us know, in an extravagant fit of naming, are like an Italian sky, unclouded, unrivalled), nor the inquisitive Clockmaker who, with soft sawder that is usually effective, calls him Squire, 'shall extract that secret!'

That secret remains a recurring theme in Canadian writing. Haliburton announces it and complicates it. His narrator, who is the Stranger in No. 1 and the mystery and the Squire, is also Haliburton. That trace of the autobiographical is to persist in later renderings of the nameless figure. Haliburton is himself, astonishingly, the man of law—lawyer and judge—creating at once the carnivalesque energy of Sam Slick and the contained lawlessness of his status-seeking narrator. Haliburton himself, when he could no longer live with his own contradiction, his own tension, his own dialogic involvement, went to England and became a member of Parliament and opposed the movement of the British North American colonies toward independence. And in his later writings, in a further bizarre paradox, he turned against his own character, Sam Slick, as if that character must be a real person and not his creation.

But Haliburton, in his first 'refusing to name' scene, was brilliantly aware of the ironies of his posture. 'Would you like, Mr—' the narrator quotes again, after his own longish digression. And then he continues to narrate the incident:

> 'Indeed, I would,' said I, 'Mrs Pugwash; pray be seated, and tell me what it is.'
> 'Would you like a dish of superior Shittyacks for supper?'
> 'Indeed I would,' said I, again, laughing: 'but pray tell me what it is?'
> 'Laws me!' said she with a stare. 'Where have you been all your days, that you never heerd of our Shittyack oysters? I thought everybody had heerd of them' (pp. 43-4).

The man who withholds his name himself comes to a name that for him names nothing. Haliburton sees, comically, the necessary and absurd implications both of naming and of his own refusal to name. He is, there in 1835, the writer, the namer, in the new world, come to the old genesis problem, the old genesis moment. Where Melville's narrator could speak so richly and powerfully, 'Call me Ishmael', Haliburton's narrator could only insist, with ambiguous laughter, on having no name.

If we look to the invisible characters in American writing, the invisible man, or the voice that says 'nobody knows my name', those are the voices of people who feel they are being made nameless by others. The Canadian narrator makes him- or herself invisible. And that Canadian is often, as was Haliburton's narrator, from the dominant force or class in society.

The paradigmatic text in Canadian writing may be Sinclair Ross's 1941 novel *As For Me and My House*. The prairie world of Ross's novel is without boundaries—instead of a boundary it is crossed by a railway that suggests a meaningless infinity. The name of the town, Horizon, suggests a no-place that is tantalizingly visible but always out of reach: a version of namelessness.

Mr and Mrs Bentley move into a nondescript house of their own, and are hardly ever seen in the house next door where God seems to be either too often absent or too often ignored—and seldom named. The minister, Mr Bentley, in his inadequacies as a carpenter, is announced as a near-nameless Joseph-figure.

The novel is presented in the form of Mrs Bentley's diary. This fascinating woman, while keeping something as intimate as a diary, never reveals to us her first name, her maiden name, or her family background. We know at best that she once entertained thoughts of a career in music—and hers is a version of European music that does not transport a lot of personal information. It serves almost to elaborate her disguise or her fate, her condition of namelessness.

This same 'nameless' Mrs Bentley—and that is our name for her; she toys with the stereotype of 'minister's wife' but won't name herself as such—is quite possibly the most discussed fictional character in Canadian writing. She, in a sense, writes about an unwritten novel which we as readers must imagine or reconstruct while reading her diary entries about the missing text; the novel itself as a larger act of naming is called into doubt.

Mrs Bentley, while carefully not naming herself, with equal care explores and records the names of all the people and even the animals around her. A major figure in Mrs Bentley's diary, the schoolteacher Paul Kirby, is an amateur etymologist and philologist so caught up in the meaning of names that he cannot get beyond them to people. Her husband Philip, the minister, after taking in a stray dog, bathes it in a mock-baptism (naming), and Mrs Bentley reports carefully that the 'drowned-looking Philip named him [the dog] El Greco—because El Greco was an artist who had a way of painting people long and lean as if they'd all been put on the rack.'[3] While on a potentially Edenic vacation on a ranch she notices a picture of a Hereford over her bed and writes in her diary:

> I looked at him [that is the Hereford, not the husband; he is absent] closer when I got up today, and found that his name was Gallant Lad the Third. His son, Annie tells me, is here now on the ranch and carrying on. As a calf, though, he belonged to Paul, and instead of Gallant Lad the Fourth he's Priapus the First (p. 99).

This might be a clue to the paternity of the fatherless son who is born to a dying mother, Judith West, and adopted by the Bentleys. But it also reduces naming to a kind of absurdity. And the novel ends with still another ambiguous naming act, when Mrs Bentley names the adopted baby boy Philip. 'Another Philip?' her husband, Philip, protests. 'That's right, Philip,' she thinks to herself. 'I want it so' (p. 165).

Mrs Bentley will settle for either too little or too much naming. But she won't herself be named. Like Haliburton's narrator, she engages in vast and devious verbal design to give herself at least margins of freedom, while finding herself tagged as the minister's helpmate in a claustrophobic small town on a limitless prairie. She names her world in great detail in order to keep herself nameless. She is the taboo-keeper, not of God's name, but of her own. Perhaps she is first of all a nameless figure in her husband's world, but she wins through that preserved and nurtured namelessness a complex humanity.

That rural or small-town setting—not the wilderness, but its edge—somehow remains the basic place of Canadian fiction, as if there must be a doubt even about where the place is. Place threatens to become mere space. From Susanna Moodie's *Roughing It in the Bush* to Ernest Buckler's *The Mountain and the Valley*, from Sheila Watson's *The Double Hook* to Margaret Laurence's *The Diviners* and Jack Hodgins' *The Invention of the World*, there is a resistance to centres. The rural or small-town setting remains the test place, the energy source, for those sophisticated writers. They are all tempted to set their stories in 'Horizon'. Nature itself becomes an undeciphered text as the old names fall away or prove to be inadequate or false. And with that emptiness at the centre of sign comes the feeling of guilt about our innocence that is so characteristic of Canadian writing.

We do, of course, have in our canon urban novels. Quite possibly the best of these is A.M. Klein's *The Second Scroll* (1951). Klein was a Montreal writer who had a distinguished career as a poet, as a political activist, as a student of Joyce, and as a lawyer. The narrator of his only novel is a Jewish-Canadian writer-journalist who goes to Europe on a double quest. And that narrator is nameless.

He is sent to Israel by a publisher to produce 'a volume of translations of the poems and songs of Israel's latest nest of singing birds'. That is, he is to investigate the emergence of a literature newer even than Canada's; and again, as in Canada, there is a vast prior literature to confront. But the nameless narrator is also in search of an uncle, Uncle Melech, a great but mysterious Hebrew scholar.

The novel begins (and the first chapter is called 'Genesis'): 'For many years my father—may he dwell in bright Eden!—refused to permit in his presence even the mention of that person's name.' The narrator realizes that in order to seek his uncle he must engage in a naming act that assumes the proportions of a taboo-breaking. Again, the old names must somehow be made new, and the person assigned the task, the person assigned to mediate the transformation (as in Ross's novel), never reveals his own name, almost as if he has none to reveal.

Against this potentially tragic assignment, Klein plays his sense of the new-naming and the mis-naming that are a part of the contemporary urban world. In the process of finding a Catholic monsignor in Rome who knows something of Uncle Melech, Klein's narrator meets Settano, a 'polylingual autodidact'. The narrator reports:

> When after several Scotch and sodas I had ordered—out of pure thirst and nostalgia—a Coke . . . , he had scoffed at me, styled me a typical emissary of the new religion, a sound, orthodox Cocacolian. I had spitefully accepted the compliment and . . . had expatiated upon the beauty of the Coca-Cola bottle, curved and dusky like some Gauguin painting of a South Sea maiden, upon the purity of its contents, its ubiquity in space, its symbolic evocations—a little torchless Statue of Liberty.[4]

He continues in that parody of his own quest:

> . . . and the evening had ended with a quasi-friendship, both of us at last quaffing it down with Canadian V.O. As an abbreviation, he said, for vodka. He then bade me good night, *Americano*.
> 'I am not an American. I'm a Canadian.'
> 'Is there a difference? Isn't Canada the forty-ninth state?'
> 'On the contrary. The States are our eleventh province.'
> His laughter—the gall of the Canuck! the utter absurdity!—rang through the corridor (p. 46).

Klein has an overwhelming sense of the sacred and the profane, of the political and the personal implications of namelessness. His long silence at the end of his life is a painful statement of that awareness. On the one hand he could imagine, through renaming, wide ecumenical possibilities, as he does in the glosses at the end of his novel. On the other hand he saw that we cannot name our brands of booze with any sense of conviction. He could imagine the English and the French and the Jewish communities of Montreal living in harmony, yet he entertained profound doubts about the notion of the self as something whole and realizable in the urban world. He anticipates contemporary anxieties about the very notion of self, and he grounds that anxiety in a nameless narrator who goes in quest of a figure whose name is not to be mentioned. In the course of conducting that search, both Klein and his narrator move through varieties of discourse, including within the one short novel varieties of the poem, of the play, of the essay, of the gloss—not to mention a variety of languages. When the narrator finally finds at least a snapshot of his missing uncle, it turns out to be 'a double, a multiple exposure' (p. 61). There is no longer, in Klein's world, the possibility of a simple and definitive naming.

In that same Montreal, fourteen years after the appearance of *The Second Scroll*, Hubert Aquin was to publish in French his novel *Prochain Episode*. And again, it is a novel whose narrator-hero has no name.

Where Klein's hero was on a double quest, the nameless narrator in *Prochain Episode* is at least a double agent in his own story. He is in a Montreal prison, but has been transferred to a clinic where he is to be, as he puts it, 'submitted to psychiatric expertise before being sent to trial'.[5] In this condition of enforced stasis he writes a story of a frantic trip through Switzerland where he was attempting to serve Quebec's revolutionary cause by killing another double agent, a well-to-do historian who is the narrator's own double.

This book, along with being about time and history and Quebec and revolution, is about the writing act itself. We read on the first page:

> At heart, only one problem occupies me: how should I set about writing a story of espionage? And I complicate the problem with my dream of doing something original in a field encumbered by a great many written and unwritten rules. Fortunately, laziness immediately persuades me to give up any thought of reshaping the espionage format. I also feel great security, I confess, in gently yielding to the demands of a literary style already so well defined. So I decide to slip my novel into the mainstream of the spy-story tradition (p. 9).

He lays claim even to the anonymity of authorship that is offered by an adherence to convention. He grounds that anonymity in a philosophic claim that originality is no longer possible and, in any case, only barely desirable. He says, later in the story, 'It's no longer a matter of how to be original in literature: suddenly I am disillusioned by the question of individual existence!' (p. 69).

Process has replaced end in a radical way, as the title of Aquin's book would suggest. The narrator says: 'The meaning of this novel will not be the shattering novelty of its final format. I am this book from hour to hour and day to day; as long as I don't commit suicide, I have no intention of stopping. This disorderly book and I, we are the same' (p. 69).

The narrator and the book are one in a process that borders on dissolution. Aquin has written a successful description of a total failure—his book becomes the synonym for a character who is not only nameless but who finds himself unnameable.

Yet this version of anonymity generates story. There can only be the next episode, and this is possible because every character or event divides, turns against itself, doubles back on itself—Switzerland becomes a double and a contrary to Quebec; Quebec becomes its Eastern Townships and its St Lawrence River; the victim gives the same account of his life as did the would-be murderer; the blonde woman K (or Québec) sought after and longed for by the narrator might be the blonde woman K (or Québec) sought after and longed for by the historian and scholar H. de Heutz, who might be the banker Carl von Ryndt.

Writing, the narrator says, wins time: 'dead time which I cover with erasures and phonemes, which I embellish with syllables and bravado, which I shower with all my atoms, fragments of a whole they will never equal. I write automatically, concentrating on spelling to avoid the compelling logic of homicide.'

Aquin's hero finds in his namelessness a prison and a destiny, a defeat and a cause, a way of writing and a reason not to write. Aquin himself took his own life in 1977—he postponed his suicide by a day when his wife said the day he had chosen would be inconvenient for her. Aquin was true to his fictional vision. The intertext of suicide is in his books. He blurred the distinction between book and life. He entered into his own narrative of unnameability.

It remained for Margaret Atwood, in her 1972 novel *Surfacing*, to test urban Canadian characters in a rural Canadian setting. Atwood's heroine and narrator in *Surfacing* is an Everywoman figure come to an archetypal confrontation with parental figures, with garden and forest, with the city of the present and the totemic creatures of the past. The nameless narrator begins her story: 'I can't believe I'm on this road again, twisting along past the lake where the white birches are dying, the disease is spreading from the south, and I notice they now have sea-planes for hire. But this is still near the city limits; we didn't go through, it's swelled enough to have a bypass, that's success.'[6]

This woman harks back to Haliburton's narrator: she is like him a city person gone into the country; she is aware of a stronger sense of definition that comes up from the south and, like Halburton's narrator, she is attracted to and suspicious of one of those defining characteristics—success.

Atwood's character enters into a labyrinth where she has not even the reassurance of her own name. Instead of a quest for a fixed and knowable and bounded identity in the labyrinth of the world, we have the idea of identity itself as the labyrinth. Like Aquin's hero, Atwood's narrator risks being destroyed and has experienced the desire to kill. Like Ross's heroine, she finds in the (now imagined) paternity of a child a locus for her obsession: an awareness of the possibility and impossibility of connecting name and object, of putting a name on things.

Atwood's four travellers in their car enter into Quebec. The narrator says, 'Now we're on my home ground, foreign territory' (p. 11). There is not even the consolation of home as a safe place for this narrator. She returns home and sees the familiar signs in a language she cannot quite read. She meets the people she has 'known' for a long time and cannot quite speak with. In Québec, on 'my home ground, foreign territory', she is, like Aquin's narrator, only made aware of a larger failure of language to name, to signify.

'Nothing', she says, 'is the same, I don't know the way any more' (p. 12). And yet she is, like Aquin's narrator, the figure of the artist. The artist is supposed to know the way. She too, like Aquin's narrator, is the artist at the edge of dissolution. 'I can't believe . . . ' is the cry of her beginning. At the end of the book she frees herself of history, of clothing, of artifacts like scrapbooks and photographs and wedding rings. Only when she has made herself unnameable in any traditional terms can she begin what might be a rebirth, a renaming into a valid vision or version of the world.

One comes reluctantly, uneasily, to the question: What is this anonymity all about? What is the name for what is not named?

Perhaps Atwood's heroine is a new Eve, freeing herself from Adam's named world. It may well be that Canadian writing owes its first debt to the model of Eve, and not to that of Adam. Eve is created into the world after Adam has been created—and after the naming has been done.

The Canadian writer in English must speak a new culture not with new names but with an abundance of names inherited from

Britain and the United States. And that predicament is in turn doubled—by the writing done in the French language in Canada.

The problem then is not so much that of knowing one's identity as it is that of how to relate that newly evolving identity to its inherited or 'given' names. And the first technique might be simply to hold those names in suspension, to let the identity speak itself out of a willed namelessness.

The experience of feeling powerless might also be a factor in the Canadian sense of being nameless. American literature is powerfully grounded in its nineteenth-century greatness, in the implications and assumptions of American Romanticism. Canadian literature is very much a literature of the later twentieth century. The nineteenth century gave American literature special interests in and definitions of self, freedom, heroism, society, nature, happiness. The twentieth century, as the basis of Canadian writing, puts special pressure on all those concepts. It would be illuminating to contrast the 'I' of Whitman that can encompass the world with the 'I' of bp Nichol's long poem *The Martyrology*, an 'I' that yields itself to the encompassing world.

In Canadian writing, and perhaps in Canadian life, there is an exceptional pressure placed on the individual and the self by the community or society. The self is not in any way Romantic or privileged. The small town remains the ruling paradigm, with its laws of familiarity and conformity. Self and community almost fight to a draw. There seems to be little literature in Canada that tells of the small-town person going to the city—a tradition that is strong in European and American literature. The principal character in Shelia Watson's *The Double Hook* kills his mother, goes into town to a place where he might catch a train and leave—and then he turns around and rides back to the community in which he committed the murder. David Canaan in Ernest Buckler's *The Mountain and the Valley* gets into the car that would take him away from his small town and into the city—then gets out of the car and stays. The pressure of community at its strongest—or worst—is towards erasure.

But at its best, the threat of anonymity generates story. Aquin makes a labyrinthine novel of his hero's inability to fix on a name. Sinclair Ross's narrator writes a commentary on a novel that we don't have (her husband's silence) and in the process writes the basic Canadian story. Morag Gunn, that busy, troubled, interrupted, procrastinating woman in Margaret Laurence's *The*

Diviners, raised as an orphan and threatened with that version of namelessness, insists over and over that she can't get her work done, isn't getting her novel written, can't in effect put a name to her experience—and we end up having finished reading the novel just as she finishes writing it.

It may be that the villain (namelessness) turns out to be the hero in the story of the Canadian story. The nameless figure who seems to threaten us may in fact be leading us to high ground. To avoid a name does not (as Haliburton's narrator so well realized) deprive one of an identity; indeed, it may offer a plurality of identities. Like the epic hero of old, we might even lay claim to a certain virtue in our ability to withhold and deceive. In a wilful misremembering of Homer's Odysseus we might say, ambiguously, proudly, tauntingly, no name is *my* name!

Notes

[1] Northrop Frye, *The Bush Garden: Essays on the Canadian Imagination* (Toronto: Anansi, 1971), p. 220.

[2] Thomas Haliburton, *The Clockmaker* (1836; edited rpt Toronto: McClelland and Stewart, 1958 [New Canadian Library]), p. 43. Further references will appear in the text.

[3] Sinclair Ross, *As For Me and My House* (1941; rpt Toronto: McClelland and Stewart, 1970 [New Canadian Library]), p. 81.

[4] A.M. Klein, *The Second Scroll* (1951; rpt Toronto: McClelland and Stewart, 1969 [New Canadian Library]), p. 45. Further references will appear in the text.

[5] Hubert Aquin, *Prochain Episode*, translated from the French by Penny Williams (1967; Toronto: McClelland and Stewart, 1972), p. 15. Further references will appear in the text.

[6] Margaret Atwood, *Surfacing* (Toronto: McClelland and Stewart, 1972), p. 7. Further references will appear in the text.

The Canadian Writer and the American Literary Tradition

Historically, both Canadians and Americans have experienced the task of commencing a new literature in a mandarin language.

American writers in the nineteenth century found themselves swamped by foreign books and foreign magazines. They encountered smug critics and teachers who said, 'What is American literature?' They wavered between a choice of European models and the attempt to find their own literary forms. They wondered if they should speak a literary language or if they should try to capture on paper their own uncouth voices. They wondered if they should write for foreign audiences or for their own small American audience. They were in turn defensive and aggressive, apologetic and nationalistic.

Canadian writers in the twentieth century find themselves in a comparable predicament. Like the Americans before them, they find themselves caught between two worlds.

And yet, I think the subtle differences are as important as the similarities.

First of all, the American writer usually thought of himself as being caught between the Old World of Europe and the promise of the western frontier. The Canadian writer, in my experience, is a person caught between *north* and *south*.

To the south of us is a huge technocracy, a world of power. Canadians are aware of power, but they have also experienced a sense of being powerless. This has given thinkers like Kenneth Galbraith a peculiar insight into technocracy. The world of technocracy is a world of communication. But it is also a world where communication, uniquely, fails. This experience has given great insight to a thinker like Marshall McLuhan. The world of technocracy is especially a world of noise; sophisticated noise, exciting noise, destructive noise. Consider contemporary music. But I find in the Canadian writers whom I know personally a peculiar will towards silence. Something that on the surface looks like a will towards failure.

This silence—this impulse towards the natural, the *uncreated*, if you will—is summed up by the north. The north is not a typical American frontier, a natural world to be conquered and exploited. Rather, in spite of inroads, it remains a true wilderness, a continuing presence. We don't want to conquer it. Sometimes we want it to conquer us. And we don't have to go there literally in order to draw sustenance from it, any more than the American had to go literally to the west. It presses southward into the Canadian consciousness.

The settled part of Canada becomes a borderland then, and a borderland is a place of interaction. This is, characteristically, a good place to look for poets, painters—the individual as artist.

The city of Edmonton, for me, is a place—and a metaphor—that enables me to talk about the confrontation of north and south. Conveniently, we have in Edmonton a technological centre that bills itself as The Gateway to the North. I am fascinated by characters who approach the city, resist it, leave it, enter it.

But the dialectic of north and south can be found in many places in Canadian writing. See James Bacque's *Big Lonely*. See Rudy Wiebe's *First and Vital Candle*. And Frederick Grove's *Over Prairie Trails*, that beautiful and radical 'novel', is a prime example.

. . . I have a suspicion that Canadian writing tends to be Jungian, whereas American writing tends to be Freudian. And I suspect that American writing is what I call moon literature—arising out of the Romantic movements of the nineteenth century, while Canadian writing is sun literature—arising out of the twentieth century and the return to the sun as the literal source of our being. But I'm not now prepared to defend (consider Layton's *A Red Carpet for the Sun*, Avison's *Winter Sun*) either of these suspicions.

. . . Consider: the peculiar embarrassment Canadians feel about (before) their own landscape. Canadian writers like to pretend they are somewhere else. *You must find the universal in the local.*

. . . I did graduate work in the United States. From American writers I learned the high seriousness of the calling of the writer.

The Canadian writer is tempted to let himself out of the agony of commitment by pretending he isn't serious.

. . . When I completed the manuscript of *The Studhorse Man*, I sent one copy to my Toronto editor, another to my New York editor. The Toronto editor said to me: 'You've certainly stripped away the myth of the west. You show Alberta the way it really is.' The New York editor said: 'Man, that Alberta is one far-out place. It's all like a dream. It's mythological.'

The apparent contradiction is, I believe, resolvable within the text of the novel—but what struck me at the time was the difference in the two patterns of perception.

I have had the experience of seeing a TV program in the US with a group of Americans, and then of seeing it again in Canada, with a group of Canadians. I will assert this: that while the video tape or the film has not been changed in any way, the two audiences see two different programs.

It becomes a problem in perception.

Okay, yes, our concepts of perception are quite close: in both countries there is a great concern with the problem of identity. The quest, if you will, in much of the literature of both countries, is a quest not for truth or the holy grail, but a quest for the self.

But I think there is a fascinating distinction to be made between the two countries, the two literatures.

In America they ask: who am I? Am I by nature violent? Am I basically anti-intellectual? Am I condemned to go on destroying westward?

Canadians do not ask *who* they are. They ask, rather, *if* they are.

Each year somewhere in Canada a few dozen or a few hundred people meet and sit down together and wonder if they exist as Canadians. This annual activity has taken on the characteristics of a formal ritual. In one hundred years the question—do we exist?—has come to permeate our sense of personal identity, our very concept of self.

There was a cartoon in *The New Yorker* of two men in business suits shaking hands. And one says to the other, 'Gee, you don't *look* like a Canadian.'

Behind that joke is a fundamental Canadian problem.

This scepticism about our existence has ontological implications—it shapes our sense of what reality is. It has epistemological implications—it governs our notions of what we can know and how we can know it. It has immense implications for literary form. As Sheila Watson knew when she wrote *The Double Hook*. As the literary careers of Dave Godfrey and Eli Mandel demonstrate.

(And listen to Mandel on the subject of silence.)

. . . Endings. Someone should compare the endings of a group of Canadian novels. For example: *Who Has Seen the Wind, The Watch that Ends the Night, More Joy in Heaven, As For Me and My House* . . .

Problems: The temptation of the metaphysical leap . . . The sweet promise of the Icarus-fall . . . The longing for the deus ex machina . . .

. . . By some strange process we select the lives of certain individuals as models of our identity. The writer in America can choose between Poe and Whitman, Pound and Stevens.

A few paradigms of the artist have begun to emerge in Canada.

Frederick Grove comes to mind. Grove's origins and motivations have long been a puzzle. The more his literal life comes into doubt, the more we find ourselves attracted to the man. As his reality, so to speak, comes into doubt, he comes more and more to represent our own predicament. I keep a copy of *In Search of Myself* on my desk . . . Good God, maybe he was a Canadian!

But the archetypal Canadian artist is Tom Thomson. He lived between south and north, Toronto and the wilderness. He drowned. Like Knister, he drowned in mid-career. Like Icarus.

The first major artists in Canada were painters. First of all we attempt to see. Sun poets, these men who paint; flying too near the sun. Listen to daddy. Be careful.

Thomson is the paradigm. Of the man who took the risk, got free, perished. Strangely, the paintings of his that we most treasure are without people entirely. And now, with life imitating art, we learn of the delightful possibility that Thomson's coffin is empty. It is the 'if' of his life, confronting the primal wilderness, that intrigues us. The Tom Thomson Mystery. The Canadian mystery.

Again and again in Canadian writing, there is destruction by fire, death by drowning. The physical literally goes back to elemental water and air. Men vanish into blizzards, under snow. Existence and doubt. We return to the condition preceding creation.

There is, in much Canadian writing, a tension between, on the one hand, the desperate need to count, to list, to catalogue—as

Whitman did for America in the nineteenth century—and, on the other hand, the terrible modern suspicion that the counting is being done in a slightly mad dream.

We have been told by various people that Canada lacks ghosts. Ha. We are our own ghosts. Look at Margaret Atwood's poetry. Look at the fictions of Malcolm Lowry, at the novels of Marie-Claire Blais and Ernest Buckler. Look again at *As For Me and My House* and its white-lipped hero.

I used to think that the writers of Hugh MacLennan's generation had persuaded us of our reality. I now realize that under MacLennan's controlled surface is the dark 'if' of the Canadian unconscious. Do we exist?

Or to rephrase the question: must we continually face the conundrum of being an invisible people?

The heroine of Atwood's *The Journals of Susanna Moodie* arrives in Canada and learns that

> The moving water will not show me
> my reflection[1]

Yes, that's the problem. We live with the exquisite fear that we are invisible people.

And yet we are reluctant to venture out of the silence and into the noise; out of the snow; into the technocracy.

For in our very invisibility lies our chance for survival.

Notes

[1]Margaret Atwood, 'Disembarking at Quebec', *The Journals of Susanna Moodie* (Toronto: Oxford University Press, 1970).

6

Unhiding the Hidden

'Now we're on my home ground, foreign territory.'
—Margaret Atwood, *Surfacing*

Survival itself is the Canadian apocalypse. The Canadian cannot die and therefore writes fiction. He longs to be destroyed by America; in his wrath at America's failure he sets out to become the artificer of a possible destruction. It is his only hope.

At one time I considered it the task of the Canadian writer to give names to his experience, to be the namer. I now suspect that on the contrary, it is his task to un-name.

This necessity did not originate with Canadian writers. Heidegger says in his *Poetry, Language, Thought*: 'Roman thought takes over the Greek words without a corresponding, equally authentic experience of what they say, without the Greek word. The rootlessness of Western thought begins with this translation.'[1]

The Canadian writer's particular predicament is that he works with a language, within a literature, that appears to be authentically his own, and not a borrowing. But just as there was in the Latin word a concealed Greek experience, so there is in the Canadian word a concealed other experience, sometimes British, sometimes American.

In recent years the tension between this appearance of being just like someone else and the demands of authenticity has become intolerable—both to individuals and to the society. In recent Canadian fiction the major writers resolve the paradox—the painful tension between appearance and authenticity—by the radical process of demythologizing the systems that threaten to define them. Or, more comprehensively, they uninvent the world.

The most conspicuous example is the novel *Surfacing* by Margaret Atwood. In that novel the three *named* characters, Joe, David, and Anna, live constantly in danger of becoming American. Waiting for the barbarians, they begin to become, in terms of the essential American paradox, the awaited barbarians. But the Canadian who borrows this posture as an account of his condition is metamorphosed into the inauthentic fool that David makes of himself with his speech and his camera, that Anna makes of herself with her mirror and her compact and her vagina.

Atwood's heroine must remove the false names that adhere to her experience. The terror of her journey is not that she, like her drowned father, like her drowned and revived antipodal brother, almost drowns; it is rather that she surfaces. The terror resides not in her going insane but in her going sane.

Atwood signals this very Canadian predicament when she has the narrator say early in the novel. 'Now we're on my home ground, foreign territory.'[2] The truth is disguised, hidden. Camouflage, the narrator says, 'was one of my father's policies' (p. 32). And she too is good at varieties of camouflage: she says of herself as commerical artist, 'I can imitate anything: fake Walt Disney, Victorian etchings in sepia, Bavarian cookies, ersatz Eskimo for the home market. Though what they like best [her Canadian publishers] is something they hope will interest the English and American publishers too' (p. 53). And as she is able to imitate art, so she imitates marriage, imitates friendship. She can fake, has been taught to and forced to fake, not only a personal identity, but adherence to a social order: looking at school pictures she sees herself 'in the stiff dresses, crinolines and tulle, layered like store birthday cakes; I was civilized at last, the finished product' (p. 108).

But underneath this layering, this concealing, is a woman who still recognizes that something doesn't fit. Joe says, 'Do you love me, that's all,' and she thinks 'It was the language again, I couldn't use it because it wasn't mine' (p. 106).

The Roman writer borrowed a Greek word into a Latin context. The Canadian writer borrows an English word into an English-language context, a French word into a French-language context. The process of rooting that borrowed word, that totally exact homonym, in authentic experience, is then, must be, a radical one.

Atwood's heroine burns the drawings and the typescript from which she works. She takes off the ring that signifies her sham marriage, drops it into the fire. But even that is only the beginning:

Everything from history must be eliminated, the circles and the arrogant square pegs. I rummage under the mattress and bring out the scrapbooks, ripping them up, the ladies, dress forms with decorated china heads, the suns and the moons, the rabbits and their archaic eggs, my false peace, his [her brother's] wars, aeroplanes and tanks and the helmeted explorers . . . Even the guides, the miraculous double woman and the god with horns, they must be translated. The ladies on the wall too with their watermelon breasts and lampshade skirts, all my artifacts . . . [t]he map torn from the wall . . . When the paper things are burned I smash the glasses and plates and the chimney of the lamp. I rip one page from each of the books. . . . When nothing is left intact and the fire is only smouldering I leave, carrying one of the wounded blankets with me, I will need it until the fur grows. The house shuts with a click behind me (pp. 176-7).

In the marvellous extravagance of this surfacing, this uninventing of the world, the narrator must finally deliver herself of the notion that she is a human being. Bare-assed she can become bear-assed—in accordance with the outrageous, seductive, fabulated contemporary female vision of what total freedom must be. At the end of *Surfacing* the narrator has achieved a state wherein she might—with minimal help from Joe, who has in him still a bit of the buffalo, a bit of the bear—give birth to her true identity. 'The word games, the winning and losing games are finished; at the moment there are no others but they will have to be invented, withdrawing is no longer possible and the alternative is death' (p. 191).

Atwood's heroine will not die; rather, she will give birth to herself. And, curiously, a similar version of parthenogenesis marks the end of another recent novel.

David Staunton, the hero of Robertson Davies' *The Manticore*,[3] like Atwood's heroine, must begin by confronting death and the father. For eastern Canadian writers, this matter of literal ancestors is paramount. And David, named after his father's hero, the Prince of Wales (pp. 43-4), compared to Absolom, must not so much learn as unlearn family history: be it in the form of a borrowed coat of arms, a family fortune, or the English origins of the family name. His father, like the father in Atwood's novel, must literally be brought back to the surface from death by water. And, quite literally, Boy Staunton (the father) is unmasked: the dentist-artist who would make a death-mask succeeds instead in removing the corpse's face.

Where the larger process of uninventing, in Atwood, becomes a journey into the wilderness, in Davies it is a journey to the old civilization, the sum of our ancestry. And yet, for both these novelists, the condition of pre-history is necessary to valid and authentic birth.

I cannot here examine Davies' skill in taking us on that journey: his use of theatrical devices of unmasking, his exploration of the theme of illusion, his concept of the role of the fool in the unhiding of the hidden, in the speaking of the unspeakable. Davies, the sophisticated novelist, works back to notebooks, to diaries, to confession, to psychoanalytic method, to Jungian archetypes.

What is central is that his hero, David Staunton, criminal lawyer, alcoholic, Oxford graduate, archetypal Canadian fucked virgin, literally goes back into the earth. High up in the mountains of Switzerland he crawls with a mysterious woman down into a cave. He goes back into the darkness, extinguishes the last light. He finds in that darkness, in that womb-like cave, the necessary connection between Felix, the stuffed bear that was his consolation at four, and his bear-worshipping ancestors. The world has been uninvented: by this man, for this man who earlier was told 'You think the world is your idea' (p. 242). And now, reunited with his infancy, with his animal nature, with his emotions—gone back beyond thinking (p. 274)—he finds himself so close to death that in terror he shits himself.

At that 'lowest ebb,' the woman tells him: 'Go on, you dirty brute, go on' (p. 275). And Staunton, his anima recognized, his whole ancestry acknowledged, is able at last to give birth to himself. He crawls out into the cold sunshine. It is Christmas Eve. He is the newborn stranger ready to return to his 'home ground, foreign territory'. Like Atwood's heroine on her island, Davies' Staunton is ready to begin. Atwood's narrator hopes she is pregnant. Staunton is ready to look for a wife. Having uninvented the world, each is prepared—in the manner of the newly-wed couple at the end of the traditional comic novel—to invent a new one.

Atwood and Davies, using the established conventions of the novel, act out this process of decomposing the world in terms of individuals. Curiously, it has been left to western Canadian writers to act it out in a larger social context.

Grove is the paradigm of this larger mode. Felix Paul Greve he departed Europe; in mid-Atlantic he uninvented himself, unwrote his history, arrived in Canada a new self, Frederick Philip Grove, about to invent new ancestors. He is the true trickster of our prose tradition, as Layton and Birney are of the poetic. He is the fool-sage, the holy nut so pompously wise he could unlearn not just himself but a literary tradition, a civilization; he could discover the new form of *Over Prairie Trails*, the fictional reality of *In Search of Myself*. . . . And of his descendants, some of whom might not recognize their mysterious father, Rudy Wiebe is the most central to my thesis. But Robert Harlow's *Scann* is a reckless demoliton of inauthenticity towards an Easter of recognition. And Dave Godfrey, that exiled westerner, has written a novel quite literally called *The New Ancestors*.

I choose to comment on Wiebe's *The Temptations of Big Bear* because here a bear-inspired man acts out, not only mythologically, but historically as well, the uninvention of the world. By an act of imagination that approaches the complexity of Grove's own, Wiebe makes of a tribe of Crees the epitome of our Canadian selves being extinguished into existence by the British and American cultures. Hounded, tricked, robbed, cheated, shot at, starved—we prove they cannot capture us: and then voluntarily we reveal ourselves to be the destroying elements. Big Bear is the poet-creator who must himself be uncreated in order to represent our necessary fate. He must resist temptations to be anything—farmer, politician, trading-post white man, Christian—other than his fated self. He must *talk* his way into his decreated and valid self; he must, dying, become the source and creator of the unimaginable new.

In his talking—in the language of the novel—he and Wiebe decreate the literary tradition that binds us into not speaking the truth. Wiebe and Harlow and Godfrey, like Grove before them, have a marvellous ability to keep the language clumsy, brutal, unbeautiful, vital, charged. Atwood makes a fine Canadian prose style of the run-on sentence. Davies distrusts any sentence that loses its connection to his newspaperman's background. But Wiebe is determined to destroy the sentence itself back to sense, back to its ground. He says in his dedication that he 'unearthed' the story. He recognizes the problem of language: we learn that Corporal Sleigh 'never read a book because people in them never walked in mud. . . . You never got the sense of anyone being downright dirty the way Territories' mud stuck to you in globs. . . .'[4] He demonstrates how the problem of language becomes one of culture, society, identity: Peter Houri attempts to translate, to speak of the crime against Queen Victoria's 'crown and dignity'. Big Bear responds:

> . . . there is nothing true when they say I tried to steal her hat. How could I do that? Or knock it off, as Poundmaker said they told him, by throwing sticks at it. . . . I didn't know she had a hat and I never wear hats, what would I want it for to make me steal it, women's hats are nice but a man would be drunk. . . . (p. 387)

Where Davies invented documents, Wiebe quotes from existing sources, lets government records and legal debate and newspapers and memoirs and journals speak for themselves. The sheer failure of that language to confront reality is both comic and appalling. We discover, finally, why Wiebe is driven into complicity with the so-called renegade Indians. Like them, he must experience the de-composition of the world. He must, whatever the cost, go Indian himself.

It is possible that the old obsessive notion of identity, of ego, is itself a spent fiction, that these new writers are discovering something essentially new, something essential not only to Canadians but to the world they would uncreate. Whatever the case, they dare that ultimate *contra-diction*: they uncreate themselves into existence. Like Heidegger, they will accept that the root meaning of the word truth is un-concealing, dis-closing, dis-covering, unhiding. Or, to put it in prairie terms, they will, like Rudy Wiebe's Big Bear, even when locked up in the Stony Mountain pen, with the Archbishop generously in attendance—even then they will be loyal to their own first visions. Offered the consolation and pride of the old names, they will 'decline to be christened'.

Notes

[1]Martin Heidegger, *Poetry, Language, Thought*, tr. Albert Hofstadter (New York: Harper & Row, 1971), p. 23. I am indebted to my colleague William V. Spanos for his illuminating discussion of Heidegger's use of the Greek word *aletheia*.

[2]Margaret Atwood, *Surfacing* (Toronto: McClelland & Stewart, 1972), p. 11. Further references will appear in the text.

[3]Robertson Davies, *The Manticore* (Toronto: Macmillan, 1972), p. 242

[4]Rudy Wiebe, *The Temptations of Big Bear* (Toronto: McClelland & Stewart, 1973), p. 272. Further references will appear in the text.

7

Beyond Nationalism: A Prologue

Hearing the silence of the world, the failure of the world to announce meaning, we tell stories. 'Once upon a time there was . . .' 'In the village of —— in the year 183– . . . .' 'Tonight, as I drive home, a woman in a blue Volvo. . . .' We tell stories and then, hearing our stories told, we ask if their meaning is in the content, or in the telling itself. As critics we elaborate the doubt that our stories were intended to contain.

Criticism, as an extension of the text, liberates the text into its own potential. But this critical search for meaning is, as Wolfgang Iser reminds us in *The Act of Reading*, 'considerably influenced by historical norms, even though this influence is quite unconscious'.[1] In our time part of that historical norm is the actual writer, standing by, slightly uneasy, somewhat exhausted, not a little uncertain, reluctantly paying attention. The author as reader, having heard the critics, meditates on an extension of the text that is only marginally his. And yet it is that very *margin* that reconnects him with the world.

Canadian writing itself, in the past decade, has been obsessed with intimating that connection to readers and critics and to other cultures; in novel after novel, the quest is, implicitly or even explicitly, genealogical.

Genealogy is a primary version of narrative. Begat begat begat. Characters in Margaret Laurence's *The Diviners* and Robertson Davies' *The Manticore* and Jack Hodgins' *The Invention of the World* conduct searches in Europe for lines of ancestry. A number of novelists find new ancestors in Africa or in the Native history and myths of North America. Michael Ondaatje and Daphne Marlatt return to Asia for those lines of descent, and write down the literal world as a version of art. A.M. Klein, in *The Second Scroll* (1951), anticipates all these quests (a kind of reverse migration) with a quest that is religious and political and formal in its implications.

The nature of the genealogical patterns, when tested by journey and quest, becomes more and more elaborate, more nearly a maze. Janet Giltrow points to a model in travel narrative;[2] and one could place beside her maternal nineteenth-century settler's wife (Susanna Moodie) the paternal and mapping and bargaining figure of the trader-explorer David Thompson. There is no single source; rather, a multiplying of possibilities.

The compounding of genealogical relationship, in the Canadian novel of the seventies, manifests itself in complex narrative structure; this becomes the dominant characteristic in a series of major novels: Dave Godfrey, *The New Ancestors* (1970); Rudy Wiebe, *The Temptations of Big Bear* (1973); Margaret Laurence, *The Diviners* (1974); Audrey Thomas, *Blown Figures* (1974); Michael Ondaatje, *Coming Through Slaughter* (1976); and Jack Hodgins, *The Invention of the World* (1977).

In these novels we have not only myriad embedded stories, but also embedded voices. We have Conradian complexities that cause a Marlow figure to hesitate in his narrative. The voices threaten to override the voice. The moral and intellectual and emotional complexities refuse the coercion of a 'sane' speaking. Like the apprehending (and apprehensive) speaker in *Coming Through Slaughter*, losing his voice in the voice of Buddy Bolden, the would-be organizing centre can only say: 'My fathers were those who put their bodies over barbed wire. For me. To slide over into the region of hell. Through their sacrifice they seduced me into the game.'[3]

Our genealogies are the narratives of a discontent with a history that lied to us, violated us, erased us even. We wish to locate our dislocation, and to do so we must confront the impossible sum of our traditions. Like the Spanish-American writers from whom we presently learn so much, we recognize that we can be freed into our own lives only by terrible and repeated acts of perception. We are envious of the huge, ragged, contradictory visions of Borges or Márquez or Fuentes or Llosa or Cortazar.

Michel Foucault, speaking of Nietzsche's friend Paul Ree, says:

He assumed that words had kept their meaning, that desires still pointed in a single direction, and that ideas retained their logic;

and he ignored the fact that the world of speech and desires has known invasions, struggles, plundering, disguises, ploys. From these elements, however, genealogy retrieves an indispensable restraint; it must record the singularity of events outside of any monotonous finality; it must seek them in the most unpromising places, in what we tend to feel is without history—in sentiments, love, conscience, instincts; it must be sensitive to their recurrence, not in order to trace the gradual curve of their evolution, but to isolate the different scenes, where they engaged in different roles. Finally, genealogy must define those instances where they are absent, the moment when they remained unrealized . . . . [4]

The words have changed meaning for the Canadian writer; the desires have multiplied their directions. The task of criticism, now, is to examine those changes and those new directions without recourse to an easy version of national definition, and without easy recourse to old vocabularies. And the paradox is, again, that from the recognition of difference (or occasion, or signature) comes the illumination outward, as is suggested by the fictions themselves.

The figure of the artist is obsessively present in Canadian writing; the *künstlerroman* is, often, its sub-genre. In the beginning is the artist, beginning. With the difference that in Canadian writing the artist-figure is often a woman.

From the nameless (Mrs Bentley) narrator of Sinclair Ross's *As For Me and My House* (1941), female and male-obsessed and male-consuming, to Audrey Thomas's self-surrogate in *Latakia* (1979), female and writing-obsessed and male-devouring, we see the woman as the powerful artist-figure; we see the strong woman, busily writing a journal or a diary or letters, conniving the world into shape and existence, the man in the study or the bedroom or the bathroom, drawing failed pictures or pretending to write, white-lipped or crying, dreaming of his pipe or masturbating while he thinks of his 'wife', needing monotonously to be humoured or genitally 'suckled' in a parody of the nurturing source.

The nameless female narrator in Margaret Atwood's *Surfacing*, the false artist becoming the true artist, has minimal need of her Joe. The novelist-woman in *The Diviners* has a lover who is never at home, thank heavens. And in Alice Munro's *Lives of Girls and Women*, a deliberate parallel to (and parody of) Joyce's *Portrait*, the incipient woman novelist talks a lot about sex, but is 'saved' from relationships.

Ross's Mrs Bentley invents a contrary other in the figure of Judith West. Thomas's Rachel invents a failed female artist in her lover's wife. In the love triangle that leads to the writing act, the male is ultimately ineffectual, the 'other woman' doomed.

Ernest Buckler's *The Mountain and the Valley* offers us the most persuasive portrait of the young *man* as artist. But even in that novel, the accomplished artist, the artist who completes a work, is not David Canaan but, rather, his grandmother.

These succeeding female artists dwell, to a remarkable extent, in rural worlds, worlds that border on the pastoral—suggesting a concern with two subjects only: love and art. This domination of the pastoral scene by women, in Canadian writing, dates back at least to the whining and bitching figure of Susanna Moodie. Today it places Canadian writing in a position of moral leadership at an international level.

If Stendhal established the model of the bright young man from the provinces going on to success in the city, it is Canadian novelists like Munro and Atwood and Laurence who give us the bright young woman going forward on that journey, towards an uneasy urban success. But the story seldom actually takes us into the city. This is one of those places, spoken of by Foucault, where genealogy must define an absence. Unlike American literature, with its elaborate conventions of the city as nightmare, Canadian writing treats the city as an invisible presence. The stories are written for urban audiences; the metaphoric base is adamantly rural or small-town.

The place of Canadian fiction is a house, an isolated community, and Sheila Watson in *The Double Hook* (1959) announces both as paradigmatic. In these places the self is imagined as a contextual stance (sub-stance, in-stance); familiarity is the norm, or would seem to be the norm. In the city the strange is the norm. But inversions assert themselves, on this double hook. We somehow know the stranger. We misread the familiar.

Canadians are supremely at home when they travel. The departure and initiation and return of travel literature is basic to the narrative mode; the urban figures in Canadian literature, when we actually encounter them (in Davies, in Thomas, in Atwood, in Mordecai Richler) are, typically, travelling.

The force that brings together the two models, the small place and the impulse to travel, is the quarrel with Eden. Since Columbus and Cortés, the Americas have been caught in the Eden quest (be it for something that was lost or something that is to be found), and with it comes, always, the question of originality. *Origin*ality.

Hodgins' *The Invention of the World* is an elaborate search through multiplying counterfeits for some semblance of the real thing. Thomas's *Latakia* takes us to the earliest of alphabets (Ugaritic; in Syria), only to find it lost in an archaeological scrap heap of artifacts and languages and men and gods; Rachel's eastward quest (contrary to the westward longing of so much North American literature) leads only to her (now lost) lover's cryptic 'That's nonsense', and her own writing-down of the immensity of the found losses.

Hubert Aquin, in *Prochain Episode*, his hero a prisoner and a mental patient become a writer, confronts the absolute tension between the dream of doing something totally original and the fact that he must do it in one of the most rigid of narrative forms, the espionage story. Aquin, his hero travelling, seeking versions of Eden, a hero able to imagine but unable to act out the moment of revolution that would create a zero point, a beginning place, an easy definition, a time that both announced and stopped time, turns the Canadian into the hero of the contemporary world and Canada into its metaphor.

Canadians seek the lost and everlasting moment when chaos and order were synonymous. They seek that timeless split-second in time when the one, in the process of becoming the other, was itself the other. The city of such dreams is unrealizable; the poem of the occasion becomes the unendable long poem such as bp Nichol's brilliant irresolution of resolution, *The Martyrology*, or Margaret Atwood's elegiac hymn to survival, *The Journals of Susanna Moodie*.

The escape from definition excites the Canadian beyond all reason. He is the American who is contrary to the American. He is the questing figure with the blurred photograph of what he must find gripped firmly in his hands, as in Klein's *The Second Scroll*. He is the agglomerate self of all those novels that hear the multiplicity of voices. He is the figure of Odysseus answering 'Nobody' to Polyphemus' life-and-death question.

Two consequences attest to the ambiguities inherent in this response.

On the one hand: our concern with self-mockery and self-parody. The self-revelation of self-mockery. The self-protection. The *fool* self that Mrs Bentley both approaches and denies. The distrust of heroics; the imitation that turns to mimicry. . . . The ending of Munro's *Lives of Girls and Women*, where Bobby Sherriff, supposedly mad, is serving real cake in his real house to the young woman who is about to become a fiction writer: he takes her fork, her napkin, her empty plate: and then 'he did the only special thing he ever did for me. With those things in his hands, he rose on his toes like a dancer, like a plump ballerina.'[5]

The 'madman', come to a powerless wisdom, speaks his enigmatic dance. This in a final chapter called 'Epilogue: The Photographer'. And the young woman, watching Bobby Sherriff's androgynous[6] victory, has already decided: 'I would try to make lists'(p. 249).

On the other hand: documentation. The lists of names. The family records. The snapshots that at once announce genealogy and preclude finality. The pretense of authority is mocked, done away with by the amateur 'take'. The *snapshot* suggests the local, it suggests the magic of recovery, the metaphysics of time stopped, the validation of art by art denied. And it admits, through its lack of intentionality, that even in knowing we cannot know.

Foucault says that '[g]enealogy is gray, meticulous, and patiently documentary'.[7] It is a naming act, but in a special way: the documentary act precludes all generalization. Document opens up the site; it is the archaeological act that resists the overarching generalization of history.

From the elaborate documents of *The Temptations of Big Bear* to the real or imagined documents of Timothy Findley's *The Wars* to the imagined documents of *The Invention of the World*—the lesson is always the same. A reading of the world is at best a misreading of the world.

How does narrative mean?

To proceed by indirection: that meaning-obsessed novel *The Mountain and the Valley*, that story of the novelist looking for both the tale and the teller, is framed not only by the grandmother's rug but also by a recurring word.

Three times in the opening chapter, David Canaan replies to his grandmother's questions (What are you looking at? What are you doing? What do you see?): 'Nothing.' At the end of the novel the grandmother repeats her questions. Her grandson replies, again: 'Nothing.'[8]

Against this nothing Buckler posits a vision that might include the whole of human activity. He announces supremely the predicament we are in: we might exist in a cosmology that is so detailed and complete it enables us to read each object and act and expression not simply as metaphor but as symbol. Or we might live in a world that means *nothing*.

The novel, after Flaubert's word for word (not word for world) telling (a novel, ideally, about nothing), had a crisis about its own story.⁹ Daphne Marlatt turns that crisis into the stuff of her writing, and in the process, in the phenomenology of process, comes close to rejecting concepts of character and plot. She attempts a violent documentation of the perceiving body. And yet, even so radical book as *Zócalo* is, finally, a travel book, a journey into Mexico in search of narrative itself.

The question of identity is not exactly the Canadian question. That is an interpretive matter for people who already have their story. We ask, rather, what is the narrative of us? We continue to have a crisis about our own story. The very ability to see ourselves is based on the narrative mode: the I telling a story of I, of we, of the they who mirror us. We name, from the world's story-body, the recurrences and obsessions and strategies that become, in turn, the naming of a culture called Canada.

The woman's story leads often to the failure of that classical ending, marriage. In *Lives of Girls and Women*, in *The Diviners*, in *Latakia*, we end with the woman alone. The writing woman, alone, writing. The genealogy that will not allow easy resolution.

Marriage is the model for an ending in *The Invention of the World*; but the ceremony of the wedding is parodic, and death (Horseman) takes the bride and groom for a ride. Parody becomes a way into ending. The ending of Rudy Wiebe's *Big Bear*, unwittingly perhaps, parodies the novel's own moral and historical ambitions. The ending of Martha Ostenso's *Wild Geese* begins one marriage, but obliterates another.

It is no accident that a number of Canadian novels announce an indebtedness to the model of detective fiction, with its promise of a wrap-up ending, a solution, an untangling, a resolution of mystery.

In *The Manticore* we begin with the question, 'Who killed Boy Staunton?' The criminal-lawyer hero leads us into the genealogical maze of all our lines of *descent*. In *Coming Through Slaughter* (with its birth and death title) we hear the question, Who or what killed that 'first' artist, Buddy Bolden? And we are told, at the end, cryptically, that indeed ('There are no prizes.') there are no teleologies that shape our endlessness. In Aquin's *Prochain Episode* the question of who killed whom becomes the question of who couldn't kill whom; the failed secret agent (again, back to Conrad) is sitting in a jail that has become a mental asylum, and he is either writing down or making up the story of his search for his story.

Canadian writing takes place between the vastness of (closed) cosmologies and the fragments found in the (open) field of the archaeological site. It is a literature of dangerous middles. It is a literature that, compulsively seeking its own story (and to be prophetic after all: this will still be the case a century from now) comes compulsively to a genealogy that refuses origin, to a genealogy that speaks instead, and anxiously, and with a generous reticence, the nightmare and the welcome dream of Babel.

Notes

[1] Wolfgang Iser, *The Act of Reading: A Theory of Aesthetic Response* (Baltimore and London: Johns Hopkins University Press, 1978), p. 3.

[2] See 'Painful experience in a Distant Land', *Mosaic* 14:2 (Spring 1981), pp. 131-44.

[3] Michael Ondaatje, *Coming Through Slaughter* (Toronto: Anansi, 1976), p. 95.

[4] Michel Foucault, *Language, Counter-Memory, Practice: Selected Essays and Interviews*, ed. with an introduction by Donald F. Bouchard, trans. Donald F. Bouchard and Sherry Simon (Ithaca: Cornell University Press, 1977), pp. 139-40.

[5] Alice Munro, *Lives of Girls and Women* (New York: McGraw Hill, 1971), p. 249.

[6] The ex-rodeo star, Laura, in Ross's *As For Me and My House*, anticipates the recurring androgynous figure in contemporary Canadian writing. Long before the appearence of Ross's novel, David Thompson, in his *Travels*, built climactically towards his encounter with the Indian prophetess who comes into his camp, 'apparently a young man, well dressed in leather, carrying a bow and arrows. . . .' These two women are among the first of the celestial hitchhikers who travel the wildernesses of North America, be they Kerouac's sexually ambiguous heroes or the cowgirls and whooping cranes of Tom Robbins' *Even Cowgirls Get the Blues*.

[7] Foucault, p. 139.

[8]Three decades later, Hodgins, at the end of the 'Maggie' chapter in *The Invention of the World*, has Danny Holland ask if he should go or stay:

'It doesn't matter,' Maggie said.

'What does that mean?' Holland said.

'Nothing,' Maggie said. 'There's beer in the fridge if you want it. Have one if you like, but it doesn't matter' (p. 65).

[9]After the foregrounding of language out of context, perhaps we are tempted to foreground story out of context. One has an uneasy feeling at times, reading Márquez or Hodgins, that the world invented (or even, with more attractive connotations, 'created') is a world lost.

8

The Fear of Women in Prairie Fiction: An Erotics of Space

How do you make love in a new country?

In an allegorical passage in Willa Cather's novel *My Antonia*, we learn that two men who batch together on the Nebraska plains are the same Pavel and Peter who, leaving a wedding party in Russia, fed the bride to the pursuing wolves. Pavel tells his story to the newly arrived immigrant Mr Shimerda, and shortly thereafter dies. The survivor, Peter, kisses his cow goodbye, eats at one sitting his entire winter supply of melons, and goes off to cook in a railway construction camp where gangs of Russians are employed.

Young Antonia translates the story of the devoured bride from its European languages into American, from adulthood into childhood, for her willing but naïve listener, Jim Burden. She is, it turns out, posing for the potential writer and the potential culture of the Great Central Plains the question: How do you make love in a new country?

In a paradoxical way, stories—more literally, books—contain the answer. How do you establish any sort of *close* relationship in a landscape—in a physical situation—whose primary characteristic is *distance*? The telling of story—more literally, the literal closedness of a book—might be made to (paradoxically again) contain space.

Already the metaphor of sex, uneasily, intrudes. We conceive of external space as male, internal space as female. More precisely, the penis: external, expandable, expendable; the vagina: internal, eternal. The maleness verges on mere absence. The femaleness verges on mystery: it is a space that is not a space. External space is the silence that needs to speak, or that needs to be spoken. It is male. The having spoken is the book. It is female. It is closed.

How do you make love in a new country?

Most books contain the idea of world. Not all contain the idea of book. In those that contain both we get a sense of how book and world have intercourse. Two such novels are Willa Cather's *My Antonia* and Sinclair Ross's *As For Me and My House*. As paradigmatic texts in the literature of the western plains, they discover its guises and its duplicities, its anxieties and its accomplishments. They offer, finally, an erotics of space.

Both fictions begin by pretending not to be fictions; they conceal their artfulness by denying it. Cather's novel is supposedly an unpublished manuscript, a personal reminiscence left with a friend who might be male or female, who might be Willa Cather herself or a character from the town in the reminiscence. Ross's novel is supposedly a diary kept by the wife of a man who either was or wanted to be an artist—but who failed, certainly, to write the book that he wanted to write. This same failed book appears in many guises in Western Canadian—if not Western American—writing: the failure of white man's discourse in Rudy Wiebe's *Big Bear*, the anxiety about divination in Margaret Laurence's *The Diviners*; or, farther west, the encounter with muse and book in Robert Harlow's *Scann*. And possibly speaking the concealed message for all of them is Lowry's *Under the Volcano* and Geoffrey Firmin's failure to write the book that would restore magic to a forsaken world and, thereby, potency in the face of the vengeful bride.

Willa Cather's male narrator, Jim Burden, recognizes that he is somehow up against a bride-muse figure who cannot find an adequate mate. Guided by the scholar and teacher Gaston Cleric, he reads the 'Georgics' and meditates on Virgil's statement: 'for I shall be the first, if I live, to bring the Muse into my country.' Then he meets Lena Lingard, there in Lincoln, and is reminded of the laughter of the other immigrant daughters—the hired girls—in Black Hawk. 'It came over me,' he said, 'as it had never done before, the relation between girls like those and the poetry of Virgil. If there were no girls like them in the world, there would be no poetry.'[1]

But how to make love in a new country?

Gaston Cleric, the failed poet—the poet, incidentally, who talked his talent away—discovers that young Jim is spending time with Lena. 'You won't do anything here now,' he warns Jim, 'you should either quit school and go to work, or change your college and begin again in earnest. You won't recover yourself while you are playing about with this handsome Norwegian. Yes, I've seen her with you in the theatre. She's very pretty, and perfectly irresponsible, I should judge' (p. 289).

That perfect irresponsibility might have been the making of a poet. Jim Burden, instead, heeds the lesson in fear of women. He leaves Lincoln and goes east. He will, thereafter and always, court the muse at a great distance.

Philip Bentley, on the other hand—the hero of Ross's novel— met the muse and married her. Mrs Bentley is almost pure talk, pure voice, her husband almost pure silence. Yet it was not talk that led to their marriage, but music. Philip attended a recital to hear her play a rhapsody by Liszt. A *rhapsody*. 'The desire to reach him' Mrs Bentley tells her diary, 'make him really aware of me, it put something into my hands that had never been there before. And I succeeded. He stood waiting for me afterwards, erect and white-lipped with a pride he couldn't conceal. And that was the night he asked me to marry him.'[2]

Philip Bentley marries the muse and becomes not a writer but, if we are to believe the promise of the novel's ending, a dealer in secondhand books. Jim Burden meets the muse and flees and later travels for a great western railway and writes a reminiscence. In both novels the essential awe that might have produced the great artist of this prairie space is distorted by a fear that exceeds the wonder. The male who should be artist is overwhelmed. The bride expects to receive as well as give. How do you possess so formidable a woman?

By transgression. By substitution. . . . Philip Bentley cannot have a child by his wife; he has (apparently) a son by Judith West (and consider her *last* name; her last name), the farmer's daughter. That woman dies giving birth to her illegitimate son. Jim Burden, in approaching Lena Lingard, has already substituted her for Antonia Shimerda. Antonia has been got pregnant by a railway conductor; she is abandoned before the wedding; she, like Judith West, returns to the family farm—to the land and unmarried—to have her child.

The male is reluctant to locate and confront the muse. He works by trespass. The writer becomes the thief of words. And his fiction—the book that conceals and denies its bookness—is written as much from fear as from love. The love of woman that traditionally shaped the novel—boy meets girl (and Cather plays with that tradition)—is violently rivalled by a fear of woman as the figure who contains the space, who speaks the silence. And the resultant tension determines the 'grammar' of the western novel.

The basic grammatical pair in the story-line (the energy-line) of prairie fiction is house: horse. To be *on* a horse is to move: motion into distance. To be *in* a house is to be fixed: a centring unto stasis. Horse is masculine. House is feminine. Horse: house. Masculine: feminine. On: in. Motion: stasis. A woman ain't supposed to move. Pleasure: duty. The most obvious resolution of the dialectic, however temporary, is in the horse-house. Not the barn (though a version of resolution does take place there), but whore's-house. Western movies use that resolution. Sheila Watson treats of that resolution in *The Double Hook*. Antonia Shimerda is unhoused, almost into whoredom. Philip Bentley is unhorsed into housedom.

But the *hoo*-erhouse of western mythology is profane; against it the author plays the sacred possibility of the garden. Pavel and Peter, in Russia, might well have expected to recover their innocence by journeying to America. Even Jim Burden, American-born, playing in his grandmother's Nebraska garden, noticing the grasshoppers and the gophers and the little red bugs with black spots on their backs, can report: 'I was entirely happy.' Place is in many ways the first obsession of prairie fiction—a long and elaborate naming *takes place*; and one of the first attempts is the trying on of the name Eden—even by a boy named Burden.

He and Antonia expect to find a natural version of that Eden in a dog-town. Jim is 'examining a big hole with two entrances' when Antonia shouts something at him in Bohemian. 'I whirled around,' he reports, 'and there, on one of those dry gravel beds, was the biggest snake I had ever seen. He was sunning himself, after the cold night, and he must have been asleep when Antonia screamed. When I turned, he was lying in long loose waves, like a letter "W". . . . He was not merely a big snake, I thought—he was a curious monstrosity. His abominable muscularity, his loathsome, fluid motion, somehow made me sick' (p. 45).

This time it is Jim who translates, violently, a European story into the New World. The Eve of this version shouts a warning. But her Adam says, petulantly, 'What did you jabber Bohunk for? You might have told me there was a snake behind me!' The naming fails, the Freudian silence of America triumphs. Jim kills the snake with a spade. The boy and girl had ridden together to the dog-town on Jim's pony. Now that same Jim—or that 'experienced'

Jim—exultant at his kill, walks home carrying the spade and dragging the snake, with Antonia riding alone on Dude, the pony.

The geography of love and the geography of fear: on the prairies it's hard to tell them apart. And if Jim Burden has difficulty, the Bentleys of the Ross novel have even more. They are already in exile from anything resembling paradise when first we meet them, and Mrs Bentley must come close to being the most incompetent gardener in all of fiction. Historically, the frontier had in a sense 'closed' by the time the Canadian prairies opened to settlement. Significantly, the idea of garden finds its fullest expression at the end of the Cather novel, in the middle of the Ross novel.

Antonia, by the end of *My Antonia*, has in fact created an earthly garden of matronly delights. When Jim, in his hesitant way, visits the farm where Antonia now lives, he is taken almost immediately into the apple orchard. 'In the middle of the orchard we came upon a grape arbour, with seats built along the sides and a warped plank table' (p. 340). Jim and Antonia sit down and watch the numerous children at play. 'There was the deepest peace in the orchard. It was surrounded by a triple enclosure; the wire fence, then the hedge of thorny locusts, then the mulberry hedge which kept out the hot winds and held fast to the protecting snows of winter' (p. 341).

Antonia's husband, needless to say, is not at home. He is, we are told, 'not a man of much force' (p. 327). Jim, in the disguise of 'mere' description, can imagine he has come either to the Sleeping Beauty figure or to the *vagina dentata*—but not to a flesh-and-blood woman. He and Antonia for one last time sleep under the same roof—the artist again, by trespass, by subterfuge, by substitution gaining small access to his muse, remaining still and always the virgin, both feeding and feeding on his fear of the *woman*liness of woman, delighting in the near miss; lost pleasure becoming his secret pleasure. . . .

In the middle of the Ross novel, Philip and Mrs Bentley take a vacation from the town of Horizon. Advised by Paul Kirby, the primal couple goes west to a ranch, intending to buy a horse for the boy they've taken into their house.

Kirby is a kind of parody-double of Philip, as Gaston Cleric is of Jim Burden. But this scholar-teacher-guide is addicted to words—simply to words—not to classical authors. He clings to the last hope of naming. A man who studies sources, origins—it is he who directs the Bentleys out of town, back to nature.

'Just as Paul promised,' Mrs Bentley writes, 'there are the hills and river and horses all right, but the trees turn out to be scraggly little willow bushes that Philip describes contemptuously as "brush".' The trees will not be The Tree. 'With his artist's eye for character he says the best ones are the driftwood logs, come all the way from the mountains likely, four or five hundred miles west. They lie gnarled and blackened on the white sand like writhing, petrified serpents' (p. 92).

Paradise has once again retreated over the horizon and into the west. The snake in this place is seemingly older than the garden itself. And the labyrinth of naming and misnaming is complicated further by Paul's own boyhood fancy—he still insists that a hill across the river be called 'the Gorgon'.

The woman who is the centre and the power on the ranch is Laura: 'a thorough ranch woman, with a disdainful shrug for all domestic ties. There is a mannish verve about her that somehow is what you expect, that fits into a background of range and broncos. . . ' (p. 93). This girlish woman of forty-five was once a rodeo star. Her husband avoids her. She is almost an androgynous figure who exists prior to all coupling (or uncoupling), and the world she presides over is ambiguous indeed.

Here the women sleep in a house, under pictures of bulls and stallions; the three visiting men sleep, domestically, in a tent by the river. Mrs Bentley pays a visit one night to the male territory, because it is 'hot and close' in the house; but she cannot approach the males and their campfire; she feels her husband does not want to be 'bothered' with her. She goes past the tent and the fire into a natural world that is as 'unnamed' as the human configurations and relationships. Death and life, natural and supernatural, pagan and Christian, male and female, heaven and hell—her binary categories collapse. Like draws to like, she says, unable to make distinctions. The original place is chaos. Mrs Bentley looks into that dark. With 'a whole witches' Sabbath' at her heels, she makes a bolt for the house.

Mrs Bentley, at least for the moment, returns to the house-horse dialectic. She feels relieved—at home even with the picture of a Hereford over her bed. Not until she has gone dancing will she notice that the cow is a bull, none other than (perhaps by an error in naming) Priapus the First.

Anyone who grew up on the Great Plains knows that the one night that offers a smidgen of hope for sexual harmony (be it ever so chaotic) is dance night. In a world where the most pleasurable activities—hunting, fishing, drinking, swearing, athletics, story-telling and work—are homo-erotic, the one occasion where men and women might freely 'act' together is at a dance. There are dance scenes in both *As For Me and My House* and *My Antonia*.

The cowboys on the ranch take Philip to a bunkhouse and fit him out 'in a dark blue shirt, ten-gallon hat and red silk handkerchief' (p. 96). But Laura takes one look at him and says it's a pity he can't dance.

On this Saturday night a stripling cowboy, as tall as Philip, on a bet dances with Mrs Bentley. He ends up taking her for a bite to eat (at the Chinaman's I trust), and then for a walk to the outskirts of town to have a look at his horse—'Smoke, he called him, a little ghost-horse in the stray flickers of light from the street, a light mottled gray, with pure white mane and tail' (p. 98). A minister's wife should know her pale horses when she sees one. She returns to the dance to find Philip back from his shopping, sprawled on a bench along the wall, the boy Steve asleep on his shoulder.

Young Jim Burden sneaks out of his grandparent's town house to go to the dances and worship the young women, the country girls who make the dances a success with their energy and enthusiasm. His grandmother finds out about his nightly activities. He ends up sitting 'at home with the old people in the evenings . . . reading Latin that was not in our high-school course'—learning, by heart, a 'dead' language (p. 227).

The failure of the male protagonists, at the centre of each book, to enter into the dance, is symptomatic of what is wrong. The women can dance. Their appropriate partners cannot. The harmony suggested by dance—implications of sex, of marriage, of art, of a unified world—all are lost because of the male characters. The males are obedient to versions of self that keep them at a distance—the male as orphan, as cowboy, as outlaw.

Jim Burden leaves Virginia for Nebraska because he lost both his parents in one year. He reads a 'Life of Jesse James' on the train, and finds it 'one of the most satisfactory books I have ever read' (p. 4). His closest male companion on the homestead is Otto Fuchs, a cowboy who tells great tales of the frontier; an Austrian-born all-American cowboy who every Christmas writes a letter home to his ma. Jim acquires traits that are parallel to those of the cowboy, especially the ability to be both devoted and distant. And already in the introduction to his reminiscence he is a version of Jesse James; he works for a western railway at a time when railways were not renowned for their integrity. He is somehow orphan, cowboy, and outlaw.

The case of Philip Bentley is possibly more extreme. He was born out of wedlock, to a waitress whom he despises, out of a vanished father whom he admires. The house of his childhood is close to the horse/whores' house. The father (the Christian God?) is pure distance.

Philip, a version of the orphan, temporarily adopts the orphan Steve, whose mother abandoned him. Through the orphaned boy and Paul Kirby's faith in horses he has a shot at being a cowboy. But finally he is mostly (or almost) an outlaw—against religion, against society—even, in his silence, against art.

The male as orphan or cowboy or outlaw is drawn to and threatened by the house. The house is containing, nurturing, protecting, mothering. But the house is closed to the point where it creates, even in Mrs Bentley, a terrible claustrophobia.

Or perhaps her claustrophobia is a clue.

Both Mrs Bentley and Antonia Shimerda, out on the plains, are capable of doing both women's and men's work. Neither will, finally, quite accept the assigned role—the assigned 'name'.

In the first paragraph of *House*, Philp Bentley has thrown himself across the bed and fallen asleep, his clothes still on, one leg dangling to the floor. He is both the spent man and the tired boy. In the next paragraph his wife says: 'It's been a hard day for him, putting up stovepipes and opening crates, for the fourth time getting our old linoleum down. He hasn't the hands for it. I could use the pliers and hammer twice as well myself, with none of his mutterings and smashed-up fingers either, but in the parsonage, on calling days, it simply isn't done. . . . It was twelve years ago, in our first town, that I learned my lesson, one day when they caught me in the woodshed making kindling of a packing box. "Surely this isn't necessary, Mrs Bentley—your position in the community—and Mr Bentley such a big, able bodied man—"' (p. 3).

Granted, she takes the pliers to him a bit—recalling such an incident twelve years after it happened. But she's in Horizon—a town that is place and space at once, somewhere and nowhere, always present and never to be reached. She has a problem in naming that persists right through to the last paragraph of the book. And her problem is that she is more than any of her names will allow her to be. She is as much in need of a great artist—a great namer—as her artist is of a great muse.

Antonia is sometimes called Tony. 'Oh, better I like to work out-of-doors than in a house,' she sings to young Jim Burden. 'I not care that your grandmother says it makes me like a man. I like to be like a man' (p. 138). . . . Antonia refuses any mere role, any definition that is less than the total, hurt dream of this total landscape. Song of myself as everything.

By still another paradox, the male figure, out in this space, out in the open, presumbably free, once epic hero, is now the diminished hero. The woman, in the age-old containment of house or town, is, in prairie writing, the more-than-life figure—but one who is strangely sought.

How do you make love in a new country?

Curiously, travel becomes a second obsession in these place-possessed books. Travel is possibly the true intercourse in these prairie novels: a frenetic going back and forth, up and down, in and out.

The Bentleys buy a horse from the ranch and bring it into town. The boy, Steve, riding and riding on the edge of town, acts out the ritual of desire and failure that is the life of his adopted parents. Mrs Bentley, finally, is united with her husband in their mutual desire to travel to the city that is two hundred miles away. Antonia is got pregnant and deserted by a railway conductor. Otto and Jake, the boy-men of the Burden farm, must head out to open country when the family moves into town. Young Jim Burden and Gaston Cleric leave Nebraska to have intercourse with the east and Harvard. Tiny Soderball goes to the goldfields of the Yukon, where briefly she finds a true male friend--one who has no feet. The older Jim Burden, on his iron horse, wanders restlessly and endlessly across the continent, never forgetting his Antonia. Pavel and Peter, over and over, throw the bride to the pursuing wolves; and always they are pursued.

I think it would be naïve to attribute the absence of explicit sex—of its language or its actions—merely to prudery on the part of either Cather or Ross; for the same absence is an operative presence in the works of numerous prairie writers. Space and place are not quite able to find equation. The men are tempted by friendship with other men, as in the opening of F.P. Grove's *Settlers of the Marsh*. The women are tempted by dreams of androgyny, even in a book as recent and as explicit and as travel-obsessed as Tom Robbins' *Even Cowgirls Get the Blues*.

Travel, for all its seeking, acts out an evasion. One can travel to the next room as well as to the far side of a continent. There is an absence of face-to-face confrontation in both *As For Me and My House* and *My Antonia*—either in the classic missionary position or in its verbal equivalent, the tête-à-tête. Mrs Bentley, desperate, talks to herself through her diary. Jim Burden delivers his manuscript to the anonymous and sexless figure who opens the novel. In neither book are the written accounts read by the persons for whom they might have been intended. We have only the isolation of the self—the not being heard, the not hearing.

How do you make love in a new country?

It seems to me that we've developed a literature, on the Great Plains, in which marriage is no longer functional as a primary metaphor for the world as it should or might be. The model as it survived even in Chaucer (for all his knowledge of the fear of women), through the plays of Shakespeare, through the novels of Jane Austen and D.H. Lawrence, has been replaced by models of another kind. What that kind is, I've only begun here to guess.

The novels by Cather and Ross give us a clue with their demanding and deceitful titles: *My* Antonia, *My* house. For, in spite of the attempts at possession—in spite of the pretence at possession—we know that something else was the case. We cannot even discover who is protagonist: Antonia or Jim Burden? Philip or Mrs Bentley? Male or female? Muse or writer? Horse or house? Language or silence? Space or book?[3]

This is a new country. Here on the plains we confront the hopeless and necessary hope of originality: constantly we experience the need to begin. And we do—by initiating beginnings. We contrive authentic origins. From the denied Indians. From the false fronts of the little towns. From the diaries and reminiscences and the travel accounts. From our displaced ancestors.

Here the bride, so often, without being wife, turns into mother. The male cannot enter into what is traditionally thought of as marriage—and possibly nor can the female. The male, certainly, to make his radical beginning, takes on the role of orphan or cowboy or outlaw. He approaches the female. He approaches the garden. He approaches the house. . . .

And only then does he realize he has defined himself out of all entering. If he enters into this marriage—and into this place—it will be he—contrary to the tradition of the past—who must make the radical change. It will be he—already self-christened—and not the woman this time—who must give up the precious and treacherous *name*.

Notes

[1] Willa Cather, *My Antonia* (Boston and New York: Houghton Mifflin, 1918), p. 270. Further references will appear in the text.

[2] Sinclair Ross, *As For Me and My House* (1941; rpt Toronto: McClelland and Stewart, 1970 [New Canadian Library]), p. 141. I ignore (evade, if you prefer) Mrs Bentley's own need of a muse-figure—assuming that the performer of a musical composition is in as much need of inspiration as its composer. And, further, I ignore Ross's confrontation with music and art. The music comes from far places. The art (drawing, painting), in a manner that is characteristically Canadian, precedes both writing and music in its recognition of what is *present*. Further references will appear in the text.

[3] By a final paradox, Cather and Ross give us magnificent books that are written about the fear that keeps writers from writing books. *My Antonia* is a novel about the making of art, against the talk of being artist: Cather's Jim Burden is married to a New York woman who acts as a patroness in that 'arty' world. *As For Me and My House* is a novel about the artist, against art. The naming has become a near impossibility. One can only *be* an artist: let the silence speak what it will.

9

The Grammar of Silence

What I am setting out to do here is simply this: I want to ask if there is a characteristic narrative of the ethnic experience.[1] More exactly, I am asking, is there, at the point where literature and ethnicity meet, a characteristic narrative structure? Assuming that such a structure does exist, what are some of its elements? Or, as I prefer to put it, what is the *grammar* of the narrative of ethnic experience?

Behind this specific intention, I am asking for a theory of ethnicity, a theory that I would locate in the idea of narrative. There is, possibly, a story that repeats itself, with significant variations of course, whether we are describing and exploring the ethnic experience as sociologists, as psychologists, as novelists and poets, or as literary critics. Not only am I limiting myself to the literary expression of that narrative—I am, outrageously perhaps, working explicitly out of two literary texts.

Frederick Philip Grove is perhaps the most complex and most instructive ethnic writer yet to appear on the Canadian literary scene. As you know, he was a writer who arrived in Canada in the early part of this century and who gave the impression that he was a Swedish aristocrat who had fallen on hard times while visiting in Toronto. He went out to the prairies and set about becoming a Canadian writer, working in English, and by the time of his death in 1948 he had succeeded to a remarkable degree, though, as we shall see, he insisted throughout his career on calling himself a failure. Only in recent years have we discovered that Frederick Philip Grove was not a Swede but rather a German writer of bourgeois background, Felix Paul Greve, who faked his suicide and migrated to Canada and became, under his assumed name, a central figure in Canadian writing.

I am going to work with two of his numerous texts. In *Settlers of the Marsh* (1925),[2] a novel that he began in German and finished in English, he tells the story of a Swedish immigrant, Niels

Lindstedt, who goes to the frontier in Manitoba to make a new home. The story is a love triangle. Niels falls in love with a Swedish girl, Ellen Amundsen, who has sworn an oath not to marry, because of the horrible example of her parents' marriage. Niels then marries a Canadian widow, Clara Vogel, and ends up murdering her. After a period in prison, he returns to his community and marries Ellen.

In his 'autobiography', *In Search of Myself* (1946),[3] Grove purports to give an account of how he himself left Sweden and came to North America and, while living in Manitoba, set about establishing his career as a teacher and writer, after years of working as a farm labourer. He marries a Canadian woman, a teacher from a Mennonite background, and sets about his heroic effort to establish himself as a writer, against what seem to be impossible odds of poverty, poor health, and publishers' indifference.

We have here, that is, two narratives of the ethnic experience, one using the conventions of the novel, the other using the conventions of autobiography (and I might add that the chapters of *Search* are titled, 'Childhood', 'Youth', 'Manhood', and 'And After'). What is interesting is the elements that occur in both. Both are stories about the migrating generation. The experience of the migrating generation, it seems to me, is granted privileged status in this literature (even while those same immigrants might have experienced a violent silence in actual life). The migrating generation is often seen in heroic terms by the later generations. Importantly, here, in the writings of Grove, we have narratives written by the person who experienced the migration.

Grove's principal characters in *Settlers*, Niels and one of the two women to whom he is attracted, Ellen, are from backgrounds that came close to making them serfs in Sweden. The hero of *Search*, on the other hand, perceivable as Frederick Grove himself, comes from a background of extreme wealth; he might indeed have become master of the kind of estate on which his fictional characters were potentially serfs. Grove imagines these two extreme possibilities, and yet both Niels and Phil (the hero's name in *Search*) come to the same narrative predicaments, often seen in binary patterns. Let me list a few of them.

There is an extreme tension between ideas of success and ideas of failure. Niels labours for years to build a large house that he believes is the emblem of success. Yet, in that same house, he discovers how totally he has failed in the new world: his wife, Clara, becomes a figure of death, haunting that house, and reminding him constantly of the failure of what he calls his vision.

Writing *Search* twenty-one years later, Grove is even more obsessive about the idea of failure. At one point, in speaking of his literary career, he says, 'I tried; and I shall shortly discuss why I was bound to fail, as I had failed in everything that I had ever undertaken with an economic aim in view; this book is the record of a failure; and its explanation: a double failure, an economic and a spiritual one, for ultimately the one involved the other' (p. 409). It seems apparent, after a while (and the word 'failure' is used obsessively in the second half of the book), that the idea of failure has become a generative force in the narrative and in Grove's own life.

The immensity of his failure becomes a measure of his success. His very failure is not only his own; it becomes a measure of and a criticism of the society into which he has entered. Like that supreme master of creative failure, Malcolm Lowry, Grove is able to force himself into heroic bouts of writing by meditating on his failure, by recording it carefully, by listing the titles of failed manuscripts and the growing total of rejections. And, like Lowry, he goes on imagining for himself ever more ambitious projects.

Where the appearance of failure might be an act of rebellion or a naturalistic element in traditional Canadian writing, for the ethnic writer it harbours darker and more complex and possibly more exciting possibilities. As in the case of Grove, it becomes the single word by which he judges both himself and the society into which he has entered. That word can be or is made, at times, to lose its traditional meaning and come to signify success.

Another essential and related binary is that of ideas of inferiority and ideas of superiority. Niels Lindstedt, from the opening page of *Settlers*, is paired with a kind of double, a fellow immigrant, Lars Nelson, a giant of a man who with ease makes a good marriage and becomes a successful farmer. Nelson has succeeded by the standards of the materialistic society around him, but it is obvious that he is, for Grove, morally and spiritually the inferior of Niels Lindstedt. Lindstedt is the superior man who brings to bear on experience the possibilities of and demands for relevance and meaning. He confronts the idea of signification. And yet it is he who commits a murder.

Phil Grove, in *Search*, represents the pinnacle of European culture. He has been everywhere, he has studied everything, he has
met everyone of artistic consequence in Europe. Then he begins
his years of work as a farm labourer on the Great Plains of North
America. He tells at some length of pairing up with a Pole who
like him looked disreputable but who, like him also, 'spoke half a
dozen European languages' (p. 206). At one point they begin to
discuss French poetry while pitching bundles into a threshing
machine. 'It was done ostentatiously, with the pointed intention
of making the other hoboes open their mouths. He [the Pole] even
dropped his perfect American speech and changed to French; and
in doing so, he adopted what, in these raw surroundings, might
have passed for aristocratic society manners, handling his pitch-
fork with the nonchalance of a fop, parodying that nonchalance
by its very exaggeration' (p. 207).

European culture has been reduced to a parody of itself, and
that largely by means of language acts. Grove and his friend are
at once superior and inferior. And on this occasion they are shortly hauled in by the local police and fleeced of all their cash, in the
final carnivalization of what they and their values represent in this
new world.

Thirty pages later Grove can write, 'I wanted to be in touch with
the finest and highest thought of my age. Instead, I was being
rubbed the wrong way, day in, day out, by those who, for the moment, were my social equals—whom others would have called the
scum of the earth. . . ' (pp. 235-6). Half a page later he can write,
'I was no longer a "good European"; let Europe take care of her
own troubles; I was rapidly becoming extra-European, partly because on account of my failure to take a sixth trip to Europe.
Europe, to me, had suddenly ceased to exist' (p. 236).

By the end of the book this arrogant extra-European can say, 'As
I have said, I was suffering from an inferiority complex' (p. 439).
The tension between superiority and inferiority must either
destroy him or make him write. Grove, moving from class-con-
scious Europe into the North American ideal or illusion of
democracy, is *unsettled*. Again, in a situation where signified and
signifier do not cohere, he might be totally destroyed, or he might
become the truly creative individual.

There are other binary patterns that Grove establishes as basic to
the ethnic experience: revelation and concealment, integration

and resistance, forgetting and remembering. But behind all these is the basic tension between signifier and signified. In a painfully moving passage Grove observes: 'That the artist is not a hunter constitutes him a cripple, physical or mental, and therefore an object of contempt as well as, paradoxically, of a reluctant admiration. For his work partakes of the nature of a miracle . . . the work of art becomes a fetish endowed with the functions of magic' (p. 431).

In the new world, the magic seems to falter. For the heroes of *Search* and *Settlers* it becomes difficult, even impossible, to tell failure from success, to tell superiority from inferiority. A gap opens between word and object. In the Europe of their past—as Grove's characters remember it—it was possible to define and locate connections. In the abrupt change to this new world, a chasm opens.

Niels Lindstedt believes he can attach the right woman to the word 'wife'. The Canadian widow, Clara Vogel, is in his perception seductive nd evil. The immigrant girl, Ellen Amundsen, is innocent and desirable. He brings with him a paradigm that makes of women whores and virgins. Somehow he manages to set a trap for Ellen and get caught by Clara. He stumbles into an immense chasm between word and object, and compounds the space by becoming a murderer, not the farmer, the nurturing man, he wants to be.

The gap in *Search* is equally catastrophic. The single-minded hero of that autobiography that might be fiction and might be fact (another threatening binary in the ethnic experience) confesses, a few pages from the end of the book, 'I have often doubted whether there is anything that I can legitimately call "I"' (p. 452). This narrator, completing an autobiography, confesses that he cannot locate the 'I' that is the subject of the book. The gap between signifier and signified has become the subject itself, a question mark over what it is we mean by the act of writing. Grove (or Greve), the bourgeois man from Germany, in writing the autobiography of the Swede, Phil Grove of Manitoba, announces a contemporary predicament and grounds it in the narrative of ethnicity.

How do these patterns of binary opposition get turned into narrative? How do we avoid a kind of paralysis with characters caught between two worlds—caught, if you will, in silence? If we take departure and return as the basic or archetypal design of the journey, then the ethnic story immediately becomes problematic in that the traveller buys a one-way ticket.

If the elements in the binaries are the nouns in the grammatical set, what are the verbs that set things in motion? How do we articulate the silence?

A principal way to establish or re-establish narrative coherence in the face of the gap between signifier and signified is through a re-telling of stories. In ethnic writing there is often an attempt at healing by the rewriting of myths. The myth most often retold, at least on the surface of ethnic writing, is the garden story. Niels Lindstedt is obviously in search of a new version of Eden. Two major scenes take place in a garden or bower. The garden is set in contrast to the house. And further, the image of the garden recalls the question of naming that is so central to the Genesis story.

Phil Grove in *Search* is also aware of this model. When he finds himself feeling like an exile in North America, he does not dream of a return to Europe. Rather, he explains, 'A new nostalgia arose . . . I would build a shack on some hillside overlooking a stream and the woods.' He even decides on the location of this edenic place: ' . . . it was in the Pembina Mountains, on the Canadian side, not very far from the little town of Manitou in Manitoba' (p. 237).

In his choice of place he is able to unite the Indian spirit of place, or at least of the place-name, with his dream of paradise. In actual fact, of course, as Grove establishes so vividly in the prologue to *Search*, he struggled in vain toward that paradise, and ended up trying to run a dairy farm in rural Ontario. That prologue begins: 'It was a dismal November day, with a raw wind blowing from the north-west and cold, iron-grey clouds flying low—one of those Ontario days which, on the lake-shores or in a country of rock and swamp, seem to bring visions of an ageless time after the emergence of the earth from chaos, or a foreboding of the end of a world about to die from entropy' (p. 1).

Grove, on his way by car to pick up a girl to work as 'a household drudge', is painfully aware that there is only one thing you do in this paradise—and that is work. And work, in this new world, is another version of silence. Grove is remarkable in his portrayal of the silencing effect of work. Even the obsessive writer, in *Search*, seems to be silenced by his own heroic efforts. He writes and he writes, and his very effort cuts him off from all chance of being heard. And, not inappropriately, he himself begins to be afflicted with deafness.

And yet this silence is enclosed in a larger silence. Grove's travelling heroes are caught between the 'silenced' old version of the garden (European in this case) and the not-yet-speaking new one. And, it seems to me, behind the not-yet-spoken garden, there is another myth trying to speak itself.

While the garden myth is often present on the surface of a narration of the ethnic experience, I suspect the concealed story is that of the necessary death—the death, that is, out of one culture, with the hope that it will lead to rebirth in another.

Grove faked his own death. And yet in a symbolic way there was nothing fake about it: he died out of one culture and into another.

Death and rebirth is a recurring pattern in *Search*. Phil Grove is ill to the point of death and wonders if it wouldn't have been better if he had died, because in that case his manuscripts would have been destroyed and the struggle to write would have been over. But the most moving and ironic death is that of his young daughter, May. A few sentences after reporting her death, Phil Grove remarks, 'And now, as if we had at last paid our dues to the fates, break after break seemed to come for me' (p. 391).

Niels Lindstedt, after shooting and killing his wife Clara, goes to his barn and kills a gelding in a curious scene that can only invite symbolic interpretation: the death of the horse is the symbolic death of the unmanned man, Niels Lindstedt. His process of rebirth is startling in its effect. After six and a half years in prison, Lindstedt emerges a man reborn. Grove himself had served a prison term. The threat of another led to his 'suicide' and his movement from German into English as a writer. Perhaps the death in ethnic narrative is, explicitly, a death out of one language into another. (And this, beyond the example of Grove, would seem to hold true even for the person who moves with apparent convenience from an English-speaking place to an English-speaking place.)

It is as if the old story forms are no longer adequate to the new experience. Silence reasserts itself. Grove himself spoke of the 'tragedy' of Niels Lindstedt, attempting to assert the appropriateness of a traditional mode. Yet he gives his story a happy ending that surprises many readers—an ending that many readers protest but that few would change. It turns out that we allow the tragedy to transform itself into something approaching comedy, in the name of a revisioning of the novel itself as form.

Grove's *Search* sets out to be an autobiography. By the end it too has become something else, with the author commenting in the middle of the book, 'I felt an exile. I was an exile. I did not live among people of my own kind; among people who, metaphorically, spoke my language. . . .' In the next sentence he adds, 'The only sort of what, with a stretch of the imagination, could be called literary art with which I ever came into living contact, consisted of the "tall" tales of the west; and they stood out in flagrant contradiction to the squalid reality I saw all about' (p. 235).

The offended Mr Grove, in *Search*, has written one of the finest tall tales in the literary history of the west. If Mark Twain admitted to stretching the story a little, Frederick Philip Grove could be said to stretch it just about as much, while admitting nothing. He explains that at one time he was sending out as many as a dozen unpublished works, each one 'copied out in six copies of fine, copperplate handwriting. Let me say that there were twelve volumes in all; then there were seventy-two manuscripts; and each of them had been sent out and received back at least three times, more likely five times a year. So that I had made, on an average, three hundred and sixty shipments a year, or one a day' (p. 234). And this, he adds, has gone on for sixteen years.

Grove, in the course of that stretching, found a story model that enabled him to speak, eloquently and validly, of what he had experienced. Language had become that literal and that isolated for him. He had transformed himself into a great hoard of repeating and circulating and unread manuscripts.

If there is a gap between word and object, the final question is language itself, and the question of naming. Perhaps the completion of the narrative is made possible, not primarily by the surface story, but rather by a narrative movement that entails a changed sense of language, a movement from the old language, through silence (a silence that might be imagined even as a death) into a new language.

Grove says, in *Search*: 'Thus, in the attempt to set down my vision, I realized that I had at bottom no language which was peculiarly my own. In a way this was an advantage to me; I had half a dozen instead. But in another way, it was a disadvantage and even a misfortune: I lacked that limitation which is best for the profound penetration of the soul of a language. I ground my teeth in my struggles; and, for the moment, all my struggles were with words' (p. 338).

The turning point in Phil Grove's life comes when he is seen in a railway station by a French priest in North Dakota reading a copy of Baudelaire's *Fleurs du mal*. Of the priest Grove says, 'He was an immigrant himself; he was French, not, as I had supposed, French-Canadian' (p. 239). This European priest talks to Grove of his circumstances and says to him, 'Why didn't you teach?' The priest, shortly thereafter, is killed in a railway accident—he is another double and a representative of European civilization and he dies the necessary death. Grove goes to Manitoba to begin his long and hellish struggle with story and language. He is ready to unname himself as European and to struggle to rename himself as Canadian.

This erasure of names is a part of the experience of migrating peoples, and part of the narrative of that experience. And that erasure becomes palimpsest, it leaves its trace—as it did when Greve changed his name to Grove, at once concealing and changing who he was and leaving a trace that would enable us to complete the task of renaming that he had initiated.

That moment of unnaming with its potential for renaming occurs twice in *Settlers*, and this in the marshland itself, that unshaped, unmapped, unnamed space. In paired scenes, one in the middle of *Settlers*, one at the end, the two adults, Niels and Ellen, are transformed into 'boy' and 'girl', and the story's past tense gives way to present tense. In both scenes the nameless 'children' approach a schoolhouse and pass it up for the natural world of berry bushes and singing birds. Both scenes end with awkward and painful attempts at naming.

At the end of the first, Niels realizes that Ellen is going to refuse marriage:

> The realization of a bottomless abyss shakes him.
> 'Ellen,' he calls with an almost breaking voice.
> The girl slowly rises. 'I know,' she says. 'Don't speak' (p. 99).

He speaks with a *breaking* voice. She speaks to command silence—'Don't speak.' Having been named herself, she then goes on to name the man in return: 'Oh Niels, I am going to hurt you deeply.' It is as if the speaking of a name is, at this point in the story, the breaking of a taboo. That breaking of the taboo brings about tragedy.

Ellen refuses to marry Niels. We move immediately to a death scene. We see old man Sigurdsen dying: 'Sigurdsen lay in his clothes, not on the bed, but on the floor, his head reversed, his legs curved back, sprawling. . . .' Niels watches the man die in what is a grotesque parody of sexual fulfilment and the narrative reports of Niels: 'Quietly he got up and drew a blanket over it that had been he' (pp. 101-2).

Niels has entered into his death journey. He is *fooled* into marriage with Clara Vogel—the Canadian woman. He is unable to understand her—he cannot understand any of her names—as Clara Vogel, as widow, as district whore, as victim of frontier morality, as an experienced woman whose dimensions mock his own fatal innocence—and now, in an explosive reversal of convention, it is the European who is innocent, the Canadian who is experienced. The paradise Niels presumed to locate by building a house turns into hell. He completes his journey into silence by murdering his wife.

Niels Lindstedt goes to prison and in that version of silence earns (too easily for some readers) a kind of redemption. But Grove is not interested here in recording the literal prison experience. Prison has been a theme since the book opened. Grove is interested, rather, in Niels' return from the prisonhouse of silence to the world of speech.

At the end of the book Niels earns parole and returns to his farm and goes to meet Ellen. Again they meet, as they did in the middle of the novel, in 'that natural bower in the fringe of the bush'. This scene is at once a repetition and a reversal of the scene in the middle of the novel. Again the narrative moves into present tense and again the two figures become nameless—they become simply the man and the woman. Again, he speaks her name, his voice almost failing him. Again she says, 'I know. . . . Don't speak' (pp. 214-17).

But now she wants Niels to be quiet so that she can speak. Speech, finally, is possible. At this point the old names have been stripped of all prior meaning. They can be spoken now as new names, as a beginning. Ellen, at last, can forswear her oath not to marry.

The repetition of the two scenes suggests a ritual unnaming and a renaming into new lives in a new world. And the paradox here is that the new names are exact homonyms for the old ones. The signifier sounds as it always sounded. But the signified has shifted radically. Now it can be joined again with its signifier; name and object come together, the new life is possible.

A genuine settling is not so much described as proposed at the end of this narrative. In the last line of the text, a paragraph that is a single, short sentence, a 'vision' arises between the two lovers, and this time it is 'shared by both'. A grammar of the narrative of ethnic experience has begun to assert itself. The silence is finding a way to transform itself into voice.

Notes

[1] This talk was delivered as the introductory lecture in a series, 'Ethnicity and Literature: Canadian Perspectives on Language, Silence and Translation,' University of British Columbia, 26 September 1984.

[2] Frederick Philip Grove, *Settlers of the Marsh* (Toronto: McClelland and Stewart, 1966 [New Canadian Library]). Page references will appear in the text.

[3] Grove, *In Search of Myself* (Toronto: Macmillan, 1946). Page references will appear in the text.

10

Carnival and Violence: A Meditation

I have proposed for myself a meditation on violence. This seeming contradiction I will attempt not so much to mediate as to allow by examining the concept of the carnivalesque. On the question of violence I am like Thomas Haliburton imagining the reality of the American Revolution—I cannot bear to look, and I cannot bear to look away. The question of violence is so central to contemporary life and art, and at the same time so unanswerable, that it threatens to become our major concern. This sideways glance, then, is a speculative, academic, autobiographical and circuitous meditation on that moment in 1835 when, in the pages of *The Novascotian*, Judge Haliburton, on his journey to Fort Lawrence, was overtaken by Sam Slick. When I seem to have lost that moment, I would ask you to remember it.

Appropriately, I see the academic conference as a contemporary version of carnival. In a world where much of the complex ritual of carnival has been trivialized, where its function has been diminished, the conference maintains a connection with a tradition that goes back at least to the streets and baths and to the marketplaces of ancient Greece and Rome; from that time forward, into those medieval and Renaissance cities where something like three months of the year might be given over to actual carnival.

For our contemporary interest in carnival and the influence of its forms and implications on writing, we are indebted to the Russian critic Mikhail Bakhtin, and especially to two of his books, translated into English as *Problems of Dostoevsky's Poetics* and *Rabelais and his World*.

'As opposed to the official feast,' Bakhtin writes,

> one might say that carnival celebrated temporary liberation from
> the prevailing truth and from the established order; it marked the

suspension of all hierarchical rank, privileges, norms, and prohibitions. Carnival was the true feast of time, the feast of becoming, change, and renewal. It was hostile to all that was immortalized and completed.[1]

Bakhtin, however, is not concerned simply with carnival as such, but rather with the literary genres that have come under the influence of carnival. For him that carnivalization produced the greatness of Cervantes and Rabelais and Shakespeare, then, by the middle of the seventeenth century, went into serious decline, and, by the nineteenth century, almost total eclipse. It recovers some of its energy in the novels of Dostoevsky and his twentieth century heirs like Joyce and Kafka and Proust. But Bakhtin makes little mention of the North American writers of the nineteenth and twentieth centuries. It is with those writers, and their connection with the carnivalization of literature, that I am concerned.

I would like here to go back and arrive in the New World in the nineteenth century. I'm going to quote at length from *Roughing It in the Bush*, where Mrs Susanna Moodie, the wife of a British army officer who had received a grant of 400 acres in Ontario, tells of arriving at a St Lawrence River landing:

> It was four o'clock when we landed on the rocks, which the rays of an intensely scorching sun had rendered so hot that I could scarcely place my foot upon them. How the people without shoes bore it I cannot imagine. Never shall I forget the extraordinary spectacle that met our sight the moment we passed the low range of bushes which formed a screen in front of the river. A crowd of many hundred Irish emigrants had been landed during the present and former day and all this motley crew . . . were employed in washing clothes or spreading them out on the rocks and bushes to dry.
>
> The men and boys were *in* the water, while the women, with their scanty garments tucked above their knees, were tramping their bedding in tubs or in holes in the rocks, which the retiring tide had left half full of water. Those who did not possess washing tubs, pails, or iron pots, were running to and fro, screaming and scolding in no measured terms. The confusion of Babel was among them. All talkers and no hearers—each shouting and yelling in his or her uncouth dialect, and all accompanying their vociferations with violent and extraordinary gestures, quite incomprehensible to the uninitiated. We were literally stunned by the strife of tongues. I shrank, with feelings almost akin to fear, from the hard-featured,

sunburnt women as they elbowed rudely past me.

. . . The people who covered the island appeared perfectly des-
titute of shame, or even of common decency. Many were almost
naked, still more but partially clothed. We turned in disgust from
the revolting scene, but were unable to leave the spot until the captain satisfied a noisy group of his own people, who were demanding a supply of stores.

And here I must observe that our passengers, who were chiefly
honest Scotch labourers and mechanics from the vicinity of Edinburgh, and who while on board ship had conducted themselves
with the greatest propriety, and appeared the most quiet, orderly
set of people in the world, no sooner set foot upon the island than
they became infected by the same spirit of insubordination and
misrule, and were just as insolent and noisy as the rest.[2]

Susanna Moodie has, unwittingly and only slightly willingly,
entered the carnival world of North America—hierarchies are
breaking, labourers and mechanics are 'infected' by the spirit of
'insubordination and misrule', the body becomes more fascinating than the mind, shame is no longer shame, sex is becoming sex,
language itself is becoming 'the confusion of Babel'—'All talkers
and no hearers—each shouting and yelling his or her uncouth
dialect. . . .'

'Carnival', Bakhtin writes, 'is a pageant without a stage and
without a division into performers and spectators.' He goes on to
explain, 'In the carnival everyone is an active participant,
everyone communes in the carnival act. Carnival is not con-
templated, it is, strictly speaking, not even played out; its par-
ticipants *live* in it.'[3]

Mrs Moodie will not enter into her own uncrowning. She tries
to re-establish the division between performer and spectator, for
the failure of that division does violence to all that she believes she
is. 'While our captain was vainly endeavouring to satisfy the un-
reasonable demands of his rebellious people,' she writes,

Moodie [her husband] had discovered a woodland path that led to
the back of the island. Sheltered by some hazel-bushes from the intense heat of the sun, we sat down by the cool, gushing river, out
of sight, but, alas! not out of hearing of the noisy, riotous crowd.
Could we have shut out the profane sounds which came to us on
every breeze, how deeply should we have enjoyed an hour amid
the tranquil beauties of that retired and lovely spot (pp. 25-6).

Hers has become a subjunctive life. If. Or if only. Then.

But matters are even 'worse' than they first appeared. Moodie remarks to a sergeant that it must be 'no easy task to keep such wild savages in order.' 'You may well say that, sir,' the sergeant replies,

> —but our night scenes far exceed those of the day. You would think they were incarnate devils, singing, drinking, dancing, shouting, and cutting antics that would surprise the leader of a circus. They have not shame—are under no restraint—nobody knows them here, and they think they can speak and act as they please.... They are a sad set, sir, a sad set. We could, perhaps, manage the men; but the women, sir!—the women. Oh, sir! (pp. 26-7)

One has the feeling of having missed one hell of a good party. But none of this for Mrs Moodie. She heads back toward the ship, through the mosquitoes and the 'squabbling crowd' to the landing place—only to meet still another Irishman, and this a truly carnivalesque figure who anticipates Haliburton's encounter with a fictional figure that is to take place three years later:

> Here we encountered a boat, just landing a fresh cargo from the Emerald Isle. One fellow, of gigantic proportions, whose long, tattered great-coat just reached below the middle of his bare legs and, like charity, hid the defects of his other garments, or perhaps concealed his want of them, leaped upon the rocks, flourishing aloft his shilelagh, bounded and capered like a wild goat from his native mountains. 'Whurrah! my boys!' he cried. 'Shure we'll all be jintlemen!' (p. 27)

Mrs Moodie is an aspiring English gentlewoman of the nineteenth century and a truly unsettling figure. She writes so powerfully about herself that her books make her as real as a fictional character. She is the closest thing we have in Canadian writing to Joseph Conrad's Mr Kurtz, and, like poor, dear, hesitating Marlow, I feel the 'fascination of the abomination'. We read her and wonder in horror—is *this* where Canadian culture comes from?

The answer is—alas! as Mrs Moodie would say—in very strong part, yes.

Mrs Moodie herself was horrified by the carnival world of Upper Canada—but she never stopped looking. She becomes the true voyeur who can at once *gaze* and *disapprove*. She points the way to a dilemma of Canadian writing and to a difference between Canadian and American writing.

Mrs Moodie cannot surrender the security of distance. She maintains by that carefully measured distance the desire and doubt that characterize what I am calling the subjunctive life. Perhaps, and cruelly, she anticipates our present lives in front of television sets, behind systems of locked doors and scanning cameras, where we either imagine or watch vague images of violence.

In her book, published in 1852 (twenty years after the actual landing), in a kind of unintentional parody of the Romantic posture, she retreats to what might be called a bower. But, confessing as well as complaining, she reports that she was, even there, 'not out of hearing of the noisy, riotous crowd'. She and her party could not or, perhaps, finally, would not shut out the 'profane sounds' that came on every breeze.

For Julia Kristeva,[4] one of the most important interpreters of Bakhtin, the carnival 'challenges God, authority, and social law'. It is a drama located in language. It is a drama of rebellion. Mrs Moodie, it turns out, cannot enter in, cannot walk away. She comes to the moment of rebellion and is—by the paradox of her own strong will—arrested. Carnival is a turning upside-down, a turning inside-out, of our elaborations of order. Mrs Moodie hides from this, but she hides within earshot. She stops exactly at the edge of violence. She stops subjunctively.

Bakhtin tells us: 'The laws, prohibitions and restrictions which determine the system and order of normal, i.e. non-carnival life are for the period of carnival suspended. . . . All *distance* between people is suspended and a special carnival category goes into effect—the *free, familiar contact among people*' (D, 101).

The structuring *distance* must be broken, violated, for carnival influences to come into play. The first time we meet Thomas Haliburton's carnivalesque figure, the Yankee clockmaker, Sam Slick—that clockmaker is violating the distance the narrator wants to impose. The narrator is riding what he thinks is a fast horse. He is overtaken by his 'inferior' who is in fact riding a 'better' horse—and cannot escape back into a safe distance. He is forced into the world of carnival. Hierarchy is destroyed. The distinction between actor and audience is erased; actor and audience, indeed, become interchangeable.

Sam Slick profanes sacred space and sacred time. He sells cheap tin clocks to a people who are still living in another kind of time. When first we see him sell a clock he sells it to a 'deacon'. He sells the clock by *talking*; that is, he is a master of the oral tradition that is basic to carnival.

Sam, while making the sale, has the gall to implicate his observer by pointing out that he is using 'soft sawder' to clinch the deal. And he can't resist adding, '"An Englishman would pass that man as a sheep passes a hog in a pasture, without looking at him; or," said he, looking rather archly, "if he was mounted on a pretty smart horse, I guess he'd trot away, if he could."'[5]

Haliburton, challenged to be an 'Englishman', can't be one. Sam has out-observed the narrator-observer, yet he is at the same time securing his role as main actor. The narrator-observer, drawn into the 'play' as an actor, is now carefully reminded of his 'other' role as audience. The securities of measured distance have been transgressed—violated—and the consequence is a rich pattern of role-playing, exchange, reversal.

The complexity of Haliburton's observations and self-exploration are so brilliantly dramatized in the opening scene of *The Clockmaker* that I can imagine North American writing itself breaking loose on those few pages. 'I was always well mounted,' the narrator begins; the narrator at once Haliburton himself and a fictionalized version of himself. 'I am fond of a horse, and always piqued myself on having the fastest trotter in the Province. I have made no great progress in the world; I feel doubly, therefore, the pleasure of not being surpassed on the road' (p. 4).

Four pages later he is engaged with his own *double*, Sam Slick, who remarks, 'I am fond of a horse; I don't like to ride in the dust after everyone I meet, and I allow no man to pass me but when I choose' (p. 7).

The tension between the two men is resolved through the misunderstanding and then the understanding of a word--the word, circuit. The narrator begins with an understanding of the word's *legal* implication. He comes to learn that clockmakers, in a carnivalesque inversion, also 'ride the circuit'.

The narrator concludes: 'This explanation restored my good humour, and as I could not quit my companion, and he did not feel disposed to leave me, I made up my mind to travel with him to Fort Lawrence, the limit of his circuit' (p. 7).

Thomas Haliburton, Judge Haliburton, the man of *law*, had

created a great pedlar, a flimflam man, a confidence man, a carney, a folk philosopher, a cynic from the carnivalesque streets of Greece and Rome. Haliburton, a Loyalist with a thorough dislike of that new nation, America, could only create his great figure by making him an American. The binaries of love-hate, friend-enemy, peace-war were, temporarily, collapsed. The king put on the clown's mask, the clown the king's. And the mask is essential to carnival. The mask enabled Haliburton to do violence to his own identity, personal and national; carnival rejoices not in our completeness but in our incompleteness; the mask allows us to partake of several possibilities; we are allowed to cross boundaries; we can at once be serious and mocking, be ourselves and caricature others, be others and criticize ourselves.

But Haliburton was at heart, or at centre, an eighteenth-century man who cherished his completeness and who could not tolerate the American sense of incompleteness, of eccentricity, of the receding green light, of revolution, of a violence that was somehow natural to the human condition.

Haliburton's struggle both to ride with and ride away from his carnivalesque double is a moment of continuing consequence in the history of North American literature. He has met the devil himself and, as in true carnival, has found him a rather endearing fellow. The encounter recalls the moment when Don Quixote and Sancho Panza set out across the landscapes of Spain.

'Familiarization,' Bakhtin writes, 'furthered the destruction of epical and tragical distance and the transferal of the material that is being presented to the zone of familiar contact . . . .'

That zone of contact, finally, is too much for Haliburton. He cannot do enduring violence to his own Tory principles, his own Tory sense of hierarchy and order. As a result, he can create a great character, but he cannot create a story for that character. He cannot create an action that will, violently, discover its own consequences.

Later in the century, Melville will destroy that same hierarchical distance, accept the 'zone of familiar contact', by putting Queequeg and his narrator into the same bed in a marriage that is carnivalistically at once mock and serious. 'In bed we concocted our plans for the morrow,' Ishmael reports matter-of-factly. Mark Twain will destroy that distance violently by putting Huck Finn and Nigger Jim into intimate relationship on a raft on the Mississippi, where they play at a shifting of roles, including that central carnivalistic shift, into representing the opposite sex.

Melville explores a carnival world in *The Confidence Man: His Masquerade*, a work that is itself, appropriately, incomplete. But his major work centres on the Pacific. Perhaps, for him, not just the *Pequod*, but the entire Pacific Ocean was a carnival. Mark Twain, the younger Samuel Clemens at least, found the whole Mississippi to be a carnival world. Twain brilliantly breaks down the audience-actor distance, with Huck constantly walking onto stage, in feuds, in duels, finally into plays themselves, in the upside-down world of the duke and the king.

For both, the act of living on water, in a ship or on a raft, in a place that is always itself and yet becoming something else, allows the world to take on its carnival aspect. And for both novelists there is an endless confrontation with violence itself: for Melville in all that whaling implies, our living by killing; for Twain and Huckleberry Finn in the violent encounters on the Mississippi— the river itself becomes street and carnival square. Water, like fire, is a dimension of the carnival, insisting on the stateless and the flux; it is the condition entered into by Moodie's Irish emigrants ('The men and boys were *in* the water . . .'), much to her disapproval. It is becoming, incompleteness; it is the verb, to carnivalize.

For Kristeva, the novel is heir to the carnival. 'Carnival discourse', she says, 'breaks through the laws of a language censored by grammar and semantics and, at the same time, is a social and political protest. There is no equivalence, but rather, identity between challenging official linguistic codes and challenging official law' (p. 65).

In the use of folk speech itself, language from the oral tradition in which the carnivalesque survived, Haliburton and Melville and Twain found a way to issue their carnivalistic challenges to the official codes, the official laws. Folk speech itself became a form of violence.

Susanna Moodie does not challenge linguistic codes. Indeed, she is quick to make fun of grammars and accents that are unlike her own. Her prose is appropriate to the distance, to the social and voyeuristic distance, she wishes to maintain. It does no violence to linguistic convention. Her prose is fascinating in its illusion of clarity; a white glare on the surface creates a kind of opaqueness.

Haliburton's prose reflects his own unresolvable division. The narrator speaks careful eighteenth-century prose. But Sam Slick speaks a violence to that precision, his language is a kind of folk poetry. He embeds in the literary prose of the narrator an equivocating series of folk narratives.

Melville anticipates the novel of the twentieth century; he dares to use a first-person narrator, in a time when the authority of the third-person was paramount. 'Call me Ishmael. Some years ago— never mind how long precisely—' Even the unsteady way in which the narrator finds his voice and loses it again, into other possibilities, is evidence of a carnivalistic energy, a doing-violence to the laws of genre.

And then Twain, in *Huck Finn*, begins with his great blast at the law-makers and the grammarians:

> NOTICE: Persons attempting to find a motive in this narrative will be prosecuted; persons attempting to find a moral in it will be banished; persons attempting to find a plot in it will be shot.

> EXPLANATORY: In this book a number of dialects are used, to wit: the Missouri negro dialect; the extremest form of the backwoods South-Western dialect; the ordinary 'Pike-County' dialect; and four modified varieties of this last. . . . I make this explanation for the reason that without it many readers would suppose that all these characters were trying to talk alike and not succeeding.[6]

Haliburton and Melville and Twain, in their major writings, invite us to laughter. Theirs is not a laughter that mocks eccentricity, thereby reinforcing the norm, the status quo, the laws of society. For Bakhtin, carnival laughter

> is ambivalent. . . . The people do not exclude themselves from the wholeness of the world. . . . This is one of the essential differences of the people's festive laughter from the pure satire of modern times. The satirist whose laughter is negative places himself above the object of his mockery, he is opposed to it. The wholeness of the world's comic aspect is destroyed, and that which appears comic becomes a private reaction. The people's ambivalent laughter, on the other hand, expresses the point of view of the whole world: he who is laughing also belongs to it. (R, 11-12)

This is the laughter of Rabelais and Shakespeare.

Haliburton, at his best, achieved this level of carnival laughter. As he began to hesitate, in the face of his own mocking double, he retreated towards a kind of parody that removed him from the ranks of those being laughed at. Haliburton's carnivalesque anticipates that of Melville and Twain. But where he finally contained his own laughter, they dared a laughter that confronted the dark nothingness, or the white nothingness, of chaos itself. They enter into that American confrontation with a violence that might annihilate as well as renew.

The promise of the carnivalesque is a promise of renewal by destruction. One of the forces that accounts for the radical development of literature in nineteenth-century North America is the encounter with the renewing energies of the carnivalesque. I am here looking at prose; I could as well look at the poetry of Whitman against that of Longfellow and Isabella Crawford. The writers in North America confronted a carnivalesque world in which hierarchies were collapsing, boundaries disappearing or shifting, opposites uniting or dissolving or changing face. Actor and audience were no longer separate. Everything was in a state of becoming, not of being. Violence was at once metaphor and reality; that distinction, too, collapsed. Violence was no longer a page-turner, a novelist's trick, a philosophic proposition. Perhaps North American culture itself became a kind of carnivalesque response to the 'authority' of European cultures and European versions of history.

It is possible that a war of rebellion is a kind of carnivalesque upsetting of the world, and it is by now a cliché to observe that Americans could successfully enter into this kind of war, Canadians could not. Haliburton is offended that Sam Slick's father at Bunker's Hill shot not just a British soldier, but an officer. Yet he describes the event with something bordering on relish. 'Well, I took a steady aim at him,' Sam Slick's father says,

> and fired. He didn't move for a space, and I thought I had missed him when all of a sudden he sprung right straight up on eend, his sword slipped through his hands up to the p'int, and then he fell flat on his face atop of the blade, and it came straight out through his back. He was fairly skivered (p. 147).

The shocked rebel then turns and flees. Haliburton could at once disapprove of and represent violence to authority. But his actor is American.

The two American writers Melville and Twain would not only observe the carnivalesque inversions of the world; they would also enter in and ask for us the twentieth-century question: Does the carnivalesque, which has in its ritual violence been an ultimately renewing force in the past, offer some understanding of, some form of rescue from, our own extremes of violence?

It may be that the great protest movement of the 1960s, against American involvement in Vietnam, was a kind of carnivalesque response to authority; whether this was the establishing of a new paradigm or a freak occurrence remains to be seen. But it was a precise example of the discrowning of the king (or presidents) that Bakhtin sees as primary to carnival.

On the other hand, it may be that Cortés, arriving in America, could destroy all before him precisely because he saw it as carnival, and not as a reality he would honour and allow to endure; the carnival was expendable because it was carnival, a mere turning upside-down of his reality.

In our own time, we have had a great novel about Mexico. Malcolm Lowry, in *Under the Volcano* (1947), writes obsessively about the carnivalesque. And the novel's background is obsessively war—the Spanish Civil War as prelude to World War II. Lowry's hero, the British consul Geoffrey Firmin, an ambiguous representative of authority, is literally turned upside down in a looping-the-loop machine. He literally loses his possessions, then has them restored to him. He might be the scapegoat figure who, through his encounter with violence, saves us. Or he might be the victim of violence, cast away. Or he might be the man who would not quite deal with his own violence, and is cast into hell.

On the other border of America, we have today the vital literary tradition of Quebec. Roch Carrier's *La Guerre, Yes Sir!* was first published in 1968, translated from the French by Sheila Fischman in 1970. Carrier's novel is another and different response to the New World, there on the shores of the St Lawrence where Mrs Moodie watched and disapproved and went on watching. It opens with a man trying to do violence to violence itself:

Joseph wasn't panting.

He approached like a man walking to work. Which hand would he put on the log, his right hand or his left? His right hand was stronger, better for working. His left hand was strong too.

Joseph spread the five fingers of his left hand on the log.

He heard breathing behind him. He turned around. It was his own.

His other fingers, his other hand, seized the axe. It crashed down between the wrist and the hand, which leapt into the snow and was slowly drowned in his blood. . . .

'Their Christly shells would have made jam out of me . . . They won't get me . . . me, I'll be making jam next fall: strawberries, blueberries, gooseberries, red apples, raspberries . . . '

Joseph burst into a great laugh, which he could hear going up very high, up above the snow. He hadn't had so much fun since the beginning of the war. The villagers heard his voice. He was calling for help.[7]

Carrier's novel combines the violence of war with the violence of laughter and the violence of sex. The war referred to is World War II, but in effect it becomes a civil war—between English soldiers and a French-Canadian village, the soldier and the civilians bound together by the violent death of a man who belongs to both groups—a man who is at once French Canadian and a soldier. The return of his coffin to his home village becomes a truly carnivalesque occasion. The coffin becomes the table to an unofficial feast. The villagers and the soldiers alike join in a dance of death— the carnivalesque dance that is the path at once to hell and to redemption. Laughter and prayer become inseparable, the most holy of prayers are corrupted into colloquial mis-translations, the flow of language turns the village into a Babel. The snow-bound village becomes the embodiment of a carnival that recalls Bakhtin—or Breughel—

Or the Canadian psyche, laced/lashed into its abominable white shroud.

Notes

[1]Mikhail Bakhtin, *Rabelais and His World*, trans. Helene Iswolsky (Cambridge Mass. and London, England: MIT Press, 1965), p. 10. Further references will appear in the text, preceded by R.

[2]Susanna Moodie, *Roughing It in the Bush* (Toronto: McClelland and Stewart, 1962 [New Canadian Library]), pp. 24-5. Further references will appear in the text.

[3]Bakhtin, *Problems of Dostoevsky's Poetics*, trans. R.W. Rotsel (Ann Arbor: Ardis, 1973), p. 100. Further references will appear in the text, preceded by D.

[4]Julia Kristeva, *Desire in Language*, ed. Leon S. Roudiez, trans. Thomas

Gora, Alice Jardine, Leon S. Roudiez (New York: Columbia University Press, 1980), p. 79. Further references will appear in the text.

[5]Thomas Haliburton, *The Clockmaker* (1836; edited rpt Toronto: McClelland and Stewart, 1958 [New Canadian Library]), p. 9. Further references will appear in the text.

[6]Mark Twain, *The Adventures of Huckleberry Finn*, ed. Henry Nash Smith (Boston: Houghton Mifflin, 1958), p. 2.

[7]Roch Carrier, *La Guerre, Yes Sir!* trans. Sheila Fischman (Toronto: Anansi, 1970), p. 5.

11

The Exploding Porcupine

English-Canadian writing is a writing that has too often avoided its own violence. The path of excess may be the road to wisdom; but the middle way is surely the way to a modest profit. I suspect that no writer in English Canada could begin a novel with a character placing his left hand on a log, picking up an axe with his right hand, aiming the right hand at the left. The axe, we are told in *La Guerre, Yes Sir!*, 'crashed down between the wrist and the hand, which leapt into the snow . . . Joseph burst into a great laugh, which he could hear going up very high, up above the snow.'[1]

Violence, physical violence, proposes an ending. Joseph, in Roch Carrier's Québécois novel, proposes to end the anxiety he feels about the war. Timothy Findley's novel *The Wars* begins with Robert Ross, its ambiguous hero, already a soldier and already in battle. He is, though wounded, alive, apparently the sole survivor of an attack, along with twelve cattle-cars loaded with horses. He lives ambiguously between the proofs and contradictions of his own experience of violence.

The theory of answers, for us, is a dangerous one. We must resist endings, violently. And so we turn from content to the container. It is the form itself, traditional form, that forces resolution. In our most ambitious writing, we do violence to form.

Something got in the way of story in high modern writing. Paradoxically, that something was language. In the works of Joyce, of Pound, of Eliot, of Virginia Woolf, the language itself became the language itself. The story became untellable. The motion of story turned into image. The image turned into word.

Contemporary criticism is full of our attempts to break out. Or, more exactly, to break in: that is, to penetrate. Behind the noun, violence, is the verb, to violate. We want to penetrate the word, penetrate the image, and uncover story.

The words violence and deconstruction are in complicity; but violence is prior to, more primitive than, deconstruction. Deconstruction implies, for all its attraction to disorder, a recovery of order, control; not so much the moment as the moment after. Story is a mode of thinking. In order to think itself, nowadays, it must do immediate violence to its own conventions.

The ultimate violence that might be done to story is silence. Roland Barthes, writing on Roland Barthes, goes farther and says, 'a cessation of language is the greatest violence that can be done to the violence of language.'[2] But that possibility of silence, finally, is only a provocation into speech. Foucault tells us that 'every language . . . erects itself vertically against death.'[3] This erection must issue into speech; speech must issue into story.

Major John Richardson's novel *Wacousta*, appearing in the middle of the nineteenth century, suggests the paradigm of contradiction that continues to shape English-Canadian fiction. The English commander in that novel, Colonel De Haldimar, is supposedly a soldier of high accomplishment. The content of the story insists that he is a soldier. The telling of that content makes him a kind of virgin, hidden away, guarded rather than guarding, in a room inside his fort, in a room that itself is unbroken, vaginal. The violator must connive an entrance. A surreptitious entrance. A dreamed entrance. And, against the silence of De Haldimar's posture of waiting and denial, a *speech* entrance. A violation by story; story violated.

The enacted violence of the novel is formulaic, conventional, derived from the Gothic fictions of European literature. Stuffy. Predictable, Repetitive. But Richardson, in his struggle to violate that material into a story, portends our later coming. In that stubborn novel (and the text is so often mutilated by editors that we hardly know what the text is), he commences the English-Canadian search for that contradictory necessity, a grammar of violence. A grammar that occasions rather than prescribes; a grammar that, against its own prescription of repetition, invites breakage.

The classic modern novels in the English-Canadian tradition are three: Sinclair Ross's *As For Me and My House*, Sheila Watson's *The Double Hook*, and Ernest Buckler's *The Mountain and the Valley*. One hears in each of those three titles a kind of opposition, a basic contrary that is implicitly sexual in its inclination towards interpenetration: the need of violence. In each there is a pastoral world that is violated out of its original innocence. In all three novels the figure of the artist is close at hand, imploding into the text the author's concern with how the text gets itself written.

The grammar of violence in these three novels I would define with the phrase 'ceremonies of disbelief'. In all three novels there are ceremonies of order, Christian in derivation, though touching on other systems of conviction (systems of family, systems of community). But conviction is indeed what the system becomes. And the convicts, in each novel, are tempted appallingly by silence, by the kind of silence that Barthes has described. In all three novels a magnificent attention is paid to language, that ultimate ceremony of culture. But that ceremony, that ceremonial speech, only enlarges the silence of the characters within the speaking.

The new worlds of these novels, the newly spoken worlds, are already decaying towards silence. The closed door of Philip Bentley is a silence as great as Mrs Bentley's speech act, her diary. The son pushing his mother down the stairs in *The Double Hook* (his sister, grinding coffee, grinding away his voice), creates a silence that all the eloquent echoes of the novel cannot blot into sound.

In Buckler's novel, Ellen, the grandmother, completes her rug, the ceremony of her rug-making, as the novel itself begins to end:

> Only one tiny circle remained. White. White . . . She picked up the scrap of fine white lace and made of it the last circle. She smiled.
> 'David,' she called, 'the rug is done. Come see.'
> He didn't answer.[4]

The hero of the novel, David Canaan, the grandson, the writer, the artist, doesn't answer. He has perished into the white and absolute silence of snow. The uttered world hears its own silence, even as it is created. Even as it is spoken. The ceremonies of this kind of novel bespeak their own disbelief.

A second and younger group of English-Canadian writers insists on another version of the grammar of violence. In all the novels of Rudy Wiebe and Jack Hodgins, and the novel *Scann* by Robert Harlow, I hear a version that I would call 'the continuing apocalypse'.

'The minimal complete plot', Todorov tells us in *The Poetics of Prose*, 'consists in the passage from one equilibrium to another.'[5] For Wiebe and Hodgins and Harlow, this passage is signalled by a disaster or calamity of apocalyptic proportion. Possibilities of sainthood afflict the heroes of Wiebe's *The Temptations of Big Bear* and Hodgins' *The Invention of the World* and even Harlow's profane *Scann*. The world obliges with catastrophe and death.

And yet what is most violated is the set of conventions that supposedly shape story. Big Bear can be neither named nor annihilated by all the official varieties of language—journalistic, legal, political, religious. Strabo, in *The Invention of the World*, like his namesake, the amateur geographer of old, invents the world by an extravagant telling of its story. Scann, the teller of Harlow's novel, locked up in his hotel room, at his writing-table, at his peephole, does more violence to story than ever he does to the chambermaid. The apocalypse of speech, the naming of the world's end, does not end the world; that act, precisely, insures its continuance. We, invited in as radical readers, participate in this murdering into life.

The Canadian critic and novelist David Williams, the author of a violent novel, *The Burning Wood*, writes to me:

> violence, like art, is just one more defense of the immortal ego, another self-saving form of expression in the face of death. For as the violent doer promotes his own life by taking another's—or lessens his fear of death by dealing it out—so too the artist destroys his materials in the very act of creating them . . .

Immortality and effacement find grammatical conjunction. The manuscript of Scann's story burns at the end of the book; even the novel has its apocalypse. But Harlow's novel of that novel goes on, it is there, we read it. The apocalypse continues.

A third version of our English-Canadian grammar of violence finds expression in the works of Michael Ondaatje and Audrey Thomas. These two writers anticipate a group of emerging Canadian writers who are, it seems to me, the gangsters of love.

In Ondaatje's *Coming through Slaughter* and in Thomas's *Blown Figures*, we journey to foreign places—to New Orleans and to Central Africa. In both novels, if we can still use that word to name such radical experiments in form, the story is specifically a quest; in each the quest is for a missing person. Because of this, the model of history (and the traditional novel was often, traditionally, the history of a person) is replaced, explicitly, by the methods of archaeology.

Archaeology, of necessity, involves violence—the uncovering of past lives. That uncovering, for Ondaatje and Thomas, involves as well the acceptance of the discontinuity of form. The continuity asserted by history is beyond, lies beyond, the truth of fiction. The reader, like the writer, becomes archaeologist, seeking the grammar of the fragments.

Ondaatje traces, finds traces of, a jazz artist whose talent was literally and violently destroyed, the music-maker turned into a silent man in a lunatic asylum. Audrey Thomas finds out the journey of a woman who went to the edge of madness in search of a child whom she supposedly lost by abortion—a child who did not ever escape from silence, into speech.

I'll concentrate on *Coming through Slaughter*, inviting the reader all the while to consider *Blown Figures* while I speak of Ondaatje's book. Let that other book be either a silent presence or a speaking absence.

Ondaatje's, the book's title: *Coming through Slaughter*. We read. Coming: as opposed to the going we would expect, through slaughter. Coming: prescriptive, hopeful. But sexual, still violent. Explosive now. The great porcupine that wards off the world (words off the world), exploding from inside. Foucault tells us: 'the work is ruined by that which initially constituted it.' Coming is, also, going. Ondaatje, by a nicely violent twist, tells us, or reports from an interview that he has unearthed, that his hero, Buddy Bolden, was 'Buried in unmarked grave at Holtz Cemetery after being brought back from the Asylum through Slaughter, Vachery, Sunshine, back to New Orleans.'[6] We must, ourselves, as readers, participate in the archaeologist's quest. And in his pleasure at this unpleasant dis-covering.

There is, in a grave-like frame on the bottom half of the cover of the book, a photograph. A faded picture, in black and white, against the brown and blue of the book's cover. *In* the brown and blue. Six jazz musicians, at this point nameless, in static arrangement. Posing. Posed. Poised. Silent. As the great musician, Buddy Bolden, is silent; because we have no record (no *record*) of his playing.

Here is the 'real thing', anticipating, refusing, creating, destroying the fiction that is to come. Photo: arrest. Killing. Going. The camera as weapon. With, but against, the novel. The positives of the negatives. Realized in acid. Ruined in acid. The reader, being read.

Bellocq. The imagined real figure, Bellocq, the photographer, as version of artist. The photographer, ignoring audience, recording the prostitutes (but only when they are *not* working; another violence), doing violence to narrative expectation.

The turning of a page, in the reading of a novel, is a kind of violation of narrative. Traditional narrative glosses over the break by insisting on its own adherence to cause and effect, to motivation, to verisimilitude. Ondaatje heightens the sense of violation by beginning a new section of the 'story' at the top of the lefthand page. By spacing his paragraphs. By inserting asterisks. The bookness of book is used, to violate the consolation of narrative. Book and text, discrete. But revealing each other. A grammar of violence.

And Audrey Thomas, in *Blown Figures*: the cover of her book is a painting, 'Lovers in a Landscape No. 7', by Claude Breeze. Art calls attention to art. The book is dedicated to Isobel; Isobel is the name of the heroine in the book. A heroine in the book. Audrey Thomas promises Isobel that oldest kind of story, a fairy-tale; but 'a new one that nobody has ever read before'.[7] We turn the pages, into the book: the pages themselves enclose silence, encapsulate. A single sentence on a page. A cartoon strip. The definition of a word. A child's verse. A newspaper ad: 'NO. 9 BLADDER AND KIDNEY TEA / LETS YOU ENJOY LIFE AGAIN.'

Audrey Thomas dares to turn the disruption into waste. Our economical, bourgeois selves look at the blankness of the pages: words are a necessary commodity to fill space. This novel borders on the indecent extravagance of poetry. Genre itself is threatened.

The violence of story. Violence in story. Ondaatje gives us that too: in the scene where Bolden and Pickett fight, in the barbershop where Bolden cuts hair [Pickett is speaking]:

> He got his left arm under my chin—like this—then he opens the razor with his other hand, flicks it open in a movement like he was throwing it away and puts it in my shirt and slits it open in a couple of places. Once the shirt's open he starts shaving me up and down my front taking the hairs off. I wasn't moving or saying anything. Thought I'd keep still. Then he slices off my nipple. I don't think he meant to, was probably an accident. But that got me shouting. Then he lets go my neck and starts shaving my face very fast now small cuts now . . . (p. 73).

What makes the slicing off of the nipple a violent act is not simply the act itself. But more: Ondaatje refuses to give the scene a traditional beginning, middle, and end. His refusal of form releases the experience of violence into the reader's experience of reading. The violent act is not contained, manipulated, accounted for.

In an earlier passage, Frank Lewis has told us, speaking of Buddy Bolden:

> But there was a discipline, it was just that we didn't understand. We thought he was formless, but I think now he was tormented by order, what was outside it. He tore open the plot—see his music was immediately on top of his own life (p. 37).

It is by this tearing apart of plot that Ondaatje too does his creating. And we are told that his story of Bolden, his making of art, is on top of his own life:

> . . . When he went mad he was the same age as I am now.
>
> The photograph moves and becomes a mirror. When I read he stood in front of mirrors and attacked himself, there was the shock of memory. For I had done that. Stood, and with a razor-blade cut into cheeks and forehead, shaved hair (p. 133).

Foucault gives us a way to read this so-called authorial intrusion:

> . . . we find the link between writing and death manifested in the total effacement of the individual characteristics of the writer; the quibbling and confrontations that a writer generates between himself and his text cancels out the signs of his particular individuality (p. 117).

The photograph becomes mirror. In the mirror Ondaatje reads not so much his own text as his own absence. In the picture of Bolden he reads not his own life but his own death. He tears apart the plot that is his life. He discovers his gangster-complicity in death.

Ondaatje is forced, forces himself, to ask: Who killed Buddy Bolden? The plot, torn apart, ironically becomes detective story. Web, a policeman in the book, pursues the musician and his disappearance. Only to discover that he was, himself, in certain ways, Bolden's fate. And as his fate one of his violators. The detective as murderer. As even the audience was one of the murderers, that day in April 1907, when Buddy Bolden returned to the streets and played with a band; and played until he burst, from inside out, poured his own blood into his cornet.

But the author, Michael Ondaatje, in pursuing the story, literally, through Louisiana, through libraries and archives, finds that he too is implicated. He is denied the traditional immunity of authorship (I'm innocent; I only wrote it). Like Web, like the audience, like the photographer Bellocq, like the women who inspired and protected and helped to destroy Buddy Bolden, he too is one of the gangsters of love.

Like Audrey Thomas, posing her riddle at the end of *Blown Figures* ('TIME! YOU MONSTROUS MOLE. WHY ARE YOU DOING THIS TO ME?'[p. 547]), Ondaatje contributes to the riddle of his pursued hero. That contribution is story. But story of a special sort. For if the ceremonies of death are diminished, if we are, in some strange way, archaeologists, grave-robbers, then we must make of that violent act a new kind of story. A story that honours the mystery.

No doubt there are writers for whom violence, of either content or form, represents merely a turning away from the act of creation to the act of annihilation. No doubt there are writers for whom violence is a striking back at determinism, a perverse assertion that free will, of a sort, does still exist. These are not the motives of the best English-Canadian writing.

The quest of narrative, finally, is for the form of its quest. In our time, this questing has taken on proportions that silence some writers, that drive others back to the shelter of banal conventions. But the best of our writers, from Watson and Ross, on through Ondaatje and Thomas (and into the future too, I would hope), accept the terrors and the obligations and the necessary violence of that questing.

It means, finally, that the form itself must violate itself. The renewal does not come from outside, cannot be brought about by the introduction of new materials into the form. This creature is a porcupine that can only be violated from within. The porcupine of ego. The porcupine of the Safeway novel. The porcupine of English-Canadian self-righteousness. . . . And boredom. And self-congratulation. And timidity. And self-deception.

The inviolate animal, daring to learn the grammar of violence. The novel itself, acting out a ceremony of disbelief. The novel become a continuing apocalypse. The novelist become, beyond the

Adam-pose of innocence, the gangster of love. . . . Not violence done, but violence in the doing. . . . Consequently, in the end that is not an end (and Buddy Bolden says of the right ending: it can mean exactly the opposite of what you are thinking): the exploding porcupine.

Notes

[1] Roch Carrier, *La Guerre, Yes Sir!*, trans. Sheila Fischman (Toronto: Anansi, 1970), p. 5.

[2] Roland Barthes, *Roland Barthes*, trans. Richard Howard (New York: Hill and Wang, 1977), p. 159.

[3] Michel Foucault, *Language, Counter-Memory, Practice: Selected Essays and Interviews*, trans. Donald F. Bouchard and Sherry Simon (Ithaca: Cornell University Press, 1977), p. 60.

[4] Ernest Buckler, *The Mountain and the Valley* (New York: Henry Holt, 1952), p. 301.

[5] Tzvetan Todorov, *The Poetics of Prose*, trans. Richard Howard (Ithaca: Cornell University Press, 1977), p. 111.

[6] Michael Ondaatje, *Coming through Slaughter* (Toronto: Anansi, 1976), p. 137.

[7] Audrey Thomas, *Blown Figures* (Vancouver: Talonbooks, 1974), p. 547.

12

For Play and Entrance: The Contemporary Canadian Long Poem

purpose is a porpoise

a conceit

is there a sea

yes

is there a cloud

yes

everything elemental
everything blue

the precision of openness
is not a vagueness
it is an accumulation
cumulous

bp Nichol
The Martyrology, Book 4

1

In love-making, in writing the long poem—delay is both—delay is both technique and content. Narrative has an elaborate grammar of delay. The poets of the twentieth century, in moving away from narrative, abandoned (some willingly, some reluctantly) their inherited grammar. Poets, like lovers, were driven back to the moment of creation; the question, then: not how to end, but how to begin. Not the quest for ending, but the dwelling at and in the beginning itself.

2

Wallace Stevens, 'Of Modern Poetry':

> The poem of the mind in the act of finding
> What will suffice. It has not always had
> To find: the scene was set; it repeated what
> Was in the script.
> Then the theatre was changed
> To something else. Its past was a souvenir.

The problem for the writer of the contemporary long poem is to honour our disbelief in belief—that is, to recognize and explore our distrust of system, of grid, of monisms, of cosmologies perhaps, certainly of inherited story—and at the same time write a long work that has some kind of (under erasure) unity.

And yet the long poem, by its very length, allows the exploration of the failure of system and grid. The poem of that failure is a long poem.

3

Our interest in the discrete, in the occasion.

Trace: behind many of the long poems of the 1970s in Canada is the shadow (Jungian?) of another poem, a short long poem.

1965: Phyllis Webb, *Naked Poems*.

A kind of hesitation even to write the long poem. Two possibilities: the short long poem, the book-long poem. Webb, insisting on that hesitation. On that delay. On nakedness and lyric and yet on a way out, perhaps a way out of the ending of the lyric too, with its ferocious principles of closure, a being compelled out of lyric by lyric:

The poet, the lover, compelled towards an ending (conclusion, death, orgasm: coming) that must, out of love, be (difference) deferred. Phyllis Webb, from *Naked Poems* ('Flies'):

> tonight
> in this room

two flies
on the ceiling
are making
love
quietly. Or

so it seems
down here

4

A place to begin (Canada):

1970: Margaret Atwood, *The Journals of Susanna Moodie.*
1970: Michael Ondaatje, *The Collected Works of Billy the Kid.*
Both are book-length poems about books, about inherited story.
Both, also, treat of *real* legendary people. This basic tension, then,
in the Canadian long poem: a) the temptation of the documentary,
b) the scepticism about history. And as a consequence: a kind of
madness in the recording:

(Dorothy Livesay, 'The Documentary Poem: A Canadian Genre':
'a dialectic between the objective facts and the subjective feelings
of the poet': 1969: a place to begin)

a pressure towards madness. And against it: photographs, collages, analyses, protests of accuracy and source, afterwords.

Poems in which archaeology supplants history; an archaeology
that challenges the authenticity of history by saying there can be
no joined story, only abrupt guesswork, juxtaposition, flashes of
insight. A perpetual delay as we recognize the primacy of the
forthcoming and as yet unmade discovery.

5

The essential difference between delay and postponement.

1972: bp Nichol, *The Martyrology*, Books 1 & 2.

The third possibility: the life-long poem. Our interest in the discrete, in the occasion, carried to the uttering of the word itself:

as there are words i haven't written
things i haven't seen

> so this poem continues
> a kind of despair takes over
> the poem is written in spite of
> . . .
> this is not a spell
> it is an act of desperation

In Nichol we have, supremely, against the grammar of inherited story, the foregrounding of language. But the limits of language are such (the spirit become flesh; The Word become words) that all should be written down. The failure of language becomes its own grammar of delay:

> I am
> this moment is
> everything present & tense
> i write despite my own misgivings
> say things as they do occur
> the mind moves truly
> is it free

6

A method, then, and then, and then, of composition; against the 'and then' of story.

> This new variation of physical poetry can be called *particular poetry*. The daily gestalt of sound, smell, and image that we perceive in a fastpaced world of rapid transit, computerization, mass produc- tion, and global communication is so limitless that we perceive fragments, rather than the whole.
> E. Quigley, 'Particular Poetry,' *Rune* (Spring 1980).

The story as fragment *becomes* the long poem: the story becomes its own narrative; i.e., our interest is in, not story, but the *act* of tell- ing the story: and Dorothy Livesay is mistaken in saying that 'the Canadian longer poem is not truly a narrative at all'; i.e., it may not be story, but it is (as we shall see, must be) narrative:

Solecki: Why did you want to make a film specifically about Nichol?
Ondaatje: At that time I was very interested in the possibilities of

concrete poetry and I'd just finished the actual writing of *The Collected Works of Billy the Kid* and there was a real sense of words meaning nothing to me anymore . . .

7

myth & map The placing of place, but not as in the American poem of (Paterson, Gloucester) place:
1974: Robin Blaser, *Image-Nations* 1-12.
1974: Daphne Marlatt, *Steveston*.
Blaser, beginning:

> the participation is broken
> fished from a sky of fire
> the fiery lake pouring itself
> to reach here
> that matter of language caught
> in the fact   so that we
> meet in paradise   in such
> times, the I consumes itself

(place: the eye
consumes itself: time)
Marlatt, beginning (acknowledging Williams' *Paterson*):

> He said they were playing cards in the
> Chinese mess hall, he said it was dark a hall? a shack.
> they were all, crowded together on top of each other.
> He said somebody accidentally knocked the oil lamp over, off
> the edge
>
> where stilts are standing, Over the edge of the
> dyke a river pours, uncalled for, unending: . . .

Marlatt's *Steveston*: a fish story:

time, here, as a function of the poetic line; fishing (the line without end?) ubiquitous in Canadian writing; the act of fishing itself (delay) as a translation of place into narrative:

Robin Blaser, in *Caterpillar* 12 (1970):

I'm interested in a particular kind of narrative—what Jack Spicer and I agreed to call in our own work the serial poem—this is a nar-

rative which refuses to adopt an imposed story line, and completes
itself only in the sequence of poems, if, in fact, a reader insists upon
a definition of completion which is separate from the activity of the
poems themselves.

Robin Blaser, in 'Statements of the Poets,' in *The Long Poem Anthology*, edited by Michael Ondaatje (1979):

The poet is not the centre of meaning, and if he were, the horror
would be his dearest subject. The serial poet chances it to think
again as if everything had to be thought anew. . . . The serial poem
is not simply a sequence. It is meant to be a narrative that trans-
figures time, our limit, mine. I have wanted to use the form because
it makes language direct and insistent without reference to a grid
of meaning, which in our time has become intolerable, a-historical,
a lie.

The caught fish, the fish, caught: explosion, conclusion, ending,
fire, home, net, night, orgasm.

8

fishing (for) (play)

1975: Don McKay, *Long Sault*.

1975: Fred Wah, *Pictograms from the Interior of B.C.*

McKay: elegy (eulogy?) as a place to begin. The town and the
rapids, submerged by the building of the St Lawrence Seaway. The
drowned city. As for Williams before McKay, as for Dante before
Williams: the descent beckons.
The

poet: gone fishing.
Death as deferral only, as another grammar of delay. The poem itself, surfacing. The poem of the place, the place lost. Things fall
into place in the poem.

Wah: the mysteries of the pictograms. The temptation to read the
scattered text (the descent, this time, to find Orpheus). Begin from
loss. The double hook. The poet (gone) fishing.

The pictograms are a language and a story; at once, a language and
a story. But we have lost the connection. Wah, desperately, reading the traces, trying to leap the gaps (signifier to signified), trying

to un-name the silence back to name:

> Only three persons and a dog survived
> and one man
> had the entire map of himself
> shot out
>
> others also
> lost what had been gained
> the winners were heroes
> thinking more to win over
> than could ever be remembered.
> Remember?

And then, on the next page:

> nv s ble
> tr ck

The poet as (inspired? shamanistic? mad?)
archaeologist.

9

You, poet, giving birth to yourself. The contemporary Canadian long poem as birth and trauma. The endless need to begin.

Novels can use story for that giving birth: Buckler's *The Mountain and the Valley* (though David moves out of narrative, into a kind of poem-meditation, on the top of the mountain), Davies' *The Manticore* (bear story), Atwood's *Surfacing* (and here, the poet herself, compelled to story).

But in the poems: the massive evasions of *The Martyrology*, the violence of *Billy the Kid*. In the poems we write towards cosmologies that cannot be (thank heavens) located:

1976: bp Nichol, *The Martyrology*, Books 3 & 4.
1976: George Bowering, *Allophanes*.

10

DANGER: proceed at once / past this point:

... it implies a form of literature that feeds upon its own impossibility: it implies an almost violently paradoxical form of literature, one which requires for its creation the failure of language. ... What turns over in Valéry's mind ... is precisely the idea of the negativity of beauty, together with the possibility that, by virtue of this negativity, the very inadequacy of a language becomes a resource. 'Ineffability: "words fail us"'—and yet literature seeks to establish itself upon this failure. Gerald L. Bruns, his chapter 'Negative Discourse and the Moment before Speech', from his book *Modern Poetry and the Idea of Language*, 1974.

—negative capability—

11

DANGER: deferral (delay delayed) of the encounter. With god. With the muse. With the lover.

Phenomenology and / or erasure:

1977: Douglas Barbour, *Visions of My Grandfather*.
1977: D.G. Jones, *Under the Thunder the Flowers Light up the Earth*.
1977: Roy Kiyooka, *The Fountainebleau Dream Machine: 18 Frames from A Book of Rhetoric*.
1977: Robert Kroetsch, *Seed Catalogue*.
1977: Eli Mandel, *Out of Place*.
1977: Daphne Marlatt, *Zócalo*.
1977: John Marshall, *The West Coast Trail Poems*.

(chancing it)

12

Place become space.

The beautiful blankness of the page.

Absence.

In the middle of the argument, of the journey, of the descent: where the traditional traveller, in the traditional story, traditionally receives the secret knowledge that enables him both to return and to go on:

we come to a dispatch of silence.

And later Bruns says that

> Barthes is saying that modern poetry is not simply 'poetic discourse' and therefore merely a different kind of discourse from prose or conversation. Modern poetry is nondiscourse: the modern poetic act is not intentional; it is a refusal to mean.

13

grandpa (and all those fucking tombstones)

Doug Barbour: the long line in the long poem.

(It is Nichol who teaches us a Miltonic scorn for economy. Many poets of the long poem hear still, inside the longness, the model of the short: perhaps one secret of the short poem is its offer of apprehensibility to the reader. The long poem, as Nichol conceives it, refuses the reader this option ['so many people saying to me they do not understand']. The possibility of *apprehension* is obliterated by apprehension itself: if nothing else is certain, the extension of the text, at least, is—)

Doug Barbour, hearing the line clear across the page. Clean across the page. Visions / revisions of a grandfather in Canadian writing, a tradition acknowledging our need for and resistance to history; our finding in the local tradition, in the oral tradition, as Purdy has it in his poem: 'First my grandfather'.

1964: Al Purdy, *In Search of Owen Roblin*

(Purdy writing the line that he shaped into the poetic line of the 60s, in Canada

(Purdy in *search* instead of in *vision*; the story intruding on the potential of the poem

(the photographs in Purdy's book edging us towards nostalgia, not towards discovery; and consider the tombstone pictures in his book beside those in *Billy the Kid*, beside those in *Out of Place*:

a new country; the fascination with tombstones):

Doug Barbour writing without clamour or blush the book-long poem, at ease with space and spacing: not typology but typography.

14

fragments / flow

And, against the fit / vision of Barbour, the fragments (Heraclitus) of Bowering's *Allophanes*: all / appearances / sound / voice:

> The snowball appears in Hell
> every morning at seven.

The poem with no more chance than. The poet as skilful alchemist who changes sound into silence.

Homer wrote poems without stanzas. We threaten to write stanzas (fragments, pieces, journals, 'takes', cantos even) that cannot become the poem.

(or: against the long ellipsis that is Bowering's poem: 1976: Gary Geddes, *War & Other Measures*: Geddes, who dares to make the poem both explicitly urban and explicitly political, moral even; Geddes who with all that daring then surrenders to the economy of a kind of narrative that excludes the invited and yet apparently extraneous detail)

15

the erotic and erratic erotic

Jones and Mandel. The war within. A generation caught between generations: post(modern) / modern.

Jones: the wonderful temptation to read nature as woman: behold (but cannot, quite) the sweet cunt of the world. The man as merest word-monger (remembering Archibald Lampman, remembering Shakespeare, writing versions of the sonnet), promising only immortality in return for entrances:

> Kisses are knowledge, Kate
> aphasia confounds us with a new
> tongue

or again

> Wild carrot, daisy, buttercup
> I scatter words in the air
> like your bouquet

        petal, sepal, leaf,
delicate explosions
   . . .
        thus fields
mimic your grace, thus words
rearticulate the trace
of outcast energy

Jones's sequence 'Kate, these flowers . . . ' (The Lampman Poems), again a book on books; but with the longing (desire?) that word and world might have touched (the short long poem; the lyric that might have been narrative).

The strength of poets like Jones and Mandel: a conflict of the poetry of Modern and the poem of Postmodern.

For Doug Jones: nature as text and world and woman; poet as reader and lover, even if the poet is blind, the text abused.

(elsewhere, a new cosmology of nature, located in science:
1973: Christopher Dewdney, *A Palaeozoic Geology of London, Ontario*.
1975: Christopher Dewdney, *Fovea Centralis*.

Dewdney: 'THE FOSSIL IS PURE MEMORY'.)

16

the Artist-artist connection

Mandel: *Out of Place*. The conflict of poem with its own design. The book of poems that is a book-long poem. The poet meets shadow, or vice versa: the double, the destruction that allows the new. The paradox of deconstruction: the man who is running out of time:

    the doppelgänger:

    ways to prevent me:

    refusing to be interrupted especially by children
    single-mindedness to the point of brutality
    in all matters of politics religion metaphysics &
    the character and lives of your closest friends
    praising the worst lines of your fellow writers

jogging followed by volley ball and cold showers
concentrated masturbation before and after sex
sleeping with a towel knotted in your back
inspired teaching ferocious tactics in rumoli
combinations of alchohol librium and   bad novels
seeing I'm here you know all methods fail
you don't even know how long it has been
what I might have said to children or others
now it's forever too late
no one could possibly know
you've been gone for days
when I make love to your wife
she will moan and praise you
asking you never to leave

where shall I say you have gone?

The grammar of narrative remembered, even if it can only occasion a mistelling

Out of Place and *The Journals of Susanna Moodie* are poems of the same loss, and the same guilty pleasure at the loss. In both books, the resort beyond language to illustration. The flight from language into photos and collages (into documentation).

The encounter with the double who can be seen but cannot quite be imagined.

It must have been, look, here's a picture, a snapshot. The snapshot, hinting of artlessness, asserting against art the reality of reality.

Canadian books of poetry with, obsessively (madly?), their photos and illustrations that do and do not fit. The phenomenology of erasure: replace language with image. Or, documentation: the presence of absence.

(Dennis Lee, throughout much of the '70s, writing and rewriting. 'The Death of Harold Ladoo'; Lee, transfixed by the meeting with the double, the aging white male dark and dangerous and wild and *poetic*. And then struggling to impose on his vision [against the sweet taste of madness] the consolation of an accepted grammar.)

The paradox become this now: that art does not quite narrate, while life, possibly, does. (the long poem as, literally, rewriting)

17

for play / foreplay

We write mandalas towards a cosmology that cannot be located. Towards a cosmology that, possibly, we do not wish to locate. Like Wordsworth, we spend years on the prelude. Like Stevens, we make notes towards a supreme fiction.

(My own continuing poem is called, somewhat to my dismay, *Field Notes*. Perhaps Olson's field is there somewhere, but more specifically I think of the field notes kept by the archaeologist, by the finding man, the finding man who is essentially lost. I can only guess the other; there might, that is, be a hidden text. Yes, it is as if we spend our lives finding clues, fragments, shards, leading or misleading details, chipped tablets written over in a forgotten language. Perhaps they are a counting of cattle, a measuring out of grain. Perhaps they are a praising of gods, a naming of the dead. We can't know.)

Perhaps we tell a blurred story because the story is blurred.

18

the book-ness of book: the book

Bowering: the poem become notation.
Kiyooka: the book become book.

Not just the phenomenology of reading, but the phenomenology of book. The Coach House Press as a phenomenal influence. Kiyooka, not the poet fascinated by art (Doug Jones), but the visual artist as poet, the sound of sight / site: Kiyooka, like Ondaatje, fascinated not only by the document in the book but by the book itself as document. We try to read, not what is in the book (that failing), but the book itself. The poet, then, not as maker, but as bookmaker.

19

The traffic report from the sky that we get in the morning on the radio.

The long poem, since the time of *The Odyssey*, has been a kind of travel book. Since its beginning, you might say. The travel book as

poem *contains* a version of narrative. The travel poem has, traditionally, a specific (if not clear) sense of goal. Of ending (eschatol-
ogy), if you will.

Further, the long poem as travel poem elaborates its own complex
relationship to the idea of love. Separation and delay and fulfilment are elements in the grammar. Surprise and temptation take
the traveller away from and towards.

Marlatt's travel book *Zócalo*, with its diagramming of the ineffable
(protomandala?) desires to become both love poem and long
poem. But Marlatt's grammar of delay is so absolute that the
poem, by a strategy of speech rather than silence, delays even its
becoming a poem. The lover is a photographer, a lover who delays
love by taking pictures (documentation); he is the book's silence.
The writer in the book, the poet ('she'), talking endlessly, endlessly endlessly talking, caught in the eroticism of her own speech act,
delays infinitely the entrance into the poem. The speech, the style,
the journey delayed by speech and style, impose on the reader the
absolute and exquisite (sexual) pain of delay. This book is pure
metonymy, a long poem instead of a long poem.

Marshall's *The West Coast Trail Poems*, poems become travel book,
works in a contrary way: the blankness of the page itself occasions
the desire: the reader's desire for words, the reader's desire to
enter the rain forest. Against all the blankness, of page, of forest,
is the counterpoint of a few words, a few verbal clues, hints that
there was a journey, there were encounters, the act of mapping did
take place:

> the balance of this
> time of evening
> the stars are, the tense
> light held
> an order known by
> not yet   about to
> begun

The poet, still, as traveller, still.

20

not a theology of travel / but travel as theology:

1978: Barry Callaghan, *The Hogg Poems & Drawings*.
1978: E.F. Dyck, *Odpoems Et* (illustrations by Bill Johnson)
(and I have here on my desk, in Winnipeg, newly discovered, not
yet explored:
1976: Wayne Clifford, *Glass Passages*.)

The tourist as visitor to God. Versions of the comic; and, more and
more, the idea of self as a cosmic joke. These books stand in opposition to the Romantic song of myself and its tradition, from
Whitman through Olson's *Maximus*. Hogg's ironic epilogue: 'Behold the whole Hogg.'

21

The temptation to write the final book.

We are everlastingly (in this our time) preparing to write the larger
poem. The impulse to write the final book (Joyce, Lowry, Pound .
. . or, before them, Spenser? . . . before Spenser, Ovid? . . .): the
book that frees us either into silence or into new possibilities.

Dyck's poem, attempting its own end (or epilogue):

> on the morning of the day
> of cre(m)ation the Poet
> at coffee raises his eye
> as she lands on the stool
> beside him   it sinks
>
> he left you his love & pulley
> he says   the latter of which
> I happen to have with me here
> & he hands her Od's pulley
>   then   he converged
>   she asks
> he died   says the poet
>   . . .

22

Or, against the poet's book, the poet's life:

the visionary poet, the hermit from Wood Mountain (living in the
city now, and in love): the poet, Andy Suknaski. All of his work

threatening to become one poem. His life and his writing become synonyms, become the life-long-poem. Most recently, the poem of his own travels, in the Canadian North:

1979: Andrew Suknaski, *East of Myloona.*

Not a sequence of poems, but an aspiration: the poet as shaman; every place an extension (narrative) of Wood Mountain; every speaking an extension of his own (language) speech.

23

entrance / en-trance!

We write poems, in Canada, not of the world, but to gain entrance to the world. That is our weakness and our strength.

Dare to enter.
Dare to be carried away, transported.

Is not the long poem, whatever its inward turn, finally the poem of outward? As we come to the end of self, in our century, we come again (consider the critical writings and poetry of Frank Davey) to the long poem. We become, again, persons in the world, against the preposterous notion of self. We are each our own crossroads.

24

delay / and after

To understand the long poem of our time would be to understand our time. I can't pretend to that understanding. I do hear in our long poems a changing sense of place, a changing sense of hero, a reluctant joy at the discovery that we can live without an Arnoldian longing for the old cosmologies. I do hear:

a voice trying to talk its way back from solitude
(from self to person?)

Old habits die hard.

Delay is the mother of beauty. Delay can become a misnaming of death. We have, we are told, in moving from Modern to Postmodern, moved from dialectic to diacritic. Thus we make new dialectics.

Delay, in the contemporary long poem (that necessary resisting towards the condition of art), has devolved upon the language itself, instead of into new resources or narrative. The language has become so foregrounded that the dialectic with narrative very nearly fails. Or else: the narrative, adhering to old grammars, refuses the excitement of its own language.

The gap between language and narrative, for our best poets, generates new possibilities, new long poems. bp Nichol names us out of a jam in *The Martyrology*. Ondaatje mocks us out of the self in his vision of child in *Billy the Kid*. Daphne Marlatt, giving us speech, even speech as a kind of silence, frees us from silence. Eli Mandel, for all of us, enacts the terrible and necessary encounter with the double. Those poets, with others of the '70s, fulfil the musing that Phyllis Webb whispered in her *Naked Poems* of 1965:

> Hieratic sounds emerge
> from the Priestess of
> Motion
> a new alphabet
> gasps for air.
>
> We disappear in the musk of her coming.

Bibliography

Atwood, Margaret. *The Journals of Susanna Moodie*. Toronto: Oxford University Press, 1970.

Barbour, Douglas. *Visions of My Grandfather*. Ottawa: Golden Dog Press, 1977.

Blaser, Robin. *Image-Nations* 1-12. London: The Ferry Press, 1974.

_____. 'The Fire'. *Caterpillar* 12 (July 1970), 15-23.

Bowering, George. *Allophanes*. Toronto: Coach House Press, 1976.

Bruns, Gerald L. *Modern Poetry and the Idea of Language*. New Haven and London: Yale UP, 1974.

Callaghan, Barry. *The Hogg Poems and Drawings*. Toronto: General Publishing, 1978.

Clifford, Wayne. *Glass Passages*. Ottawa: Oberon Press, 1976.

Dewdney, Christopher. *Fovea Centralis*. Toronto: Coach House Press, 1975.

_____. *A Palaeozoic Geology of London, Ontario*. Toronto: Coach House Press, 1973. Coach House Press, 1973.

Dyck, E.F. *Odpoems Et*, Moose Jaw: Coteau Books, 1978.

Jones, D.G. *Under the Thunder the Flowers Light up the Earth*. Toronto: Coach House Press, 1977.

Kiyooka, Roy. *The Fontainebleau Dream Machine*. Toronto: Coach House Press, 1977.

Kroetsch, Robert. *Seed Catalogue*. Winnipeg: Turnstone Press, 1977.

Lee, Dennis. 'The Death of Harold Ladoo'. *Boundary* 2, 5, No. 1 (Fall 1976), pp. 213-28.

Livesay, Dorothy. 'The Documentary Poem: A Canadian Genre', *Contexts of Canadian Criticism*, ed. Eli Mandel. Chicago: University of Chicago Press, 1971, pp. 267-81.

Mandel, Eli. *Out of Place*. Erin, Ont.: Press Porcépic, 1977.

Marlatt, Daphne. *Steveston*. Vancouver: Talonbooks, 1974.

_____. *Zócalo*. Toronto: Coach House Press, 1977.

Marshall, John. *The West Coast Trail Poems*. Lantzville, BC: Oolichan Books, 1977.

McKay, Don. *Long Sault*. London, Ont.: Applegarth Follies, 1975.

Nichol, bp. *The Martyrology*, Book 1. Toronto: Coach House Press, 1972.

_____. *The Martyrology*, Book 2. Toronto: Coach House Press, 1972.

_____. *The Martyrology*, Books 3 & 4. Toronto: Coach House Press, 1976.

Ondaatje, Michael. *The Collected Works of Billy the Kid*. Toronto: Anansi, 1970.

_____, ed. *The Long Poem Anthology*. Toronto: Coach House Press, 1979.

Purdy, Al. *In Search of Owen Roblin*. Toronto: McClelland and Stewart, 1974.

Quigley, E. 'Particular Poetry', *Rune* 6 (Spring 1980), pp. 30-53.

Solecki, Sam. 'An Interview with Michael Ondaatje', *Rune*, No. 2 (Spring 1975), pp. 39-54.

Suknaski, Andrew. *East of Myloona*. Saskatoon: Thistledown Press, 1979.
Stevens, Wallace. *The Collected Poems*. New York: Knopf, 1961.

Wah, Fred. *Pictograms from the Interior of B.C.* Vancouver: Talonbooks, 1975.

Webb, Phyllis. *Naked Poems*. Vancouver: Periwinkle Press, 1965.

13

Towards an Essay: My Upstate New York Journals

Sunday, January 11, 1970

The ironies: an editor at *Look* called me: We'd like you to do an opinion piece for a series in *Look*. Younger writers look at the world. How younger? I asked her. Under thirty. I'm a little over. Well, a little over wouldn't matter. Like twelve years over? Good grief, she said, you're *my* age. And so a circulation of 7.5 million is gone; and I'm back to Simon & Schuster's hope that they might sell 5,000 *Studhorse Man* in hard cover.

Holy Mary. My studhorse man, my prairie politicians. My dreamed reality as real as any dream: the garden and the end at once, the sky-haunted wait and the sky-brought apocalypse. The rain falls cold in Alberta.

Outside my Binghamton window today, a snowbank like a sand dune. The crest of the bank is sharply defined—defining itself as broken glass. To the windward side, a long white slope as smooth and blank as a sheet of paper.

What the hell. Write seven novels and see what happens.

Tuesday, January 13, 1970

Last night at a party given by graduate students I learned that Charles Olson is dead. He was the living master poet of this time, and now he too is only his books. Last semester I taught 'The Kingfishers' and 'In Cold Hell, in Thicket'. Next semester I teach *The Maximus Poems*. Olson found resources in our language that go beyond the discoveries of Pound and Williams. He had a special way of bringing time and place/space together; a way that spoke to me as a North American writer.

From *Call Me Ishmael*: 'I take SPACE to be the central fact to man born in America . . . It is geography at bottom, a hell of wide land from the beginning . . . PLUS a harshness we still perpetuate, a sun like a tomahawk . . .'

I set out now
in a box upon the sea

Wednesday, April 1, 1970

An April Fool's Day trick on myself: three agents, two offers for the movie rights to *Studhorse Man*—and still nothing sold.

Oh well, back to the typewriter—in three years I can have another book coming out.

There is
nothing.

There
is nothing.

There
is
nothing.

Wednesday, April 8, 1970

I went home at 5:15 (after the anguish of reviewing applications from Upward Bound students) and found that The Canada Council had phoned. Someone wanted to be sure I'm still a Canadian citizen: which can only mean(?) I'm in the finals for the Governor General's Award. At 8:15 I was helping Jane get the kids ready for bed. The phone rang. Is this the right Robert Kroetsch, the author and professor? Yes ma'am. This is Metro-Goldwyn-Mayer calling. One moment please. And a man's voice comes on and says, I've just read *The Studhorse Man*. It's a great comic novel. Have you got a theatrical agent? Has there been any interest in the movie rights? We feel we could do something good with this.

If, if and if. Maybe. Perhaps.

And I, nevertheless, was so goddamned 'up' that I talked Jane's ear off, then went to Sharkey's by myself for a dozen steamed clams and three draft and a long think. Hazard, my bad good man . . .

Saturday, April 11, 1970

Kattan phoned. Yes, I'm to receive the GG for *The Studhorse Man* on May 11, Ottawa. Went to a reading by Robert Creeley. Went to a party after. Charlie Coleman surprised me with a bottle of champagne. People smoking pot, drinking, talking with genuine pleasure about my good news.

And twenty years ago this month my first story appeared: 'The Stragglers', in the April issue of *The Montrealer*. I remembered back to the inviolate excitement of that occasion. I had spent part of the winter working in the army camp in Wainwright. The fellow I worked with never got any mail. One day I got a big pile, he again got none: I told him to open some of mine just for the fun of it. He did. He had often teased me about writing stories in the evening in our barracks when I should have been out raising hell, and he teased me about sending those stories off to magazines. Now he opened a letter and began to read aloud—We are pleased to accept your story . . . I thought he was teasing again. Then he gave a detail that I realized he couldn't have known. The letter was the real thing. And that night I did go out and raise hell.

Monday, May 18, 1970

Today our new university assembly meets for the first time; and I, hopefully, will have more free time. As Chairman of the Committee on Committees I've been running the elections. On top of that: a campus 'strike' and the killings at Kent State; more recently the killings at Jackson State. White Southerners, with Nixon at the helm, obviously feel safe. And Blacks once again are dying in the streets, in the alleys. In dormitories. And meanwhile the utter folly of the Cambodian invasion.

Canada looked awfully good last weekend. I went to Ottawa to receive a GG. The Governor General's Mansion. The Château Laurier. My daughter Laura thinks Canada is a beautiful land where people live in castles and spend their time visiting with friends.

Gwendolyn McEwen, sharing the poetry award with George Bowering, was there with her young Greek lover. George Bowering wore a green velvet suit with an extravagant silk shirt. I was introduced in French and didn't know when to stand up and receive my award.

Wednesday, June 17, 1970

Wrote a draft of Tape No. 2 this morning. Newest title for the novel: FUNERAL GAMES.

Last Thursday I flew into New York City to have a Friday luncheon with Danny Moses at Simon & Schuster. A tall bent young man who studied with Nabokov at Cornell; a fiercely contemporary young man, yet gentle, soft-spoken; spends his day in his office on the 28th floor of Rockefeller Center; goes home 30 miles to a house on a large old estate. We had lunch in The Baroque: a salmon wheeled up to our table whole, white wine with strawberries floating in same, other editors and bookmen at other tables. . . . And yet . . . I began to think fondly of Binghamton, up in the hills on the other side of the Catskills.

With all of New York around me and money in my pocket, what did I do? I looked at *Cue* to see what movies were showing, what plays were playing. But I ended up in the bookstores; from Gotham on south, wandering, reading. Friday night: dinner in Luchow's. Walked until I ached. Watching people on 7th Avenue, in Times Square.

Wednesday, June 24, 1970

Reading: Joseph Campbell, *The Masks of God*. He's fascinating on the Tristram story. Reading: Johan Huizinga, *Homo Ludens*—towards my use of games, of the festival, of art, in the novel-in-progress. Reading: Denis de Rougemont, *Love Declared*—on Tristram and Don Juan. Should get around to some Gothic novels again. Peeking into Sir Thomas Malory. Yesterday I put *The Return of the Native* on the reading list for my fall graduate course. Must go back and reconsider Hardy. He does that beautiful lonely thing with his region.

Write all morning these days. Read for a while in the afternoon and write letters. Late afternoon, go home and work on the house—putting in a downstairs bathroom. The necessary corrective to a mythological flight. Icarus on land. Icarus puts up wallboard. Icarus lowers the ceiling.

Friday, July 17, 1970

Milt Kessler and I drove to Cornell last night to hear a poetry reading by John Logan. Had a pleasant drive up Highway 81 and over to Ithaca on 79; the countryside richly green after so much rain, the sky threatening rain again. We talked about writers in our age group, especially poets in their forties: John Logan, Galway Kinnell, Archie Ammons. We both know these three men: all three achieved early recognition and were heralded as poets of promise. All three, now, seem to be at a point of crisis, fearful they cannot progress beyond the plateau on which they find themselves at this critical age. Milt and I congratulated ourselves on being late starters.

We went to a party after the reading, at Professor Hathaway's house. Bill Matthews was there, the young editor of *Lillibullero*. Logan was showing around a new issue of *Choice*. Ronald Sukenik was there; a young prose writer who teaches at Cornell this year. And Archie Ammons was there, wise, patient, considerate, trying anxiously to escape.

Tuesday, May 11, 1971

Took my class (Modern Long Poem) to hear Basil Bunting talk about his *Briggflatts*. The final class meeting and a pleasant one: Bunting mellow, vital, keen. *Briggflatts* beginning from place. Beginning from place, yes, and yet—Bunting says he was trying to write a Scarlatti sonata in words. Says also that he gave Eliot the idea for the title—*Four Quartets*—in a conversation in the 1920s.

Briggflatts about the life (autobiography?) of the poet. Bloodaxe the failed king is also the failed poet—the opposite way to the true way. Pasiphae represents the true way to be a poet—submit to the most awful things.

Submit. To the most awful things.

Bunting has strong personal feelings about his fellow northerner, Wordsworth. I asked about *The Prelude*. Bunting says the parallel in his own poem was more natural than deliberate. He admires Louis Zukofsky among American poets.

Zukofsky. Bunting. Aggressively, submitting.

Friday, June 18, 1971

I was thinking last night while trimming the lilac bushes: the problem of just what the hell is contemporary about/in the contemporary novel.

It seems to me that in the concept of narrative resides the radical future of the novel. To do away with narrative is utter nonsense: the novel uniquely confronts the human experience of time and space. Narrative is more significant than meaning.

Friday, July 2, 1971

Up with Laura who has been sick, and I heard the first birds of morning. And hearing those first birds, anywhere, I never stop hearing the prairies. The dawn sound of home.

Ritual for an Ending.

Starting a journal with Bill Spanos, *boundary* 2. Battling the administration to get 500 bucks. And hardly winning.

Calling the novel *Buffalo Woman* now. Wrote this draft in eight weeks. Take a vacation. Then into the third draft. I give the impression that I work steadily; in fact I work through a series of loafings and compulsions.

Saturday, September 18, 1971

Yaddo Artists' Colony. Woodlands—the name of my studio, deep in the woods. Prowlers causing a problem, so they've given me this studio—because I'm big! A marvellous theory of survival.

This studio built for a composer, but no composer here at the moment. The silence of the grand piano unnerves me. Now and then a pine cone or an acorn falls from a tree, hits my low roof. And I nearly hit the roof.

I've spent two long evenings with Padma Perera, from India, talking the traces of home. She's excited by the North American vestiges of wilderness. Yet she remembers always the glory—and the weight—of Indian culture. She was trained as a dancer; we were sitting on the floor in her studio when she noticed the shadows on the wall. She said, Let me make you a flower. She raised her hands and let them dance the shadow of a flower on the wall. That flower was more the experience of a flower than any flower I've ever seen. Those gestures were produced by thousands of years of human concentration. And yet their purpose is to show us the flower.

Friday, October 8, 1971

Roland Barthes, *On Racine*: 'Hence it is ultimately his very transparence that makes Racine a veritable commonplace of our literature, the critical object at zero degree, a site empty but eternally open to signification. If literature is essentially, as I believe, a meaning advanced and at the same time a meaning withdrawn . . .'

Working on a group of poems derived from Blackfoot mythology. From the trickster figure, Old Man.

Sunday, October 31, 1971

Halloween. Will take Meg and Laura around tonight, up and down the jack-o-lantern streets. Delighting in witch and ghost and bat. Gave our pumpkin a face last night.

Yesterday, mailed off my sequence of Old Man stories. Then attended two lectures that were part of a conference on the Black experience. That Black experience a parallel to my own, as it relates to the movement from rural to urban. The old/new struggle in the capitalistic West: land as earth and land as commodity. The connection lost, we find it. My deep longing of recent days for the west of my blood and bones. My ancestral west, the prairie west, the parklands.

Wednesday, November 17, 1971

Tonight a reading in honour of that great Greek poet, George Seferis. Miriam Leranbaum gave me today a new translation of Neruda, a book she picked up for me in London. Nowadays, we learn so much by translation. And yet, and yet—the strangeness of reading the poem that isn't there. I look at the text facing the text, in Greek, in Spanish, and I am happily confounded again by the mystery of a poem.

Wednesday, December 29, 1971

Loften Mitchell, the Black playwright, and his wife Marjorie were over last night. We drank rum and I listened to Loften thinking aloud about his Harlem life, and I realized my vision is so little of the urban experience, so much of man and nature meeting, man and animal, man and machine. I have never felt in my bones the total city.

Loften was to make his famous barbecued spareribs; Jane had talked him into it. A summer dish, Loften says; and then we set the charcoals to burning in the garage. Drank rum and ran out to the fire and turned the spareribs and returned to the kitchen and drank rum. The significance of the story, Loften says, resides outside the story.

Friday, January 21, 1972

Laura and Meg, these days, riding brooms around the house, calling them horses. As a boy on the farm I had a stable of stick horses. There were days when I must not have walked a step: always galloping. Through the stand of poplars that now has vanished from south of the barn. A slough there, in my boyhood, the classic ring of willows and poplars. The willows full of nesting blackbirds. The poplars home to a pair of orioles, to robins and crows. I stabled my stick horses there in that grove, where I had to begin with found them. Where my father's draft horses sought protection from flies, and slowly destroyed the grove itself.

Had a beer with Bill Spanos at Pancho's Pit, on our way home from the university; we got to talking about World War I, Bill's fascination with it, the commencement of mass killing in the twentieth century.

Wednesday, April 19, 1972

American B-52s dropping bombs in North Vietnam. Twenty years ago, in Goose Bay, Labrador, I often went to work and saw those same planes parked in long lines hardly a stone's throw from my office window. I met crew members in the officer's mess, on that base where I was a civilian, and I feared then their eagerness. Their seemingly endless rehearsals. They wanted to drop real bombs on real people.

As if the idea of fiction itself is only a fiction.

Friday, June 23, 1972

Third day of rain. Hurricane Agnes. The Susquehanna continues to rise. Evacuating Elmira, on the Chemung. And the rain keeps pouring down. I'm hankering today for the Mackenzie. The Slave in full flood: driftwood, trees, coming downriver. Thinking about my planned trip down the Red Deer: head west around July 12. Must find out what kinds of floods they have in the Badlands: sudden rain and flash floods.

Took another look at Frye, *Fables of Identity*: 'The darkness, winter and dissolution phase. Myths of the triumph of these powers; myths of floods and the return of chaos, of the defeat of the hero, and Gotterdammerung myths. Subordinate characters: the ogre and the witch.'

Sunday, July 9, 1972

Rain without end, and rain, and more rain. No one remembers the sun. All yesterday I wandered about, to chores in my office, to a fire in the fireplace at home, to listening to Haydn, a trumpet piece, over and over, to walking in the hills behind the college (in the rain), to coffee and bagels in the snackbar, to writing a note to Pat Battin on pain and poetry, to hearing, hurray, for the first time, a new narrator's voice. . . . I got the first signals: an old Indian woman giving her account of the downriver trip of the fossil hunters, a ribald old woman, natural, lusting, garrulous, garrulous . . .

Sunday, August 21, 1972

Got up at seven: made myself a breakfast of one boiled egg, two slices of toast, a glass of milk. Read the *Sunday Press* while waiting for the *New York Times* to arrive. It was on my doorstep by 8:30. I opened the book section, read William Gass on Valéry—and felt

I had to go to work. Jumped into my VW and drove to Howard Johnson's, across the road from the campus, stopped for two cups of coffee and worked on my novel while drinking them. To my office a little after nine: beautifully, monkishly quiet, the fog not yet burned off outside my window.

Thursday, September 7, 1972

Little Meg went into grade one yesterday. Her first day of school. Her excitement is beautiful: she can hardly wait in the morning until it is time to depart. She comes home reporting how she likes her teacher, her classmates. My sense of the overwhelming importance of that first experience compels me to listen in silence.

Thursday, November 2, 1972

Ezra Pound dead now. The old order done.

> Le Paradis n'est pas artificiel
> > but is jagged,
> For a flash,
> > for an hour.

The old order gone. But still everywhere present. Last night at a poetry reading, the young poet unaware, we learned that Pound is dead. We drank wine. We listened to new poems. There was a party after the reading, but I did not go to the party, I went home and listened to Mozart and wondered about the making of poetry, the poet's life. Old Ezra telling us, without curiosity there is no art.

Wednesday, November 22, 1972

Over coffee with Jane this morning: she telling me of my own background, of my growing up in a closed society in Heisler, my struggle to escape that society. The struggle of individuation so intense, so prolonged, that I cannot bring myself to trust interrelations. A kind of painful truth there. My novels of escape, of loners. The intense life all in my head. My distance, my slipping away when people get close. And yet my longing back to that closeness, my fascination with that lost place.

Dinner with Gerry and Kathie Kadish this evening. And a friend of theirs, Jodie O'Leary, and her young son coming along to play with Meggie and Laura.

Thursday, December 7, 1972

Out of the earth's orbit and into whatever it is when you have escaped our little night. I, watching TV past 12, the children asleep
unaware, Jane home late from a PTA meeting, three men thrust by
rocket towards the moon. The TV coverage broken by a Gulf Oil
ad that kept reminding us of the national fuel shortage, real or
manipulated. Perhaps, once again, in still another way, only the
sun can save us; technology burns up the fuels, burns its way back
now to the sun.

Imagine a space traveller, the earth gone, finding on the moon a
handful of unnatural objects and trying to construct from them the
civilization that left them there. They were a people without
stories. Or so it would seem. And he who has no story is outside
of time. Maybe the sungod tells itself a story by pretending a
universe.

Wednesday, January 10, 1973

Worked on the basement walls for a while last night, then went up
to my attic study and finished reading Harold Bloom's *The Anxiety
of Influence: A Theory of Poetry*.

Tells me what I mean when I tell students the best critique of one
poem is other poems. Bloom is immensely sophisticated (sophis-
tical?) in the matter of 'swerving': the way in which a poet
deliberately (?) misreads a great precursor in order to be able to
write his own poem.

p. 107: 'In poetic vision, guilt comes from repression of our middle nature, the ground where morals and instincts must meet and
subsume one another.'

Here we go round the buffalo berry bush.
So early in the coulee.

Sunday, January 14, 1973

The bomb is the American weapon. In WW2, in both Germany and
Japan, now in Vietnam. Our technology delivering an impersonal
destruction, impersonal death.

Reading Clark Blaise's *A North American Education*. The careful
language, the attention to quiet authenticity, that characterizes the

best eastern Canadian writing. In the west we are possessed of a curious rhetoric. A rhetoric that goes back to religion and politics, to the outcry, to the curse, to the blessing, to the plea, to the song. Not to the educated man imagining himself to be reasonable.

Another dimension of Blaise's book: his use of the self as character. He has lived an ordinary life, an *intensely* ordinary life, especially in his relation to Montreal as place, as a season of the soul, and out of that life and place he produces fictions that will survive both the originating self and the changing place. . . . But I am drawn, finally, to the excesses of invention. . . . Of self . . . destruction?

Wednesday, January 24, 1973

'PEACE' in bold letters across the top of the morning newspaper. I was reading it at the check-out desk in the library, having found myself unable to watch Nixon on TV last night. Two librarians came by to read the paper—and both mentioned their doubts, their suspicion that the announcement did not mean what it seemed to mean. Then two more came—and they would not even look at the 'top' story—they checked the stock market and went away.

And does 'peace' mean peace? We have lost our ability to trust language. There is no excitement at all; only, at best, a willingness to wait and see. Nothing is what it seems to be. Or, nothing is indeed what it seems to be.

Thursday, March 22, 1973

Diane Wakoski read on campus last night: a beautiful performance. Innocence as guile. The naked honesty that is art. As she says: the problem, the task, is to turn your own life into mythology without not living it. I like the sheer *pluck* of that. And she does it too: masochism, sadism, the plethora of lovers, the lonely woman dreaming her lost father, her men on motorcycles.

Sunday, March 25, 1973

Friday Bill Spanos and I drove to Syracuse to the airport to pick up William Gass. He met a class in the afternoon, lectured in the evening 'On Being Blue' and attended a party at my house; Bill and I drove him back to Syracuse and the airport yesterday. A fine, even rare, experience.

Gass is relaxed yet intense, gives of his energy, shares his ideas. Both modest and sure of himself, he knows where he is going and quietly goes about becoming one of the best fiction writers in America. He abhors the New York City scene and delights in his St Louis life.

Gass telling my class: he wished he could eat delicious food without becoming full—he wished the aesthetic experience could be freed of the physical limit. And then I realized how that would spoil the experience for me: because I delight in the food but also in the sense of my complex (and erotic?) bargain with the immensity of the pleasures offered.

Monday, September 3, 1973

Laura's birthday today. Tonight we dine at the House of Yu. Yesterday I took Laura and Meg and two of their friends to an amusement park and my birthday gift to Laura was an airplane ride for all of them. Their beautiful faces in the windows of the small plane. Laura 9.

Today, Labour Day. I'm supposed to be boning up on Berryman's *The Dream Songs*; instead, I'm toying with the basis for a long poem of my own—'Winter Count'. Berryman at work for fourteen years on his *Songs*. That's really what interests me . . .

Sunday, September 6, 1973

Yesterday: to work early. The essay that is to be the paper I give at Chicago MLA this Christmas. My thesis: 'My thesis is simply this: it is the first task of the Canadian writer to uninvent the world.' Reading again in Heidegger's essay, 'The Origin of the Work of Art'.

Home to mow the lawn. Painted the putty on a window I fixed: Laura broke a pane in a basement window. Listened to Beethoven's Sixth and some clarinet music. Drank two glasses of sherry.

To uninvent the world. To unconceal. To make visible again. That invisible country, Canada. Our invisible selves.

Monday, September 17, 1973

Played with Meg while Laura did her homework. Our copy of the *NY Times* didn't arrive. The newsboy was short of copies. I wanted to read about the situation in Chile. My sympathies all with Allende at the moment. With the homeland of Parra and Neruda. To what degree were the Americans meddling?

Thursday, September 20, 1973

Preparing to teach Ginsberg's *Kaddish*. Stopped in to see Miriam and tell her I'd escaped the chairmanship. Because she, as dean, thought I should take it.

Phone call from Eli Mandel at York. He wants me to read when his class is studying *Studhorse Man*. I agreed. November 30.

Wednesday, September 26, 1973

Neruda dead. Assassinated? The great communist lover surrealist poet. The voice of courage. Gone into that new Chilean catastrophe.

Friday, October 12, 1973

Finished Olson classes yesterday morning. Students finally responding well. Olson once again capturing me, even while I resist. Don't like his great man view of himself: the prairie radical democrat in me resisting—and yet I admire the daring to go for greatness. He will write the text for explication, live the life for explication. . . . In Canada, uncertain of the canon, we write commentaries on the process of creation itself . . .

Monday, October 14, 1973

Colour change of the leaves at its height over the past week end. A delight beyond category.

Today, must prepare Nicanor Parra's poetry for class tomorrow. The appeal of the Spanish-Americans—their courage, their commitment, their wrestling with a predicament that traps them between nature and the Americanized urban.

Wednesday, February 27, 1974

Studying *The Bridge*, or rather, talking about it with a graduate student. The failure of the poem. Fails at myth-making because the old gods win. The new gods have to win in the making of the myth, goddamnit. . . . And more, you need story/people, not object. The bridge, the spanning object, is not enough.

The sheer, outrageous daring of that failure . . .

Monday, March 4, 1974

8 am. Laguardia Airport. Waiting for a flight to Toronto; then to North Bay.

Flight delayed to 10:30. Hydraulic pump to be replaced on the plane. Faces of waiting passengers gone slack, immobile. Only a group of actors (I eavesdrop) beautifully alive: vain, bright, aggressive, self-conscious, pleased to be their various selves, each of them.

The only survival: art. The imagination. The artist in the self. Kept heroically alive in some who do not write or paint or act . . .

. . . the temptation of a five-year poem . . .

Wednesday, April 24, 1974

No mail from Canada for days, because of the mail strike. A curious sense of being cut off from my sources. In America and alone. A far connection missing these days.

Two days ago, got started on a long poem. After months, years, of waiting for the poem to begin itself. Trying to force it and knowing I must wait. And hearing it now, that penitential and reckless blend of sex and wine and words.

Monday, June 3, 1974

Laura fell off her bike Saturday evening, fractured her skull. . . . The beauty of Laura. In the hospital and yet so alive to the new experience. An older girl in the room, and Laura imitating her, learning. Meg and I went together to have supper in The Villa last night, little Meg so grown up, taking charge of herself, ordering her meal.

The horror of being a writer: there is nothing good enough to be worth doing after you've written for a few hours. The sheer descent, after. The collapse.

All apart today. No centre. Trying to rewrite the last section of 'Badlands'. Get Anna's voice into the clear.

Sunday, June 9, 1974

Playing softball yesterday, I hurt my left ring finger. Had it X-rayed last night; nothing broken. Hit a homerun with the hand injured. Old macho.

I have written for many thousands of hours. And I can't remember one of them. Not one. There is that terrible separation between life and art.

I said to Jane, What is the subject of a love poem? She said, There can only be one subject of a love poem. What? I asked her.

14

Learning the Hero from Northrop Frye

1

Here in Rome[1] I am, even now, far beyond what it was I intended to say. Rome is always a labyrinth of memory, a place we knew before we arrived, a place we, arriving, hardly recognize at all. To reread Northrop Frye is to have an experience similar to that familiar and surprising arrival in Rome.

I was a young writer for a long time. I was born into a country where we cling to, proclaim even, the fiction of our prolonged youth. This becomes a protracted (or delayed) destiny, marked by a longing for the disguise of an early but only apparent death. In Canada, we long to die young, but at an old age.

Harold Bloom, in *The Anxiety of Influence*, writes: 'The young poet, Stevens remarked, is a god, but he added that the old poet is a tramp'.[2] That double vision of the poet as god or tramp, as god and then as tramp, speaks eloquently in the careers of Canadian writers and in our major texts.

Having decided at the age of seventeen to become a writer, I stopped writing. My youth was too absolute for anything but silence. In that godly view of the poet, I could not go tramping into mere words.

Perhaps this is a necessary stage, the potential writer becoming author who will one day write: it is a necessary process of letting the nerve endings shift toward an abiding discomfort, of letting the body and the vision meld into a stir of fictions, of keeping one's language sense free of the atrophy of prescribed adulthood.

I might have gone on being a young writer all my life, unwilling to learn that terrible dialogue of god and tramp, had I not come finally to a recognition that exhausted me into language.

Northrop Frye, writing in 1943, describes the experience I was to have over a period of two decades. Though I had not yet read him, he had already described, forecast, the condition of the spirit, the weather of design, that I was about to endure; his act of writing, then, had already offered the long lesson in narrative shape and prophetic foreclosure that I had yet to hear:

> The colonial position of Canada is therefore a frostbite at the roots of the Canadian imagination, and it produces a disease for which I think the best name is prudery. By this I do not mean reticence in sexual matters: I mean the instinct to seek a conventional or commonplace expression of an idea.[3]

I was already then vehemently anti-colonial. The spent narrative of empire (at least of the British Empire) haggled in my bones, and I longed for absolute frontiers. I was a homesteader's son, an only son, already weighted with hints of the responsibilities of smaller kingdoms that imitated their larger masters, kingdoms of fields of wheat, of herds and lands that expected generations to recite the story onward. I was caught in a story that I did not even recognize as story, because I did not know how stories retell themselves. I did not know then, as my father and grandfather did not know before me, or seemed not to know, that their small empires were inherited or filched from the Cree Indians, who had in turn inherited or taken by force from the Blackfoot that same empire of grass and poplar bluffs and herds of buffalo.

I was at once resisting and caught inside a story of empire. My political instinct, for all its appalling Canadian innocence, was unswerving. What I lacked was a story against the story I was in, a correction in the compass reading. And then I heard again, in the reflection that Frye had written but I had not yet read:

> But even when the Canadian poet has got rid of colonial cant, there are two North American dragons to slay. One is the parrotted *cliché* that this is a 'new' country and that we must spend centuries cutting forests and building roads before we can enjoy the by-products of settled leisure (p. 135).

He was right, of course. I had bought that one, lock, stock and barrel. There on a homestead, on the edge of culture, I was seeing only the frontier, the edge of nature, the version of story that offered itself as 'new'. 'But Canada is not "new" or "young",' Frye understood, 'it is exactly the same age as any other country under a system of industrial capitalism; and even if it were, a reluctance to write poetry is not a sign of youth but of decadence' (p. 135).

On that homestead, back then, I somehow knew the illusion of frontier pastoral was an illusion. I had no word for what I knew. Reading Frye years later, I knew the word I wanted then was decadence. I lived not in a new country but in a decadent country. That decadence, I came to understand, was represented not by an absence of appropriate forms but by an exhaustion of forms.

I was, as that insistently young writer on the Canadian prairies, aware that the forms at my disposal had spoken their piece and were into a recitation of content and form that not only told me little, but that, further, concealed from me what it was I wanted to say.

For the writer in that predicament, for the young writer conceiving himself a god, there is the further temptation to give birth to oneself, to speak *ab ovo*, to give birth blatantly, at once and complete. But Frye had written his lesson against that temptation too. He says:

> The other fallacy concerns the imaginative process itself, and may be called the Ferdinand the Bull theory of poetry. This theory talks about a first-hand contact with life as opposed to a second-hand contact with it through books, and assumes that the true poet will go into the fields and smell the flowers and not spoil the freshness of his vision by ruining his eyesight on books (pp. 135-6).

I had spent six years in the Canadian north, in the wilderness, working on riverboats on the Mackenzie, working on an air base in Labrador—and for all the wonderful experience I had collected, I began to sense that I had learned very little about writing. I should say in my own defence that I did at some point, somewhere in my cabin on a riverboat somewhere above the Arctic Circle, one day attempt, somehow knowing the model of Virgil, to write an Alberta Georgic. I had that small instinct to tell the story over, but didn't quite know the story that I would tell, didn't quite know how to go about retelling it, into the newness that I knew as desire.

I decided to go to graduate school. I went to the States and earned an M.A. Still dissatisfied with what I didn't know, resisting fiercely now the Ferdinand the Bull theory of writing, I began my Ph.D. studies in 1956, a young writer then of the age of twenty-nine.

Frank Lentricchia, in his book *After the New Criticism*, describes the state of graduate studies in English at that time. 'By about 1957 the moribund condition of the New Criticism and the literary needs it left unfulfilled placed us in a critical void.' Lentricchia goes on to say, 'Even in the late 1940s, however, those triumphant times of the New Criticism, a theoretical opposition was already quietly gathering strength.'[4] He lists the books I had actually studied while an M.A. student: Ernst Cassirer, *An Essay on Man*; Susanne Langer, *Philosophy in a New Key*; books by Richard Chase, R.W.B. Lewis, and, of course, Sir James G. Frazer.

Like many graduate students, I had been unwittingly prepared for the appearance, in 1957, of Northrop Frye's *Anatomy of Criticism*.

In that year I gave a seminar report on Milton using *The Anatomy of Criticism* as my critical starting point. The Milton professor, in a kindly way, asked me to explain briefly to him and to the class who this new Canadian critic might be.

I began, in answering that request, to talk about the hero, the nature of the hero, in literature, in the modern world, in my Canadian world, and in a way I haven't stopped, and here, today, thirty years later, I'm still giving the report, though now Northrop Frye himself has become the hero under discussion, a peculiarly Canadian hero, in a modern world that has assigned to critics and theorists a hero's many tasks. We live at a time when the young critic as tramp faces the uncomfortable fate of becoming the old critic as god.

2

But to go back for a few moments those thirty years. I very quickly discovered that I was not the only young Canadian writer being instructed by Northrop Frye's writings on narrative and poetry, on Blake's prophecies and Canadian poetics.

Canadian writers like Eli Mandel, Margaret Atwood, Doug Jones, James Reaney, Jay Macpherson, and Dennis Lee, to name only the most obvious, were changing Canadian literature because they had in turn been changed by Northrop Frye.

Within a dozen years, the basic fissure, the Lacanian gap perhaps, that so informs the Canadian psyche, had become the subject of intense critical speculation, and this in response to a recognition by Northrop Frye of the complexities of 'I' and 'other' in the Canadian literary experience. Ours indeed is a fearful symmetry. Ours is the bush garden, as Frye would have it, in turn quoting from his student Margaret Atwood. Ours the double hook of Sheila Watson's novel, the mountain and the valley of Buckler's title, the second scroll of A.M. Klein's difficult text, at once novel and poem, text and commentary, book as scroll attached to and separated from the scroll as book.

By 1970 two of the poets in the Frye school had themselves become critics.

In 1970 Doug Jones published his study *Butterfly on Rock*, with a title taken from a poem by Irving Layton, a title reflecting the quality that Eli Mandel would later name duplicity. In that study Jones says, ' . . . Canadians have developed a kind of cultural schizophrenia, a division between their conscious aspirations and their unconscious convictions, which undermines their lives and leads to the development of a profoundly negative outlook'.[5]

Jones's chapters, with titles like 'The Sleeping Giant', 'Eve in Dejection', and 'The Sacrificial Embrace', reflect a direct indebtedness to Frye's myth criticism, yet they surely resist what I would find in Frye to be a comic vision.

Margaret Atwood's sequence of the same year, *The Journals of Susanna Moodie*, contains a much-quoted 'Afterword' that lays the same charge of schizophrenia against the Canadian psyche. 'If the national illness of the United States is megalomania,' she writes—reflecting still another dimension of the divided Canadian consciousness—

> that of Canada is paranoid schizophrenia. Mrs Moodie is divided down the middle: she praises the Canadian landscape but accuses it of destroying her; she dislikes the people already in Canada but finds in people her only refuge from the land itself; she preaches progress and the march of civilization while brooding elegiacally upon the destruction of the wilderness; she delivers optimistic sermons while showing herself to be fascinated with deaths, murders, the criminals in Kingston Penitentiary and the incurably insane in the Toronto lunatic asylum.[6]

I need hardly add that this wonderful state of schizophrenia makes for much of the energy and excitement and accomplishment of such Canadian poems as Atwood's own *The Journals of Susanna Moodie*, Jay Macpherson's *The Boatman*, and Dennis Lee's *The Death of Harold Ladoo*. But the poet who speaks most tellingly to me of complex involvement in the lessons of Northrop Frye is Eli Mandel.

I can only wish that good health would permit Eli to speak here for himself. His most recent book of criticism, *The Family Romance*, acknowledges his involvement in Freudian theory, in the literary family, in the anxiety of influence, and in a lifelong study of the writings of Northrop Frye.

Eli Mandel's poem 'the doppelgänger' turns that latent schizophrenia into a statement about love, into a statement about being in the world, about art itself. About the predicament of the Canadian artist.

'the doppelgänger' appears in a longer book called *Out of Place*,[7] a poem that explores and dramatizes much of what Northrop Frye has told us about Canadian writing. That larger poem is at once a statement of Mandel's own recognition of himself become his own other and an answer to Northrop Frye's celebrated question to Canadians: 'Where is here?'

Eli Mandel, in that long poem, in the company of his wife Ann, visits the site of his childhood. The empty site proves to be truly a ghost town, full of absence and presence, a place testifying at once to Mandel's removal and to his presence in the guise of stories retold. Content, for the poet, as for his teacher Northrop Frye, must submit to the instruction of form.

3

While much of this speculation was in progress in the environs of the University of Toronto, I was, in a Hemingway way, seeking experience by working on riverboats and in the wilderness of Northern Canada. I had spent six years in this fashion when I read in Frye, ' . . . Canadian poets have been urged in every generation to search for appropriate themes, in other words to look for content.' And in a way that was my predicament. Frye goes on, 'But the poet's quest is for form, not content. . . . I mean by form the shaping principle of the individual poem, which is derived from the shaping principles of poetry itself' (pp. 176-7).

I had been on the poet's quest for a long time. Now I began to understand that like other questors before me, I was looking for the holy grail without quite knowing what the holy grail looked like. And not that I know now, or should. The quest itself dictates the unknowability of the quest's object.

The question for the questor is: How are you to know a form, a form that doesn't manifest itself until your moment of writing, when you see it?

Confronting this question, the poet in his conundrum might stay falsely young forever. In this predicament, all art, as Frye would have it, must be radical.

Frye suggests, in my reading, in my wilful misprision, that the moment of recognition of the possible departure is available only at the moment of recognition of the departure's impossibility. Realizing that we are already where we propose to go, we are free to go originally. Ideally, he imagines a moment when the poet, by knowing everything, is at last free to know the unknowable as well. Incompleteness is made possible only by completeness. Completeness, allowing incompleteness as its other, allows for the gap, the rupture, that is the space on the shelf, the space in the complete library, that desires the poet's arrival as fully as the poet desires to arrive.

The 'young' poet expects to work simply from his ignorance into knowing, from his 'newness' into a 'being there'. In fact he must work in the opposite direction, from his knowing to his 'ignorance', from his condition of 'decadence' to the possibility of the 'new'.

It was Frye who articulated (in every sense) my suspicion that no story can be told only once, that a story to be a story at all must be a retelling of itself, and, at the same time, a retelling of a story that it can no longer be, because of that very retelling. At the impossible centre of this maze of story is the impossible story that once and forever decentres all story into periphery. It is as if there were a god who told himself/herself out of existence, into existence, by telling *all*. The young poet, then, is a god, a god created in the image of that enduring absence. Learning to *tramp*, that young poet moves from the stasis of wistful longing that is the contrary of desire. Desire is outward. The young poet must resist the *gravity* of the centre and learn to tell profanely.

Writing must be scandalous.

4

My concern is with the master narratives—the hidden narratives, often—that are assumed in a culture. While teaching for years in the United States I had occasion, quite often, to visit my home in Canada and to watch television programs I had already watched in the US. It struck me that in Canada the audience was looking at the same images but seeing a different narrative. It was that recognition that led me to speculate about the assumed narratives that made the understanding of a particular telling possible.

The question of what those assumed narratives might be in Canada is especially vexing, in part because we function a good deal of the time by saying what we are not. Many Canadians—artists especially, perhaps—are versions of what we call Red Tories: people who at once believe and radically disbelieve what they believe in.

Again, it is Northrop Frye who articulates this predicament. In a wonderfully telling title, he announces our design and our resistance to that design. The title of the essay is: 'Preface to An Uncollected Anthology'. He proposes, in effect, a preface to a collection of poems that is and is not there, and in that act he situates his own critical writing as a preface—pre-face, one is tempted to say—to written Canadian poetry and to its unwritten texts, the texts that are implied in the patterns of lyric and narrative that, while 'hidden', are heard nevertheless in the culture that encodes them, in the country that is their encoding. Canada is vastly a country of silence, the natural silence of snow and winter, but also the stubborn and wilful silence of a people who work hard at hearing only a trace, even an absence of themselves, by hearing the sound of others. He writes an actual preface to a dispersed—an uncollected—anthology. That unbound—and possibly boundless—anthology contains texts of the past and texts of the future, texts by Canadian poets, texts by the many poets who speak intertextually in the written and unwritten corpus of Canadian poetry.

In a very real sense I find myself writing into and against that anthology, trying wilfully at times to include myself in both its sound and its silence, trying wilfully at times to write myself out of it. In the conclusion of the preface to his singularly unconcluded collection, Frye writes: 'We are concerned here . . . not so much with mythopoeic poetry as with myth as a shaping principle of poetry'.[8]

It is precisely there that I am able to enter inside of and to escape from Frye's boundaries. It may even be that, confronting those boundaries, guessing their demarcations, their very existence, I become Canadian.

The narrative quality of myth, its narrative reliance, not its inherited or defined meaning, is what defines me. I find in the narrative necessity of myth not meaning at all, but a potential for meaning, a potential that locates me and loses me, a potential that is present in my telling of a story, yet beyond that telling.

The master narratives of our own time, in their rigidity and in their force, are sternly political. Ideological, in Frye's terms. It's a commonplace, I suppose, to observe that the two narratives of empire that nowadays dominate our lives—the American and the Soviet—contend with each other for the possession of all. What may be less obvious is the way in which each contends with itself.

Within each of these two current narratives of empire is a double plot, one that argues and plots continually toward the dominance of all by a powerful centre; another that remembers, however wistfully or embarrassedly, a moment of escape—of revolution.

In both narratives of empire, the powerful centre attempts to neutralize the plot-line of revolution by turning the moment of revolution into a sacred moment, a moment of birth that, by that metaphor of birth, should happen only once, should ignore—forget—the ritual implications, the ritual of repetition implied in the making sacred.

Frye, in his decent and quiet and radical way, tells the Canadian poet to be anti-colonial. We are a nation made of the waste of the narrative of empire, a nation made of wars won and lost, of peace treaties and their humiliations and their prophecies, of retreating people tempted to glorify their retreat, of the acquisitions of land and resources under the disguise of pastoral utopias.

To resist, to aspire toward a condition now described as post-colonial, asks for a radical act of imagination. Frye, in his offering of 'myth as a shaping principle', offers a place to locate and to release that imaginative energy. Simply put, by the act of retelling we can tell ourselves both out of and into story.

Guile and violence, Frye tells us, are the basic stuff of narrative. Guile, I hear him implying (in what may be, again, my misreading), is preferable, in the retelling of any master narrative.

As a young writer I believed I was stymied by being born into a country without a tradition of revolution; for one thing, revolution is a history (a story) easy to memorize, and Canadian students often know early American history better than they know their own. At worst, having no moment of birth to recall, we dwell on the possibility of the death that will authenticate our existence. In Canada at times, in disguises (guile) as various as trade schemes and international wars, death is the beloved, the sweet other that mothers, that mutters, our being in the world. We are tempted even to reverse the myths of agriculture. Winter, then, is the fair embrace of that assuring death, our ragged spring is another betrayal into the mere continuance of life.

But at its best, this same unrevolutionary predicament, this absence that destroys the metaphor of birth and its attendant narrative, frees us from the appalling ignorance celebrated by that birth, celebrates instead our life-inspiring decadence. Coming always to the end, we are free, always, to salvage ourselves, not by severance, but by the lovely treachery of words.

Come to this condition as hinted at by Frye, we are surprised into freedom. We are carnivalized into the possibility of our own being. That carnival condition, so eloquently put for us now by Bakhtin in his anatomy of Menippean satire, was announced for me—became the theoretical account of what I was doing by violence as well as by guile—in Frye's discussions of what is essentially the comic vision, the comic mode.

By the time I began to write *What the Crow Said* I had been much and directly influenced by Frye's *The Secular Scripture*. It had become a kind of bible to me.

In *What the Crow Said* I play with the story of a foundling child being raised by animals, a story not unfamiliar to Romans. Vera's strange son, Vera's Boy, is, it would seem, the offspring of her own sexual union with a swarm of bees. Vera, in the way of folklore, on a dark occasion in snow, throws her son off a sled (a cutter, we call it) and leaves him to the pursuing wolves. That son, to be named simply Vera's Boy, is raised by coyotes and returns to his community with messages from the unknown world.

This, for me, smacks of the tradition of romance. Frye tells us in *The Secular Scripture*:

> . . . romance presents a *vertical* perspective which realism, left to itself, would find it very difficult to achieve. The realist, with his sense of logical and horizontal continuity, leads us to the end of his story; the romancer, scrambling over a series of disconnected episodes, seems to be trying to get us to the top of it.[9]

Romance enacts the very undoing of story that makes story. Frye gives us the necessary clue when he says later: 'The real hero becomes the poet, not the agent of force or cunning whom the poet may celebrate. In proportion as this happens, the inherently revolutionary quality in romance begins to emerge from all the nostalgia about a vanished past' (p. 178).

Ours is a continuing revolution, Frye is willing to suggest. In *What the Crow Said* I allow that the real hero might be the poet. Liebhaber, setting type for his newspaper, might be the poet as hero. Vera Lang, writing her column of gossip, just on the edge of scandal, might be the poet as hero. The crow itself, nameless, and always talking, naming those others, the humans who trouble its life—it too might be the poet as hero.

But to go back to Vera's Boy. Frye says in *The Bush Garden*: 'The myth of the hero brought up in the forest retreat, awaiting the moment when his giant strength will be fully grown and he can emerge into the world, informs a good deal of Canadian criticism down to our own time' (p. 221).

I can only add that much Canadian narrative as well as much Canadian criticism is caught in a story of the hero of potential strength, emerging from that forest retreat. Frye gives us that discouraging insight. And yet it is also he who revises the story that at times seems so unrevisable. In the face of that version of hero, he stands at times as the only other hero.

It is difficult, almost impossible, to imagine a nation without its epic poem. Northrop Frye's work is an extended commentary on the great Canadian epic poem, a poem whose text we do not have, but whose intention and design and accomplishment he makes everywhere present in his elaborate response.

Frye's long discourse, the single book that all his many books imply, is at once taxonomic, encyclopaedic, the epic tale of the tribe. The very *all* of the story he tells inscribes another story.

Northrop Frye becomes, by that inscription, by that revealing of prophetic presence in absence, by that locating of the denied or at least concealed story in his own commentary, the voice of the epic we do not have. In his collected criticism, he locates the poetry of our unlocatable poem. In talking about that poem, he becomes our epic poet.

Grazie.

Notes

[1] Convegno Internazionale Ritratto di Northrop Frye, Rome, 25-7 May 1987.

[2] Bloom, Harold, *The Anxiety of Influence: A Theory of Poetry* (London and New York: Oxford University Press, 1973), p. 152.

[3] Northrop Frye, *The Bush Garden: Essays on the Canadian Imagination*

(Toronto: Anansi, 1971), p. 152. Further references will appear in the text.

[4] Frank Lentricchia, *After the New Criticism* (Chicago: University of Chicago Press, 1980), p. 4.

[5] D.G. Jones, *Butterfly on Rock* (Toronto: University of Toronto Press, 1970), p. 14.

[6] Margaret Atwood, *The Journals of Susanna Moodie* (Toronto: Oxford University Press, 1970), p. 62.

[7] Eli Mandel, *Out of Place* (Erin, Ont.: Press Porcépic, 1977).

[8] Frye, 'Preface to an Uncollected Anthology', *Bush Garden*, p. 179.

[9] Frye, *The Secular Scripture: A Study of the Structure of Romance* (Cambridge, Mass., and London: Harvard University Press), pp. 49-50.

Hear Us O Lord and the Orpheus
Occasion

Hear Us O Lord from Heaven Thy Dwelling Place.[1] With this apostrophe, Malcolm Lowry cautions us that his collection of related stories, circuitously and directly, is a meditation on the relationship between a lyric strategy and the narrative desire.

We as readers become eavesdroppers on an address to the sacred. We hear Lowry addressing God. We hear the writer addressing the deafness of God in the only way possible: by narrating the deaf God into the story as hearer. And then, the hero made hearer, we as readers find ourselves written out of all innocence, into complicity, into the violence of the telling. And now we too, in our deafness and in our listening, transgress our way *away* from indifference, proposing ourselves at once as gods and fools.

Geoffrey Hartman, in his 'Preface' to Maurice Blanchot's collection of essays *The Gaze of Orpheus*, writes: 'According to Blanchot, writing is a fearful spiritual weapon that negates the naïve existence of what it names and must therefore do the same to itself.'[2]

Lowry, always, in writing, negates the naïve existence of what he names. His act of writing, always, negates its own naïve existence. And to read that writing is to share the risk that that writing undertook.

I am a reader writing my reading. In typing the title of Lowry's story, I wrote, by accident I believe, Hear Us O Lord from *Heavy* Thy Dwelling Place. Already, I propose my own signature, and Lowry as mediator becomes in turn usurper, the deaf mediator who will not hear me, and I must write his stubborn story into my story. Hey. Malcolm.

To continue with Hartman's comment:

> Literature runs the danger of denying its own desire for presence, although it cannot (as Hegel thought) become anything else— philosophy, for example. Hence writing is a self-disturbed activity: it knows itself to be, at once, trivial and apocalyptic, vain yet of the greatest consciousness-altering potential (pp. ix-x).

Fooling around, we god our loins. Transgressing as readers, we speak the title *with* Lowry (Hear Us O Lord), re-citing those words 'From the Isle of Man'.

We hear, in our own apostrophe, the terror of a double distance. Literature indeed runs the danger of denying its own desire for presence. The very act of speaking announces space. The apostrophe is addressed quite possibly not to God the Father but to the gap itself, the gap that separates the speaking voice from the listener, the mouth from the ear, the spoken word from the longed-for signification.

The boat in 'The Bravest Boat' is a small and gone boat, slow in its vast returning. The finding is a treasure beyond all hope of treasure. But the message is gnarled. It is a written message. 'Hello,' it begins. 'Thanks,' it ends. 'My name is Sigurd Storlesen,' it begins. 'Sigurd Storlesen,' it ends. Against the vast narrative of 'Hello' and 'Thanks' is posited a solipsism that makes even the ordinary language of communication problematic. The distance inheres even inside the namer naming his own name.

Jonathan Culler, in *The Pursuit of Signs*, writes heroically on the idea of apostrophe. Culler says that apostrophe 'makes its point by troping not on the meaning of a word but on the circuit or situation of communication itself'.[3]

We live at a time when poetry—Canadian poetry at least—is full of the etymologies of words, as if an earlier version of a word had a privileged status against all the problematics of meaning in our fumbling century. Lowry returns us from that false innocence to the circuit or situation of communication itself. He reminds us, continually and radically, that we are always, as writers, as readers, in the predicament of Orpheus, listening across his shoulder, hearing first and only the silence of Eurydice, who might or who might not be following, behind his uncertain head. Lowry and Orpheus, like few other poets, it seems to me, address compulsively the complicity of eye and ear. Distance is at once our vocabulary and the denial of its efficacy.

Hear Us O Lord is somehow full of couples, a man and a woman. Inseparable couples. Joined couples. Page 24:

> 'And we've been married seven years.'
> 'Seven years today—'
> 'It seems like a miracle.'
> But the words fell like spent arrows before the target
of this fact.

The Orpheus predicament speaks its silence. Eurydice announces the life-in-death, the death-in-life concern of so much of Lowry's writing: the will toward the unreachable recovery, the problematics of any action occasioned by that will.

The circuitry of Eurydice's fate includes at once the will toward that unreachable recovery and the act that refuses it. It is the very acting itself, not the not acting, that sends her back to hell. We move from gap to gape to gap. Hear us O Lord. From Heaven. Thy distant place. The indifference, addressed, becomes true *différance*.

Or does the indifference, addressed—given an address—confound all distancing?

Culler goes on to write of a level 'at which one must question the status so far granted to the thou of the apostrophic structure and reflect on the crucial though paradoxical fact that this figure which seems to establish relationships between the self and the other can in fact be read as an act of radical interiorization and solipsism' (p. 146).

Lowry is profoundly writing Lowry. Not writing *about* Lowry. Writing Lowry in a way more deceitful and correct than any autobiographical act. It is the very daring to address God's improbable ears that locates Lowry himself as the questing voice in the fictionality of his fiction. He dares the impossible gaze. Inventing outward, he becomes the possibility of himself.

But—does he then run the risk of realizing himself at the cost of losing that very cosmos which he so longs to narrate into visibility?

'This internalization', Culler goes on to say, 'is important because it works against narrative and its accompaniments: sequentiality, causality, time, teleological meaning' (p. 148).

It is this very resistance to narrative, this temptation of solipsistic discourse with the other, that gives Lowry's narratives their special poignancy. By our act of reading, we write with him. The journey that never ends cannot end because the story as he conceives it allows, even predicates, its own resistance to story. There is a movement toward the impossible complete cosmology that, centring on the authenticity of thou, reduces the probabilities of 'I'. There is a movement towards the realized 'I' that, by the process of internalization, forfeits the assurance of a cohering and intelligible 'thou'.

That dance, that quarrel, that play of seduction and resistance in its complexity and contradictions and Don Juanish promises, is what commits us as readers to the embarrassment and the irresistibility of our reading. It is the prospect of our own dismemberment that excites us with that further prospect of our re-membering.

Near the end of the opening story in *Hear Us O Lord* we read: 'It was like gazing into chaos.'

We think of Orpheus turning to look backward, into the night, into that version of chaos which is the underworld. For even chaos, it would seem, has its shapes, its laws of randomness. Orpheus, turning to look back at the ghostly presence he has sung so hard to rescue, looks to his other and by his willing and not willing creates the gap that his other must now become. That gap will bind him to Eurydice as no mere rescue ever might. His gaze is a betrayal, and yet it is a fulfilment too. For it is the task of the artist, as Blanchot tells us, to dare to *look*.

In Lowry we have Orpheus in the moment after he looks back, in that appalling and sacred moment when he believes still in the possibility of union (and unity) and realizes nevertheless that dismemberment is his fate. To look, even to look back, is to look forward. For Lowry, the writing of a narrative becomes the writing of a discourse against his own will to narrate.

The chaos that was a version of other becomes in the apostrophe of Orpheus' gaze a condition of the interior. From the opening of 'Through the Panama':

> Frère Jacques
> Frère Jacques
> Dormez-vous?
> Dormez-vous?

The sacredness of Frère Jacques and the profaneness of Brother Jack sleep together and at once. If they 'give in' to sleep.

The surrogate writers in 'Through the Panama' seem occupied chiefly in gazing. And now even gazing doubles on itself, becomes ambiguous. These writers in their gazing threaten to abandon the gift of time, they threaten to confound the narrative whose ends they would pursue.

But . . . And yet . . .

The duplicity of their 'looking' in its confounding of narrative renews the narrative. Lowry, the part of Lowry that is 'pure' artist, is tempted by the power of song, as the trees and rocks were seduced by the songs of Orpheus: a diabolic solipsism whereby the artist is tempted out of narrative by the hearing of his own power of narrative.

Page 30:

> The further point is that the novel is about a character who becomes enmeshed in the plot of the novel he has written, as I did in Mexico. But now I am becoming enmeshed in the plot of a novel I have scarcely begun.

The 'I' threatens to become the merest shadow of the world it would initiate, and even that shadow a hindrance.

Page 31:

> —The inenarrable inconceivably desolate sense of having no right to be where you are; the billows of inexhaustible anguish haunted by the insatiable albatross of self.

Malcolm Lowry thinking of Sigbjørn Wilderness thinking of Martin Trumbaugh thinking. The surrogate writers in Lowry's story compounding in their conspiracies the resistance to the seductions of art, asserting the making of art by resistance, the story itself becoming journal entries, asides, marginalia, letters, history; all those forms of non-art discourse that in their discourse make art of art. Art, in the purity of art, sacred or profane, as sleep. That sleep, as night, as the chaos of the underworld, as mere sleep, a sleep that must be entered and broken.

That sleep as other. The other is the not-me that is me. It is also the me that is not me. And that sleep, like chaos, is insufficient, if for no other reason than its refusal to let us share its inexpressibility. For to speak at all, to write, is to render 'undecidable' the absolutes of chaos and sleep. The large boat moves, in 'Through the Panama', as did the small boat in the preceding story: we deliver our small, absurd messages from ourselves to ourselves. The hermeneutic sleep is somehow breakable, even when art itself becomes the lullaby, when art becomes the endless song against awakedness.

The gaze of Orpheus, in its affirmation and betrayal, recognizes the Lacanian fissure between self and other. The gaze is an act that announces distance, an act that in its announcing turns space into a relentless quality of time. That transformation from space into time allows the narrative to resume its energy. The pressure of narrative, in Lowry, arrested by the gaze, in the instant of its recognition and denial employs that condition of *arrest* to move itself forward.

The past, always, for Orpheus, for Lowry, is the as yet empty sign of the future, a sign that is at once full of the possibility of meaning and full of the potentiality of emptiness. Page 44:

> . . . and even at this moment Martin knew it to be no dream, but some strange symbolism of the future.
> —The French government falls again.

Every act of 'being there' is at the same time a passage. That passage of course might be to mere death. If death is to be found only in the future. And that too is undecidable.

Lowry and his writers travel in the company of writers: Pirandello, Strindberg, Fitzgerald, Edgar Allan Poe, Robert Penn Warren, Wallace Stevens. A ship of holy fools. Samuel Taylor Coleridge, that earlier Orpheus, having met death in life, life in death, Christ crossified, signs a letter dated 22 November 1947. Wilderness Carlos Wilderness signs a poem.

The passage is down as well as forward:

> passing San Pedro, forgetting Point Firmin (sic) down, down, at 404 fathoms at Carsbad on November 16 at 1,045 fathoms off Cape Colnet, at midday on the 17th at 965 fathoms, still going down . . . (p. 52).

One way or another, we must go down. We must gaze across, and then cross—to chaos. To sleep. To death.

But I almost forgot, Lowry writes.

> But I almost forgot the Lighthouse Keeper of Aspinwall. And there he is. Or rather there he once lived. In the imagination of another novelist . . . he [The Lighthouse Keeper] failed to provide illumination for his lighthouse, in fact went to sleep, which no lighthouse keeper should do even if spiritually advanced enough to have an illumination in Aspinwall (pp. 64-5).

Down is up, up down. Future is past, past future.

Hear Us O Lord. Hear us O Lord. Circle circle circle.

Inside this book, in this story, we are inside another story, in another book. But the paradox of the book is this: entering in, we are taken outside.

Is the book itself, then, another other?

In the margin of the story, in 'Through the Panama', we are in a marginal story that refuses, quite possibly refutes, the notion of centre. The story itself composes itself as stories. Or the stories compose themselves as story.

Dismemberment, Lowry seems to say, is the plenitude of the self; the self is the fissure, the gap that all roads lead from. It is that O that in Lowry's title is the apostrophic O. It is the circle, the O of nothing. Or the O of everything. Naught. Or the naught that is not. Setting out is somehow the setting of *out*, like a gopher trap, a bear trap, those zero jaws of a trap, O-ing. Owing.

Self abounds in its own othering. The Ancient Mariner, for Lowry, is manifold. Page 73:

> (Mem: Discuss this a little: problem of the double, the triple, the quadruple 'I'.) Almost pathological (I feel) . . .

The writer's 'I' multiplying out, trapped. Just to begin with, in that same paragraph: De Voto, Thomas Wolfe, Mark Twain, Joyce.

Just to begin with: Wilderness, Trumbaugh, Kennish Drumgold Cosnahan. Stories, again, containing stories, contained in stories.

Page 176:

> Roderick McGregor Fairhaven sat listening to his wife describe the scenes from the train yesterday (not this train, which was the Circumvesuviana, but the Rapido, the Rome-Naples Express), how fast it went, past the magnificent Claudian aqueducts, a station, Torricola—och aye, it was a rapido indeed, he thought, as once more in memory, bang: and they flashed through Divino Amore. (No stop for Divine Love.)

Once again, a happy couple. A woman and a man. Listening. Not listening. The gaze.

'No stop for Divine Love.'

And yet there is, perhaps. If we allow for that contrary, that rapido exchange of in and other that is the world's only order. Or the world's dream of order, allowing that chaos too has its other, perhaps in its dream of a dreamer.

If the Father is the primal Other (Hear Us O Lord), the Mother is that which contains the Father's primacy. That there can be no story that is not em*bed*ded in story is amply suggested by now. Why should the father, then, be an exception? (O Dad, poor Dad.) Is the mother really the Terrible Mother, giving all, returning all to herself? the all-giving cannibal source of all?

Page 73:

> —frightening thought occurred to me last night, when Primrose says I woke her up saying: 'Would they put Mother back in the sea?' What awful thing did I mean?

Was Eurydice, perchance, not Orpheus' wife at all, but rather his Mother? Thus the indiscreet and destructive glance, an outrageous glance in place of gaze, allowing magnificently for the moment of individuation. Even the archetype is made unstable in the postmodern ferocity of Lowry's imagination, let *her* then become the many who will do the dismembering.

Even Mother cannot escape indeterminacy. She too *owes* something to the O that she is. 'They' comes to collect. The small puzzle, the riddle, of that shaky pronoun includes all else. Who the hell were 'they' and what were 'they' up to?

Lowry must have plot and must not have plot. The very will of plot to complete its own circle fills that circle with emptiness. The plot unravels because of plot. The story, even in its pastness, signs the future. What was it you said will happen? What was it you said will happen.

Page 85:

> . . . for example, he has never been able to follow the plot of even the simplest movie because he is so susceptible to the faintest stimulus of that kind that ten other movies are going on in his head while he is watching it.

Not the possibility but the impossibility of completing the story is the force that keeps Lowry writing. Discouraging as that might be. Each telling toward completeness announces itself, belatedly, as fragment. Even the tellers in their election to write share this impossible condition, recognize in the other of chaos, sleep or death the not-me that is me—and the other that is inviolately other.

Dismemberment of the story into stories reflects the dismemberment of Author into authors. And then those smaller names, too, are dismembered.

Page 109:

> Kafka—Kaf—and others . . . And Flaub— . . . George Or— . . . hieroglyphics, masterly compressions, obscurities to be deciphered by experts—yes, and poets—like Sigbjørn Wilderness. Wil—

The names themselves become fragments, the authors fragmentary, caught and lost in moments of naming that unname as well.

Lowry's work is full of the impossible and necessary task of the search, the finding, the losing again, the will to assemble, the being enabled to speak by the failures, the being caused by those failures, one's own, the failures of the speaking itself, to speak too late, too soon, in the wrong place, on the wrong occasion, to the wrong listener.

Dissembling. Even to the Mother, dissembling.

Page 124:

> I'll write Mother and explain why I couldn't write her before she died . . .

He couldn't write *to* his Mother before she died. But further, he couldn't *write her* before she died. The completeness, now, is possible only in her definitive incompleteness. Within his statement of intention are two statements in dialogic contention: 'I'll write Mother'; 'I couldn't write her.' This equivalence of the me and not me is the analogue of his own being. He can only *be* here on this edge of solution and dissolution. And speaking too late, his

Mother already dead, preparing again an apostrophe, Hear Me O Mother, he at once recognizes the collapse of narrative into solipsism and the possibility of narrating that predicament. Here again, this occasion is 'no dream, but some strange symbolism of the future'.

Even to avoid looking is to look, apparently. And Lowry, with Orpheus before him, looks more intently at that predicament too.

As poets have been dismembered into survival, so have cities, so have cultures. In the opening of 'Present State of Pompeii' we read (page 175):

> Inside the restaurant during the thunderstorm, there was one moment of pure happiness within the dark inner room when it started to rain. 'Now thank God I don't have to see the ruins,' Roderick thought.

That thunderstorm connects to the end of the opening story, to the statement, 'it was like gazing into chaos', where the chaos translates into the world as a violent storm. Roderick, unwittingly and innocently, a 'liberal-minded and progressive Scotch-Canadian schoolmaster', believes he has been spared the gaze.

A few pages into the story we hear again that fateful (or fating) song:

> Frère Jacques!
> Frère Jacques!
> Dormez-vous?
> Dormez-vous?

The doubled lines of the song, redoubled here, double the occasion as well. The deaf God listens now to Roderick's not listening. And this is the same Roderick who will observe so wonderfully later, 'It was a silly place to put a volcano.'

Lowry is the poet of ruins. Ruins of place, of culture, of visions of self, of visions of paradise. There was indeed 'one moment of pure happiness'. Even paradise must submit to the time of narrative. Even Roderick must submit. And the city, in its submission, instructs both paradise and poet. The city, dismembered, enters into the incompleteness and the temptation of completeness that make story possible and unavoidable.

Page 192:

> . . . Roderick found himself suddenly hating this street with an inexplicable virulence. How he loathed Pompeii! His mouth positively watered with his hatred. Roderick was almost prancing. It seemed to him now that it was as though, by some perverse grace, out of the total inundation of some Pacific Northwestern city, had been preserved a bit of the station hotel, a section of the gasworks, the skeletal remains of four or five palatial cinemas, as many bars and several public urinals, a fragment of marketplace together with the building that once housed the Star Laundries, what was left of several fine industrialists' homes (obscene paintings), a football stadium, the Church of the Four Square Gospel, a broken statue of Bobbie Burns, and finally the remains of the brothels of Chinatown which, though the mayor and police force had labored to have them removed right up to the time of the catastrophe, had nonetheless survived five thousand nine hundred and ninety-nine generations whereupon it was concluded, probably rightly, that the city was one of the seven wonders of the world, as it now stood, but wrongly that anything worthwhile had been there in the first place, with the exceptions of the mountains.

Pompeii, its absence, its presence, its ruins, its endurance afflict Roderick at once with loathing and with the need to attend, to pay attention, to *look*. Precisely because (a passage I skipped, page 187)—

> . . . 'On the other hand—If you compare it with Bumble, Saskatchewan—'

I was a youngish if not young writer when I first read *Hear Us O Lord*. I had earlier struggled with *Under the Volcano* and given up and then been drawn back, and had then discovered its unutterable beauty and my own compulsion to go on looking. But in *Hear Us O Lord*, which I came to early in the 1960s, I recognized my own 'I', my own will towards utterance.

In so far as I recognized myself as the writer from Bumble, Saskatchewan, Lowry was my other. Perhaps because he offered me the ruins that I so badly needed in order to become a writer.

In my version of Saskatchewan—in the rural Alberta landscape where I was born and grew—I mistakenly read that world as original, unwritten, uninscribed. Of course it was those things too. But it wasn't. I believed in a version of newness that came out of what we now, looking back, call the modernist tradition. Lowry pointed me towards the tradition we now call, so uneasily, postmodern. Perhaps his task was to sing me, not out of hell, but out of heaven. Or are those *others* of each other simply the boundaries that mark the rift where all writing occurs?

When I first read *Hear Us O Lord* my favourite story was 'The Forest Path to the Spring', and one day I noticed in that story:

> One day when we were out rowing we came across a sunken canoe, a derelict, floating just beneath the surface in deep water so clear we made out its name: *Intermezzo*.

I won't pretend to know why that sentence picked me out the way it did. Perhaps I heard in its directness the impossibility of innocence. Perhaps I heard in its duplicity the duplicity of what passes for discovery.

In our strange faith in nature, as nature is practised in North America, we fail to recognize that nature and culture, from the moment when nature is named as nature, engage each other with tenderness and loathing. That troubled hold, half stolid embrace, half dance, was apparent to Lowry from the Columbus-moment when first he set foot in the New World.

Christopher Columbus, returned from his voyage, from his voyages, insisted to his dying day that he had sailed to the Indies. Malcolm Lowry proves him half right.

Europe made an easy other of the New World. Lowry complicates that easy binary by going and looking for himself. Lowry, sailing home for that other Columbus, sailing home again and again, sailing home to the essential eviction, the eviction that is all, ever, that allows for entry, delivers again the message that Columbus did and did not deliver. No, I have come to the Indies. Yes, I have not.

If we let go for a moment of that sacred name, New World, we see our familiar world with a startling freshness. Malcolm Lowry invites us, dares us, to take that risk, for a moment to unname what it is we think we are, where it is we think we are.

The ruins were ruins, he tells us, before we so gloatingly ruined them. Before the Spanish and the Portuguese, before the French and the English, death was waiting to recognize itself in the arrival of death. Death had built its earthly cities, as Cortés discovered, even if Columbus would not. To discover paradise is to discover the idea of paradise contained in the idea of ruin that is contained in the idea of paradise.

To read 'The Forest Path to the Spring' as conclusion is to resist Lowry's elaborate positing within his book of cities, numerous cities, cities in their multitude, in their incompleteness, in their continuous ruin, in their eternal othering embrace of nature. The city—*polis*—in its sheer inability to complete itself, is the embodiment of the uncompletable fecundity of human story-making.

In the strange mathematics of a book, I'm more inclined to look at the middle than at the end.

Kennish Drumgold Cosnahan, the writer in 'Elephant and Colosseum', has written the story of his shipping an elephant to the ancient and ruined and vital city of Rome. He could write this story because he did ship an elephant to Rome, he insists on that too. And he trusts us to remember that others before him shipped, marched, drove elephants to Rome and its promise of a Colosseum and glory.

But now Cosnahan has himself come to Rome, as author, not as writer. He is here to discuss with his Italian publisher his novel *Ark from Singapore*—again, the completed book within the incompletable book, the completed book being translated out of completedness first by a literal translation, then by the experience that follows on what was the 'end' of the novel.

Kennish Drumgold Cosnahan, in the city, is again the hesitating male come to the gap or fissure, resisting the gaze and tempted to have a look, drinking his way between the narrative of action and the discourse of inaction, obeying and revising Ortega's dictum that he invent himself as he goes along, concentrating on and avoiding the other that is the silence at his back. For this, again, is a love story. Cosnahan, in the complex silence of his life, is tempted to glance just once in the direction of his first great love, Rosemary.

Kennish Drumgold Cosnahan, the author, here becomes reader. He reads the city. He reads the novel he carries with him but won't open. Cosnahan, now, after the lapse of so many years, after failure and success and the ambiguity of both, after his own transport from The Isle of Man to America, reads the elaborate story of his own career as writer.

This Nantucket man (for that is what Cosnahan has become), just as Ishmael learned to love one whale, learned to love by loving an elephant. A female elephant named Rosemary.

He is distracted or instructed in his reading first by the cosmological lure. Cosnahan, we are told, having imagined a flight of angels that became real, then (page 170)

> seemed to detect Mother Drumgold floating upwards on her celestial journey. His mother? But the answer came before Cosnahan had time to question.

And now we read the answer that anticipated his question (pages 170-1):

> For was not Rosemary a signal *from* his mother, nay, was it not almost as if his mother had herself produced Rosemary or at least guided his steps to her, his meek and impossible elephant, to a meeting in its gently buffoonish manner nearly sublime.

That meeting, buffoonishly sublime, is not only the marriage of heaven and earth. It is also the uneasy marriage of nature and culture, of the elephant and the book about the elephant, of the earthly city and the mother who in her containing is not yet mother, who only in her emptying-out becomes the container of all.

Cosnahan, in his moment of recognition that 'now at one of those rare points where life and poetry meet, Rosemary had appeared;

Rosemary, so to say, *was* his work—', resorts again to apostrophe.

And now his apostrophe is a promise, not a request, a ritual kind of profane prayer:

Page 172:

> Tomorrow, to that uniqueness of yours, I shall make an offering of the choicest Roman carrots, a bouquet of the freshest and crispest cisalpine celery. And sometimes it is true, so hapless does man seem to me, that I feel that if there is evolution, it must be to such as you. But great and wise though you are, Rosemary, I am bound to point out, our star being low, that man is more various.

Apostrophe, finally, is an appeal to the muse. Rose Mary. We remember. Those names name us into Dante's ultimate poem, into the seeming inclusiveness of the Christian story. There in Christian and pagan Rome. The elephant herself, at once tearing loose and imprisoned, naming the writer into the task of writing. In memory and forgetfulness we begin by saying, dangerously:

Hear us O Rosemary!

Notes

[1] Malcolm Lowry, *Hear Us O Lord from Heaven Thy Dwelling Place* (Philadelphia and New York: Lippincott, 1963; copyright Margerie Bonner Lowry, 1961).

[2] Geoffrey Hartman, 'Preface' to Maurice Blanchot, *The Gaze of Orpheus and Other Literary Essays*, translated by Lydia Davis, edited, with an Afterword, by P. Adams Sitney (Barrytown, N.Y.: Station Hill Press, 1981), p. ix.

[3] Jonathan Culler, *The Pursuit of Signs: Semiotics, Literature, Deconstruction* (Ithaca, N.Y.: Cornell University Press, 1981), p. 135.

16

The Veil of Knowing

1

To reveal all is to end the story. To conceal all is to fail to begin the story. Individuals, communities, religions, even nations, narrate themselves into existence by selecting out, by working variations upon, a few of the possible strategies that lie between these two extremes.

Where do Canadians locate themselves on the spectrum between the extreme possibilities (or impossibilities) of telling all and telling nothing? What might be the narrative strategies that locate the Canadian experience and psyche and language in a body of writing?

George Bowering, the enigma of his talent veiled in assertion and parody, in semi-quotation and quasi-translation, offers a clue. In his *A Short Sad Book*, which in the book is referred to among other possibilities as a novel, a collection of stories, a history, an autobiography, and a critical study, we read:

> American literature is above the ground or on top of the water don't shoot till you see the whites of their eyes. Canadian literature, well Canadian literature. One is walking into the lake & becoming an ancient fish, one is hitting an iceberg & going down, one is looking for her father's words on a rock face under the surface, it was a Canadian publisher, business as usual. . . .
>
> I said American literature was also on top of the ground, but Canadian literature is under the ground not underground but under the ground, under the ground or under the snow or under the ice. What are we doing under here.[1]

For all the echoes of Gertrude Stein and the references to Canadian works by E.J. Pratt and Margaret Atwood and who knows who else, Bowering is making a serious statement of his own about the place where he finds his stories. This writer who claims to have no unconscious is an archaeologist of the Canadian dream-world. Dream-world, not dream. And as the archaeologist of that version of world, he insists on giving us the bare facts. And the bare fact is that the story is hidden.

Bowering begins the quoted passage by telling us that American literature is up-front, above-board. He in effect quotes when he writes 'don't shoot till you see the whites of their eyes', reminding us of the immediacy of American narrative strategies. He writes or speaks in a voice that is at once explanatory and parodic of itself. He tells us about himself by hiding behind the force of American literature and the up-frontness of assertion. He hides behind a form that might or might not suggest the fictional, a voice that might or might not mean what it says. He hides behind the word 'or'. He hides behind grammar and rhetoric.

'I said', he says, beginning the second paragraph of the quotation. He's immediately present, quoting himself to make what he says more immediate. 'I said American literature was also on top of the ground . . . ,' he says, using the rhetoric of repetition to drive home his point. Except that the repetition begins to call all into doubt, and we hear him saying, 'I *said* American literature *was* also on top of the ground . . . ' And what about that switch to the past tense? ' . . . American literature was also on top of the ground . . .' And what about that word 'also'?

The second paragraph calls the first paragraph into doubt. Or into hiding. He continues his sentence, 'but Canadian literature is under the ground not underground but under the ground . . .'. Three 'unders' and two 'buts' and one 'not'. And this is only the middle of the sentence. It goes on, 'or under the snow or under the ice'. Two 'ors' and two more 'unders'. 'What are we doing here', the paragraph concludes. Without a question mark.

And it goes on. These two paragraphs are embedded in a section of the book that is called 'PART FOUR: The Black Mountain Influence'. These two paragraphs, in this section of the book, are shortly followed by the passage:

Sometimes when people ask me about the Black Mountain Influence I tell them the closest I ever got was Montenegro.
I had two Yugoslavian friends when I was in high school.

I went to Montenegro in 1966 & lookt across the mountains at
Albania. Albania is a mystery to me (p. 120).

2

George Bowering is one of the models of what the Canadian narrative strategy is: he is that model in his writing and in his career.
He writes under the name of George Bowering, and he writes
under pseudonyms. Or at least the brilliant young critic and editor
and scholar Roy Miki assures me that George Bowering writes and
publishes under pseudonyms. But at the same time he invites us,
if only through the indirections of criticism and scholarship, to
find him out. Unless George Bowering itself is, in a way, a pseudonym. Of George Bowering.

In a way the Canadian writer, writing, writes from behind a
pseudonym. That's the narrative strategy. We assume that one of
the Georges, *at least* one of the Georges, in *Burning Water*, is
George. We assume that.

In that novel someone named George makes an outrageous exploration of the expeditions and the life of George Vancouver, the
English explorer who gave his name to George Bowering's home
city. Or to the city that George Bowering lives in now; the town
that was his home town is, like his authorship, veiled in pseudonyms. Or Penticton, BC, is an actual place that gave him his fictional birth. In the novel, the George who writes the novel, and
George the explorer (and that too is a concept rife with ironies of
concealment and revelation), along with King George the Third
(whose understanding of centre and margin turned margin into
centre), become related and carefully confused as George Bowering struggles with something as simple and impossible as the archaeology of the narrative of his given name.

The truth is veiled. Except that we are, perhaps, being teased
into looking behind the veil. Or under the veil. Except that, perhaps, we should be looking at the veil. The truth shall make you
veiled.

That's the way it is, in Canadian writing.

3

Perhaps we can only read a narrative, any narrative, by reading
with or against a meta-narrative that is assumed, often uncon-

sciously, by the reader or by the culture or by the writer. George Bowering, in *A Short Sad Book*, makes effective use of the assumed fiction of American fiction, along with the various fictions that are assumed about such explicitly narrative genres as autobiography and history. At the same time, he points, in his short sad book, to a continuing dilemma.

Canadians, from the beginning of their history, have been unwilling or slow or even unable to locate the overriding stories, the persistent and recurring narratives, that allow for the development of a national meta-narrative. By contrast, for instance, the Americans, in the New World, quickly hit on the American Dream, with its free enterprise and its frontier manifestations. Or the Australians, with their seizing on the convict moment, the complex moment of transport, find an abiding narrative in that doubled occasion of bondage and release.

In Canada we insist on the archaeological sense of narrative. We find, in our experience and in our psyches, fragments, traces, possibilities, remains, shards. Timothy Findley's *Famous Last Words* is an example of this archaeological mode applied to history. Michael Ondaatje's *Coming through Slaughter* is an example of this archaeological mode applied to the individual life. Martha Ostenso's *Wild Geese*, in its obsession with secrets and trickery, seems intent on making the archaeological mode literally an act of re-covering.

The story is concealed from us. Only by a careful acknowledgement of that concealment do we allow for a revelation of the story.

The novel I'm going to look at most intently here is Howard O'Hagan's *Tay John*. That novel, published in 1939, elaborates the paradigm. Recognizing as it does, through the fur trade of the western mountains, the meta-narrative of empire, and recognizing through the processes of conversion the meta-narrative of the Christian myth, it goes on to explore an acceptance of the 'hiddenness' of narrative in a manner that we now call, loosely, postmodern.

Tay John begins with an act of authorial omniscience that would be the envy of a nineteenth-century novelist:

> The time of this in its beginning, in men's time, is 1880 in the summer, and its place is the Athabasca valley, near its head in the mountains, and along the other waters falling into it, and beyond them

a bit, over Yellowhead Pass to the westward, where the Fraser, rising in a lake, flows through wilderness and canyon down to the Pacific.[2]

Granted, this opening does announce the enormous shift of literary (not to mention economic and social) power from the Atlantic to the Pacific, a process that was hardly to be perceived, at least in Canada, in 1939. But while the Great Divide is at the centre of this passage, the perceiving eye is still godly if not God's; the speaking voice quotes itself from what is apparently a pretty reliable source. The language assumes its own authority and hardly raises the question of signifier and signified—unless we hear in 'Yellowhead Pass' a careful dislocation of the subject and origin of the book's title.

But all in all, we get through that first paragraph pretty much unscathed; the verities hold.

The second paragraph is more problematic, but slyly problematic. 'In those days Canada was without a railway across the mountains,' it begins; this in a section of the book called, 'PART I: Legend.'

And the question of legend is here, even before we meet Tay John. Or because we are about to meet him. O'Hagan begins his story of 'untiming' in 1880. Canada does not yet have a transcontinental railway. It has in mind, and under construction, a supplanting story of a railway. And that railway, and that story, we learn in the second paragraph of the novel, were about to miss the Yellowhead by a good 200 miles.

We are about to hear, not the up-front story of the building of the railway, but the delayed story, the near-miss of a story; we are about to hear the concealment of the story of Tay John.

The omniscient voice fades. We tune in on Jack Denham. He seems a self-effacing man, obsessed with telling not his own story, but that of Tay John. He is willing, it seems, to put his own invisibility in place of Tay John's silence. And even that willingness he qualifies:

Not that I feel any responsibility to Tay John, nor to his story. No, not at all. His story, such as it is, like himself, would have existed independently of me. Every story . . . only waits, like a mountain in an untravelled land, for someone to come close, to gaze upon its contours, lay a name upon it, and relate it to the known world (pp. 166-7).

So far so good. But then he (Denham, O'Hagan) goes on:

> Indeed, to tell a story is to leave most of it untold. . . . You dig down—and when you have finished, the story remains, something beyond your touch, resistant to your siege; unfathomable, like the heart of a mountain. You have the feeling that you have not reached the story itself, but have merely assaulted the surrounding solitude (p. 167).

Tay John's story is veiled in the irony that while he works often as a guide, he works always to disappear. Jack Denham, by a comparable irony, working always to tell a story, believes much of the time that the story he would tell is untellable.

Not the raising of the veil but, rather, the lowering of the veil, the acknowledgement of the untellability of the story, is the generative moment, the enabling act.

Early in *A Short Sad Book*, Bowering's narrator, or Bowering, or Bowering disguised as Bowering remarks, 'Do you know I am keeping secrets from you & I want you to discover them. & I will be disappointed with myself if you do' (p. 16).

4

In the story that Jack Denham tells, in any available bar, to any available listeners, a man named Red Rorty (a man nicknamed Red Rorty) arrives in Edmonton from the Athabasca valley to sell his furs. Like Denham, this man drinks for the company of drinking. He too likes the bars of Edmonton. But then one night, passing a church on his way to the bar, he is held by the singing. Red Rorty, quickly, is tempted by the absolutes. Soon he is sitting with a minister, talking. 'Their knees touched as they talked,' we are told. And while Red Rorty talks with this dark-haired minister, they engage in a verbal duel that becomes a litany:

> 'Do you believe?' the minister asked . . .
>
> . . .
>
> 'Do you believe?' the minister asked again . . .
>
> . . .
>
> 'I believe,' Red Rorty answered . . .
>
> . . .
>
> 'Do you believe . . .'
>
> . . .

'I believe . . .'

. . .

'Do you believe . . .'

. . .

'I believe . . .'

. . .

'Do you believe . . .'

. . .

'I believe.'

. . .

'We who believe . . .' (pp. 16-17).

And Red Rorty is on his way to attempting an assertion of a metanarrative among the Indians.

It might be instructive to compare *Tay John* with Shelia Watson's *The Double Hook*. Both are novels about the challenging of belief. In both, the Old World's beliefs come under pressure from the physical experience, and the gods, of the New World. Both challenge the wisdom of the past by recitals of that wisdom, whether in rituals or aphorisms or legend or myth. Both tease us into discovery by a subtle play with veiled sexuality—or by a veiling of sexuality.

Sheila Watson's title *The Double Hook*, in all its complexities, announces the double bind, including that of love and sex.

By what these novels conceal we shall know ourselves. That includes, in *The Double Hook*, the killing of the mother, the absence of the father, the breaking of the incest taboo. In *Tay John* too, the characters venture out of sight, into the veiling mountains.

The whippings in *The Double Hook*, with their dark glow of sexuality, somehow remember the violence of Red Rorty's death; that death, at once crucifixion and parody, is the result of his having sex with the Shuswap woman Hanni; that violated woman, we are told, however, 'did not resist'. The Great Mother, there in both books, with her doubled and doubling lure, only darkens the veil. Or darkens the veil into a knowledge that both men and women try to, and try not to, read.

Tay John goes to the aid of Ardith Aeriola when she is molested by the man who is boss and owner of the resort, to be called Lucerne, that is under construction, there in the mountains. Tay John, like Baron Heyst going to Lena's aid in Conrad's *Victory*, acts out of an impulse whose complexity he himself is not likely to understand. But the consequence is immediate. Dobble's men make a violent attack:

> Johansen the Swede was there. Pete, the blacksmith from the prairies; Scottish teamsters, French-Canadian axemen. Tay John was assailed by all at once. It was not only what he had done to Dobble. It was what was different in him—the heritage of his ancestry, the challenge of his hair, which gave fury to their assault. That fury would pull him down, change his shape, make him one of those who fought against him (p. 240).

Tay John, in acting to protect Ardith, has revealed not only his attachment to her; he has revealed the workmen's fear of the woman, their attraction to the woman, their devotion to Dobble. In his uniqueness as a blond Indian he has named their secrets. In his uniqueness he is supposed, also, to conceal their secrets.

In this scene, we recognize Tay John as an Orpheus figure. Or as an inverse Orpheus figure. He has come up from under the ground, not with speech or poetry, but with silence. And Tay John infuriates not with his unwillingness to love, but with his willingness to love. He threatens to violate the taboos that hold among the men in the camp. His silence is their story; to keep it intact the men will break him back into silence.

Jack Denham explains that he had been as willing as Tay John to go to Ardith's aid. He goes on to explain: 'Before I could move I was shoved aside.' All this while Ardith has already begun 'to beat [Dobble's] head, his shoulders with her fists' (p. 239).

Denham, throughout the novel, is in fact covertly wary of Ardith, of other women. He goes to the aid of Tay John. And in that aiding he proposes to put back together the dismembered Orpheus.

Denham wants to keep intact his own version of Tay John's silence. He will put Tay John together in such a way that he will be larger than life, a mythic figure, a figure more symbolic than real. Where Dobble's men would disguise Tay John as nothing, Denham will disguise him as everything. In both intentions, the realization of self is impossible. In both, the story is veiled and, by that veiling, transformed into text.

5

The dismemberment does not depend entirely on those male

Furies, furiously at work in a bush camp. Tay John is busy, some of the time, dismembering himself, and in this he approaches a symbolic realization that Jack Denham does not intend. Or does intend.

Tay John, cutting cards in a trader's cabin, gambling to win a mare that he madly wants (desires to possess), cuts the *jack* of spades against his rival's queen of hearts. The Terrible Mother plays that kind of game. Tay John, responding, reaches with his right hand and takes hold of an axe that the trader, McLeod, has left against the wall.

> Tay John, before they could reach him, swung the axe high, its blade gleaming for an instant above his yellow hair, stooped, and brought it down in one clean sweeping blow upon his left wrist resting on the table. McLeod said you could hear the click as it bit through bone.
>
> . . .
>
> Tay John pointed [at the severed hand]. '"If your hand offend you,"' he quoted, '"cut it off"' (pp. 108-9).

Revealed truths are dangerous stuff. But is metaphoric language the guise of the literal, or is literal language the guise of the metaphoric? Fooled by a language act from the past (if we can agree that he was indeed 'fooled'; he does get the mare), he responds now with a language act of his own. Tay John renames himself, The One-Handed. That would seem to be literally true. He believes that is the game he enters into, now. Except that the Terrible Mother is not yet finished playing with her son.

As for the severed hand—McLeod reports to Jack Denham: 'His hand . . . oh, he took that somewhere, some place, back into the hills. Buried it perhaps. I don't know' (p. 110).

'I don't know,' McLeod says, unwittingly. McLeod feels safe again. The story is under the ground again. And everything will be fine again, Tay John might simply be a tall tale, a myth about a god-man figure, a story to tell on a slow night in a trading post...

Except that McLeod (one hears a pun in Mc Loud; and *Rorty*, earlier in the novel, was trapped in the sound of his own voice: even voice serves to cloak, to veil)—McLeod on occasion, unable to make the bloodstain on his table go away, hides it. He feels he must hide it. From others. From himself.

In Canadian fiction the traditional idea or the convention of suspense is threatened by the idea of secrecy. Suspense points towards the ideal of revelation.

Sheila Watson's *The Double Hook* plays with the conventions of the murder story. Even there, suspense turns to secret. An American friend of mine on reading that novel became furious: Why does Watson withhold so much information? she wanted to know.

I don't know that I know. Or perhaps I do, and I don't want to tell. Or perhaps, as a Canadian reader, I don't for a moment expect to be told more. I don't want to be told more. The method of the novel precludes a further telling. The themes of the novel preclude a further telling. In a small community it isn't polite to ask. And besides: the person's not-telling tells you all you have to know.

Even nakedness conceals, in Canadian writing. Consider the immense secrecy of Phyllis Webb's *Naked Poems*. And yet no reader is likely to ask for an uncovering of the secrets, not even the un-covering of naked secrets; knowing the secrecy, we know what it is we know. Consider John Glassco's *Memoirs of Montparnasse*. He is telling us everything, he tells us. Of course we know he's lying, he made it all up, he didn't write the book in a hospital bed, as he claims; he wrote it in a lover's bed. He didn't tell us that, when he told us everything; but we know that too.

We write books, not in search of our identity, but against the no-tion of identity. The paradox is, however, that the Canadian iden-tity states itself in, by, its acts of concealment. What we insist isn't there is exactly what is.

Jack Hodgins, in *The Invention of the World*, explores the life and legend and possibly the myth of a man who leads a group of set-tlers from Ireland to the West Coast of Canada—shades of *Tay John*. That hero digs his own grave by burrowing under his own house; he makes of himself the absent father, a father under the ground.

Rudy Wiebe, at the end of *The Temptations of Big Bear*, says movingly of the dead figure of his Indian hero: 'He felt the granular sand joined by snow running together, against and over him in delicate streams.'[3]

Margaret Atwood, in *Surfacing*, centres her story on the search for a missing father who is under the water, and that in a story told by a narrator who has hidden her name, who keeps secret her very name.

George Bowering ends his own *Burning Water*: 'A gust of wind punched into the mainsail, and every man took a little shuffling step to stay erect, save their captain who seemed to be lifted by some strength unwitnessed, over the rail and into the unsolicitous sea.'[4]

David Canaan, in Buckler's *The Mountain and the Valley*, ends up snowed under:

> And then [the snowflakes] clung, without melting, to his eyelashes and his hair. And then they did not melt on his eyelids or on his cheeks or in the corners of his mouth or anywhere on his face at all. And then they grew smoothly and exactly over him and over the fallen log that lay beside him until the two outlines were as one.[5]

The end is not an unveiling but rather a veiling. And in the veiling we *know* indeed what it is we know. In the erotics of that disguise is our ultimate erotics. Buckler ends his paradigmatic story, not with the image of the two become secretly one, but with the orgasmic flight of a partridge, straight and exact, up over the mountain and down. In the lovely obscenity of his refusing to show, we know what it is that he and we are not, and are, showing.

6

Language itself is a version of plot.

A woman named Yaada calls Red Rorty a liar. 'See,' she says, 'he was a great liar and the word has choked him!'

There are all those *a*'s in the novel *Tay John*. Yaada. Ardith Ariola. Those repetitions of the beginning of the alphabet. Those repetitions within names, repetitions from name to name. Red Rorty. Denham and Dobble. Dobble who is almost double. Jackie and Blackie; and Jackie's Tale that contains or doesn't quite contain Blackie's tale. More *a*'s, there. And Denham: den him? And Tay itself—head, eh?

The letter, the name, hesitating to name a difference, hesitates to name itself out of hiding. We will make you look like us, say the Furies. We will make you like us.

Art becomes the politics of disguise. Consider the secrecies of Callaghan, of MacLennan, of Livesay, of Lampman, of Crawford. Consider the secrecies of Susanna Moodie—just what *was* her husband good for? Consider the secrecies of Major John Richardson's *Wacousta*—just who was making it with whom in the secret places inside the secrets of the garrison? And of course they blamed the white Indian—more shades of Tay John.

The play between the possibilities of revelation and conceal-ment, with a revealed inclination toward concealment, becomes the trope by which Canadian literature speaks itself and questions itself. Concealment becomes the shared ground of writer and reader.

This trope opens the way to questions if not to answers.

7

There is in Canadian writing the fascination with multiple nar-rators. That narrative method becomes as much a way to cloak as to reveal, as we see in *Tay John*.

There is in Canadian writing the troubled or at least troubling tension between the symbolic and the documentary. Novels like Grove's *Settlers of the Marsh* and Margaret Atwood's *Bodily Harm* transform that 'trouble' into passionate disguise. A poem, if it is a poem, like Michael Ondaatje's *The Collected Works of Billy the Kid*, deconstructs both document and story towards a version of revelation that stands at the opposite pole from Joyce's version of Modernist epiphany.

Notions of nature and self come under violent pressure in this troping of the obscured. Not the obscure. The obscured. The self is not obscure in bp Nichol's *The Martyrology*. It is merely impos-sible. Or, as a result of that impossibility, totally possible. Nature is not obscured in *The Double Hook*. In that text it becomes blind-ingly clear that nature is the text by which we read either God or Coyote. Or possibly both. Or do I dare add—possibly neither? 'Above her [Ara] the sky stretched like a tent pegged to the broken rock.'[6] Yes, of course. But how do we read the simile? Assuming it is a simile.

Listening to Jack Denham in *Tay John*, we come to the question of the place of the reader in a literature that would speak its truth by a veiling. With the meta-narrative in doubt, there develops a new anxiety: an anxiety about subject matter itself. The writer communicates that anxiety to the reader.

Canadian writing is obsessively about the act of writing. I am asking now if that obsession, too, is a version of veiling.

The long poem for a long time has been one of the principal bearers of culture in world literatures. A number of recent Canadian long poems inherit that burden, and with a vengeance.

George Bowering, in his *Kerrisdale Elegies*, conceals his fear of self-revelation (and of middle age, and of death, and of language, and of poetry) by hiding under Rilke's elegies; and that Bowering, in his wilful and surrendering (mis)translation of translations, reveals what it is he conceals. Frank Davey, in his poem *The Abbotsford Guide to India*, by his deconstruction of the narrative of travel writing, both conceals and reveals his anxiety about subject matter—this in the face of an ancient and frightening and compelling and somehow female civilization. He begins with the marvellously clear, unlikely sentence (or stanza), 'Abbotsford is the centre of Canada & India is the centre of the world.'[7] Once again, a Canadian writer both conceals and reveals himself by a surreptitious 'glance' at another culture. He uses documentary information to construct an impossible binary that is at once intimate, distant, grammatically reassuring, hallucinatory, erotic. The 'I' in David Arnason's *Marsh Burning* narrates his present self backwards in a long glissade of memory and document; the figure that looms in the poem's opening by the poem's end has disappeared into the myriad strategies of his own poetic.

What is the reader to do?

Fred Wah, in his recent long and continuing poem *Music at the Heart of Thinking*, turns the act of writing into a dazzling sequence of linguistic postures, not as metaphors for life, but as life itself. And in those mysterious, erotic exchanges between hearing and the unheard, saying and the unsaid, he challenges our very grammar of being. Dennis Cooley, in his book-sized poem *Bloody Jack*, writes the autobiography of the criminality of our individual and our national innocence, insisting all the while (in the midst of his documentation) on a vernacular that would make each word, each line, as momentarily real as utterance itself. John Krafchenko, the bank robber and murderer and Robin Hood figure, becomes a cunning linguist. The very fleetingness of speech becomes the disguise of a radical poetics, a radical politics, that, in its Menippean strategies, is willing to haul down every meta-narrative that ever there was.

How and to what degree is the reader implicated in these poems? Does the author (or writer, should I say?) distance the reader or invite complicity? What becomes the ethos of this writing, of this reading? How do we read at all, as readers, when the meta-narrative that guides most reading (and writing) is called into doubt?

The answers to these questions will, I have a suspicion, occupy

Canadian readers, and critics, for decades to come. Let me get back, simply, to something as newfangled as a novel.

Howard O'Hagan, in *Tay John*, at once describes a paradisal state of not yet being named, a state of total potential without even the blur of a name to contaminate it into mere being, and, along with that, a state of utter madness in which one is deprived of a name, cannot so much as cling to the consolation of the constancy of one's own 'given' name.

That concealing of one's self from one's name, then, along with the revealing of one's self in that namelessness, offers the temptations of pure potential along with a potential for a fall from time into madness.

Canadian writing, by that trope of concealment, reveals to the reader a readerly predicament that is, in Roland Barthes's terms, writerly. The reader reading Canadian becomes the reader writing the writer, then writing the reader.

By the end of *Tay John*, Jack Denham is writer and reader both. Or I should say, reader and writer both. Because there is a reader here before there is a writer. Jack Denham, in effect, 'reading' the story of Tay John, realizes to his exquisite horror that he is reading an 'unwritten' story.

By the end of the novel Jack Denham is telling one last yarn, a story he heard from a trapper who strayed into the larger story just six pages from the novel's end. Denham, by what seems an evasion of the problem of ending his own story, by this act of self-veiling, reveals the story that he read, then became the writer of, then became the reader of.

'This trapper's name', we are told, as listeners ourselves, as readers, 'was Blackie—just that, no more' (p. 259).

That black-bearded man had a tale to tell about a yellow-haired man, Tay John. That Blackie had other tales to tell as well, 'of where he had been, of what he had seen, of the things he had heard. Albino bears, hybrid creatures born of the union of a moose and a caribou, a pack of wolves led by a collie-dog gone wild, wolverines that could outwit a man—' (p. 259). Tall tales. Except that even as tall tales they hint, profanely, of what transpired in the novel's opening: stories of man-god unions, of failed leaders, of sacred bears and transforming colours.

Blackie's tale hints guardedly of Jackie's Tale. We hear it, not directly from Blackie, but in a version retold, retailed, by Jack, over drinks in an Edmonton bar. The certainty of the novel's opening has become the uncertainty of this end.

Blackie saw Tay John. More exactly, he saw his tracks.

Blackie had, before this last ending, met Tay John in the middle of a lake in a blizzard. Tay John was harnessed to a toboggan that he was pulling through the snow. On the toboggan was a woman, a pregnant woman. 'Then I saw snow in her mouth,' Blackie told Denham. 'It was chock-full of snow. . . . She was dead' (p. 262).

Blackie fled the scene; then, next morning, he went back, as compulsively as Denham goes back to the story he is telling now. It was dusk by the time Blackie found the trail:

> Cold. A tree cracked. Blackie's breath hissed, rose yellow as grass smoke before his eyes. There was no wind. The snow fell in great wavering flakes without cessation, as if it would go on snowing for ever, as if all the clouds had been upended. The trees, the mountains, the ice on the rivers, all the familiar world, the sky itself were gone from sight.
>
> Blackie stared at the tracks in front of him, very faint now, a slight trough in the snow, no more. Always deeper and deeper into the snow. He turned then. There was nothing more he could do. He had the feeling, he said, looking down at the tracks, that Tay John hadn't gone over the pass at all. He had just walked down, the toboggan behind him, under the snow and into the ground (pp. 263-4).

We are back at George Bowering's story that 'is under the ground not underground' eighteen years before Bowering got there.

What happens to Tay John?

The story of Tay John is what happens. The remittance man, Jack Denham, reading the unwritten story, is compelled to read himself into the story as the story's writer. Written in as writer, confounded into blackness (or Blackie-ness) by his own disguise, he finds he must write himself out, for the written story to have a reader.

Canadian literature, at its most radical, is the autobiography of a culture that tells its story by telling us repeatedly it has no story to tell. Jack Denham—or perhaps Tay John—is the emblem of this condition. Jack becomes John becomes Jack. Becomes John. Becomes Jack. . . .

In the story's going under the ground, not underground, it cries out: Reader, please. Open this grave book. Dig me. Accept the contradictions of my suppressed intertextuality. Read with a pleased and luminous and violent desire.

Text is a three-letter word. We like it.

Notes

[1] George Bowering, *A Short Sad Book* (Vancouver: Talonbooks, 1977), p. 111.

[2] Howard O'Hagan, *Tay John* (1939; rpt Toronto: McClelland and Stewart, 1960 [New Canadian Library]), p. 11.

[3] Rudy Wiebe, *The Temptations of Big Bear* (Toronto: McClelland and Stewart, 1973), p. 415.

[4] Bowering, *Burning Water* (Don Mills: Musson, 1980), p. 258.

[5] Ernest Buckler, *The Mountain and the Valley* (New York: Henry Holt, 1952), p. 301.

[6] Sheila Watson, *The Double Hook* (Toronto: McClelland and Stewart, 1959 [New Canadian Library]), p. 134.

[7] Frank Davey, *The Abbotsford Guide to India* (Victoria: Press Porcépic, 1986), p. 3.

17

My Book Is Bigger Than Yours

A Mazing Space, in its 438 pages, is a collection of 38 essays with the subtitle *Writing Canadian Women Writing*[1]. I experienced the making of this book in a personal way. One of its editors is a friend; Shirley Neuman, along with Robert Wilson, conducted with me a book-length interview that was published under the title *Labyrinths of Voice*. The other of its editors, along with being a deconstructionist and a critic of the Canadian long poem, is my wife.

Most of the time I shared the sense of discovery, even of revelation, felt by the two editors. I also shared their discomfort and their edge of dismay when manuscripts came in late or only barely decipherable.

But as a male writer living in the presence of this feminist enterprise, I at times felt a variety of anxiety that was all my own. It is from that anxiety that I begin this response.

In the book's long period of gestation, I at times felt what many fathers feel. I felt that, while I might somewhere in the recent past have made a small contribution to what was happening, I had become, in any larger scheme of things, irrelevant. I was, at best, simply in the way. I was, at worst, an embarrassment that must be, sometimes politely, sometimes blushingly, endured.

When the published book made its appearance I read with the feverish pride and genetic curiosity that many fathers must feel, pressing their noses to the glass that simultaneously lets them see and keeps them from approaching the object of all the attention. In this extreme predicament, to feel paternal in any way at all was to become suspect; and by the same token, not to feel paternal was to become suspect.

This is the stuff of modern anxiety. A reviewer looking at Irving

Singer's *The Nature of Love: The Modern World*, remarks that '[t]oday one wants a theory of love to come to terms with love's close relative, anxiety.'[2] To which I can only respond: yes.

In a daring way, *A Mazing Space* is a look at that close relative of love. In the course of occasioning my anxiety, it confronts its own.

The first confrontation is quite literally physical. The beautifully designed and produced book has the dimensions of a telephone directory. I cannot imagine two male editors nowadays coming up with a book this size. Neuman and Kamboureli, in their exuberance, in their flirtation with abandon, indeed produce a book. The book, in its announcement of abundance, exceeds our expectations. It presents itself as a sign of the future.

We are shown here, right off the bat, that art is being politicized. This politicizing, along with the art that it will examine or elaborate or recover, is part of the feminist endeavour.

The book, through its editors and its authors and the authors under discussion, dares to ask: Does art really matter? It poses the question to an establishment that wilfully uses art to its own ends, patriarchal, capitalistic, bourgeois.

Against that questioning of the Other it inquires of itself: Is it legitimate to ask if art is or should be or must be politically correct? It inquires of its own enterprise: Is there of necessity one answer to that one question? Is there a single right way to be a feminist, a single correct political response?

Between these two groups of questions, those to the Other, those to the self, is a disputatious third group that finds its focus in the nagging and abiding question: What is the relation of art to life?

We have heard the past answers, the pat answers. Neuman and Kamboureli set out to determine, or to guess, what the answer to these questions is going to be. They ask, in this intimidating yet intimate volume: What is the history of the future? Where do we find the texts of and for that paradoxical reading?

Criticism, it would seem, narrates its own intention. Traditional critical writing narrates the history of the literary past. Only in the late twentieth century has criticism attempted a narration of the future of the literature of which it is the mediating force. Neuman and Kamboureli, in their orchestration of critics, writers, and texts as tropes, and moving beyond the pessimism of much feminist writing, record the history of what must come to pass.

In spite of the ambitious and misleading title of *A Mazing Space*, we soon discover that its hidden title is *The Mazing of Time*, and in that turn we make our first entry into the maze.

Male critics in our recent past contrived the elaborate strategies of New Criticism in order to keep nasty old time at bay.

First of all, that criticism took for granted a tradition, a canon, which in its assigned and unchallenged authority was beyond time. Second, it took for granted the completeness, the finality, of the privileged text in such a way that the life of the author need not be mentioned, indeed should not be mentioned, though the 'he' of the assumed male author was often implied.

Neuman and Kamboureli not only choose to ignore the literary canon: they specify in their Introduction that they have chosen to exclude even the established women writers of Canada from their text: 'we asked contributors to extend their consideration beyond Margaret Atwood and Margaret Laurence.' That their contributors so enthusiastically complied is testimony to the editors' careful reading of what is to be.

The second strategy of Neuman and Kamboureli is to undermine the New Critical assumptions about the text as artifact, as Grecian urn, as space made independent of time. The life of the author and the presence of the writer are both relevant to the text. Behind both the act of writing and the productivity of the text is indeed a life. This life is not to be treated in a simple thematic way. This life is somehow to be valued, and, further, this life is to be recognized as one that has been marked by extremes of dismissal.

Janice Williamson begins her essay on Marjorie Pickthall:

> The following writing is more story than history, a textual fantasy about a body of poetry and letters written by Marjorie Pickthall (1883-1922), a Canadian poet long ago abandoned by the literary community. If sexuality is a combinatory of 'biological roots, psychological constructs, and social meanings', this narrative provokes a reading of a particular moment in the history of female subjectivity and desire. Written within a series of moving frames, borders occasionally blur between inside and outside, the texts and her life.

The notion of a frame is emblematic of the relation between the biographical and fictive elements in women's writing, and also suggests the woman writer's doubled relation to the dominant male literary tradition (p. 167).

Williamson announces a resistance to canon, to genre, to notions of the separation of life and text. She locates emphasis in 'the history of female subjectivity and desire'. She inscribes in her history of the future the inevitable play, thematic and formalistic, between versions of desire and versions of writing.

In place of the timelessness of New Criticism we find in this book a concern with 'the continuous present'. Helen M. Buss traces this line from Gertrude Stein, recognizing Shirley Neuman as a critical mediator, and goes on to say:

> . . . the idea of the continuous present is enormously important in studying the works of women whose lives are anchored in relatedness, whose ground of being insists on abandoning the historical view of the world because they cannot leave the various versions of themselves in the past. Needless to say, their use of the continuous present is most often an instinctive reaction and is likely to be at war with the stylistic demands of traditional autobiography (p. 163).

Lorna Irvine, in her reading of stories by Mavis Gallant, pushes the new versions of the autobiographical toward their fictional implications. Kristjana Gunnars, in her reading of Laura Goodman Salverson, examines the ways in which autobiography veers toward the confession. But more persistent in *A Mazing Space* is a concern with that dislocated version of autobiography which falls under the loose heading, travel writing. Indeed, my own wilful misreading of the title comes very close to being corrected.

Travel becomes central, has been central, to women's writing. How do we read travel? This is the concern of critics as various as Bina Friewald, who writes on Anna Jameson's *Winter Studies and Summer Rambles in Canada*, and Heather Murray, whose speculations on 'Women in the wilderness' become a speculation on the very nature of nature.

Travel becomes a release from the male confinement of the female in space. But that confinement also served to render woman 'timeless'. So, in effect, travel does occasion the woman writer's entry into the maze of time. Travel becomes a version of exploration. Linda Hutcheon points out that 'the ages of exploration were ages of imperialism, and Alice [of Audrey Thomas's novel *Intertidal Life*] argues that it is only women who can put a stop to the modern age of male imperialism . . .' (p. 221).

Few fictional characters travel as much as do the women in the novels of Audrey Thomas. In that travelling they point away from traditional male imperialism toward new perceptions, new versions of language, new discoveries.

Travel emerges, in *A Mazing Space*, as one of the recurrences that speak the future.

To travel, to explore, is to be willing to go beyond traditional visions or at least versions of unity. These essays reflect a willingness to let the fragment speak its moment, its 'take' on experience, its own separateness and uniqueness. Three of the male critics in the book, Laurie Ricou and Doug Barbour and Fred Wah, seem vaguely uneasy, apologetic, about their use of the fragment. The female critics, writers like Gail Scott, Donna Bennett, Pauline Butling, Louky Bersianik, and France Théoret, seem to delight in the fragmentation of design and intention. The female critics arrive at the fragment with a sense of release. The male critics arrive at the fragment with a sense of anxiety.

The postmodern impulse in its radical resistance to a governing narrative is, for the female critics, a way to politicize the aesthetic question. The release, the exuberance, the abundance, make the book polyphonic. The answers to the questions are many; the unity is not in the answers but in the enterprise that occasions this multivoicing, this talking together, this talking at and to and with and against each other.

The male critics ease themselves uneasily out of solitude, out of a solitude that in its very solitariness inscribed in their world the unity loosely named as the One. They dare, carefully, to look away from the blinding Platonic assurance to the actuality of the real shadows on the real walls of the real cave. Laurie Ricou, in his quoting of many voices, asks himself in pain and anxiety: How does a male critic talk about women's writing? Doug Barbour, in his 'day thoughts' on the poetry of Anne Wilkinson, finds that 'her poems argue an erotics of living'. Fred Wah, in his high praise for the poets, especially the female Language poets, who have helped shape his own poetic intention, acknowledges the importance of 'talk', of 'the list', of 'the language of uncertainty'.

It is the fourth male critic in the collection, E.D. Blodgett, who, with his title 'The Father's seduction . . .', locates the male reader/critic's anxiety in the Lacanian transformation of penis into phallus.

Or is it the other way round?

To venture into travel, to go beyond male fantasies of unity, to rejoice in those parts which are more than their sum, is to redefine the self. The female critics in this fat volume undertake just that. Their redefinition of self into its contradictions and surprises involves, recurrently, a direct confrontation with Freud, and with his misogynist disciple, Jacques Lacan.

The female critics, instead of trying to silence the men who silenced women, quote them. Again and again, they quote Lacan. And by this deconstructive strategy, they speak against the idea of woman as gap, as lack, as blind spot, as silence. In essay after essay, the women critics make essential use of theory in order to 'practice' themselves into the complexities of self and history.

Shirley Neuman, in her essay 'Importing Difference', names the ambiguities of the predicament:

> Jacques Lacan, the unnamed absence, the void at the centre, the hole in Irigaray's 'The Blind Spot in an Old Dream of Symmetry', sets the feminist writer a different problem than does Freud. By displacing the Oedipal scene to the arena of language, by transforming the penis into the phallus, that transcendental signifier, Lacan's theory denies women a discourse in which to articulate their own experience (p. 395).

This is what Neuman *says*. But she and Kamboureli, in *A Mazing Space*, quite simply outgun the merely transcendental. 'My book is bigger than yours' is here the transformative reply. This book, in its size and beauty, raises all hell with (against) the missionary position.

Sarah Murphy, in the essay that opens the book, 'Putting the Great Mother together again or how the cunt lost its tongue', speaks cheekily the volume's secret motto. That motto derives, deconstructs one might say, from Murphy's title and essay, and is, with a mixture of force and ambiguity: You Watch Your Tongue.

The book itself, *A Mazing Space*, is a maze. The book deconstructs the idea of book; it becomes its own multiplicity. The motto implied by Murphy's essay implies the ways in which female presence is inscribed in the individual text, in the individual writer, in the canon.

That motto says that you women writers are the kinds of writers who watch the language, who see the glass in the window, who can never be literary, only meta-literary. Language itself, speech and writing, speech or writing (and that debate too has a place in the book) will undo Jacques Lacan. The impossibility of discourse makes possible the discourse.

In another way, the motto puts the emphasis on the physicality of the tongue: it insists that the body is present, giving voice. Smaro Kamboureli, in her essay 'The body as audience and performance in the writing of Alice Munro', insists that '[i]n order to be able to host its own language, to engender its own genre, the feminine body must negate its fe-maleness, its male double, and feel at home with itself' (p. 33).

In still another way, the motto admonishes: you watch your tongue! It says that only by the most acute sense of discipline, only by a careful attention to the politics of speaking, and writing, will women writers in Canada, anywhere, enter into the maze of time.

What is at the centre of this maze?

There seems to be a utopian promise at the centre, a promise, a prophecy hinted by Louise Dupré when she writes: 'Never again to be alone writing, reading, thinking, remembering the past' (p. 357).

Dupré gives us a vision of plurality, not unity, a vision of an eroticism that goes beyond phallic simplicity and order.

What is at the centre of the maze?

This book celebrates a new kind of literature of exhaustion—a literature that goes beyond the phallus, or the penis—to become a literature of the heart.

Aritha Van Herk, in her essay 'Double Crossings: booking the lover', says of the male name-calling at the end of Betty Lambert's *Crossings*: 'It is a gift because the destruction of the novel has given the narrator words, words that she takes and shapes into a woman's epic, a woman's story . . .' (p. 286).

Again, Constance Rooke, in speaking of a phrase from a Mavis Gallant story, writes: '*Fear of the open heart*: I began to think and even to dream about it. I started, that is to say, romancing the text' (p. 256). And she goes on to comment, dryly: 'Depersonalization does not strike me as altogether a good thing, in literature or elsewhere' (p. 257).

What is at the centre of this enclosing and releasing maze?

Against all anxieties: hope—that tenuous and scattering (that generative) centre.

Lorraine Weir, in her essay 'From picture to hologram: Nicole Brossard's grammar of utopia' writes a reading of Brossard's *Picture Theory* that becomes, as *mise en abyme* and prophecy, the grammar of a larger intention. A utopian intention is made real by the reality of grammar: the future becomes history.

Under the disguise of a book of sorrows, *A Mazing Space* is a book of joy. Criticism, to these feminist critics, is a disguise that allows the critic to sing a new declaration of desire—and especially of the body desiring. And because of that, the impossible is possible.

In *A Mazing Space* the terrors of the maze of space become the hope that lives at the centre of the maze of time. And in the maze of time, the centre is everywhere. Entering that maze, we leave behind the varieties of death that are embedded in patriarchal history. We enter into the living history of the future.

Notes

[1] Shirley Neuman and Smaro Kamboureli, eds, *A Mazing Space: Writing Canadian Women Writing* (Edmonton: Longspoon Press/NeWest Press 1986). This talk was written for presentation at the VII Convegno Internazionale, Associazione Italiana di Studie Canadesi, Catania University, 18-22 May 1988.

[2] Michael Vincent Miller, 'Romance, the Saving Remnant', review of Irving Singer's *The Nature of Love* (*New York Times Book Review*, 27 Dec. 1987), p. 23.

Index